Lovers Muggers & Thieves

A Boston Memoir

Jonathan Tudan

Hawk Nest

Copyright © 2008 by Jonathan Tudan

All rights reserved, including the right of reproduction in whole or in part in any form.
Published in the United States by Hawk Nest Press.

Front cover photograph, "The Dive" by Jerry Berndt
Jerry Berndt was working in the Combat Zone at exactly the same period this story takes place. He was a twenty-three year old photographer shooting for Harvard University under the direction of urban anthropologist Dr. Neil A. Eddington and an endowment from the National Institute of Mental Health. Jerry served as Dr. Eddington's point man, meeting the pimps, hookers, strippers, bar tenders, and cops while sneaking photos to compliment Dr. Eddington's research.

Back cover photograph, by Mary Poudrier

Cover design by Archer Ellison

"If You're Goin' to the City" © 1967 All rights administered by Mose Allison, Audre May Music, BMI, 82 Ballad Court, Eastport, NY 11941. All rights reserved. Used by permission.

"Get Back" © 1969 (Renewed) Sony/ATV Tunes LLC. All rights administered by Sony/ATV Music Publishing, 8 Music Square West, Nashville, TN 37203. All rights reserved. Used by permission.

"Happiness Is A Warm Gun" © 1968 (Renewed) Sony/ATV Tunes LLC. All rights administered by Sony/ATV Music Publishing, 8 Music Square West, Nashville, TN 37203. All rights reserved. Used by permission.

Library of Congress Cataloging-in-Publication Data TXu 1-584-065
Tudan, Jonathan, 1950–
Lovers, Muggers & Thieves – A Boston memoir/
by Jonathan Tudan
ISBN 978-1-60702-396-8

Printed in the United States of America

Author's Note

In 1969, as an eighteen-year-old college freshman, I lived inside Boston's Combat Zone, the most bizarre neighborhood the city has ever known, and managed a six-story flophouse that rented rooms by the week to the purveyors of the neighborhood sex trade. The seedy marquees of Boston's notorious adult entertainment district, along with its strip clubs, triple X peep shows and adult bookstores, have passed into history. That part of Boston the locals now refer to as the "former Combat Zone" has become gentrified, transformed as the city's stylish Theater District, lined with luxury condominiums, lavish high-rise hotels, institutions of higher learning and Starbucks. In this story, the dancers, musicians, drug dealers, pimps and prostitutes that once dominated these streets return to the scene to join a boy stepping into a man's world.

Although this is a work of nonfiction, most of the names and other identifying characteristics of the persons and places included in this memoir have been altered to protect identities. The experiences detailed are all true and have been portrayed as I remember them, to the best of my ability, but I would be dishonest if I did not confess to slight distortions of the finer points which lay beyond the clouds of reminiscence. Some details, drawn with lines through decades of memory, may be inaccurate. Conversations throughout the text may not always be word-for-word transcriptions of actual dialogue, but rather are meant to bring the emotional entanglements of this time to life.

To my friends and neighbors of the Combat Zone who shared with me a brief moment in time and forever changed my life, this memoir is dedicated to you.

Jonathan Tudan

March 2008

In spite of Mary

"It was an adult portion... taken in an adult dose."

Levon Helm

PROLOGUE
Boston - May, 1969

Kitty tipped me off: The vice squad will hit our building in twenty-four hours. This dump would get five stars should the Boston Chamber of Commerce decide to rate the hot spots in the city where conventioneers can go to get laid. In the past we've had a couple of girls who quietly turned tricks, coming and going without incident, leaving nothing behind but a reputation, but ever since the new girls moved in, that reputation has picked up speed. Something has to be done.

Last week, while taking the stairs up to my room, I rounded the corner on the fifth floor and confronted a greasy gang of Johns queued up against the wall in front of the door to Apartment 5A, Tomas's place. One slimy stud with acne scars on his face spotted me coming and stretched his leg across my path, resting his pointy-toed shoe on the banister to block my way, exposing a patch of pasty skin above his limp sock. "Who the hell are you?" the punk grinned, a gap between his two front teeth wide enough to hold a peanut. I stopped beside the leg and took a deep breath, "I'm the building superintendent. And while we're on the subject, move your fuckin' leg before I break it.

I want you, hotdog, and the rest of you assholes out of my building in two minutes." The pointy shoe dropped to the floor. This is the kind of shit I have to deal with every day.

I share the maintenance of our building with my roommate, Robert Van Helden. For some reason, the crowd here recognizes us as their official leaders. Running this show is a mind-blowing business; a bit like being mayor in the Land of Oz, on acid.

Kitty, Apartment 6C, has been screaming in my ears for weeks to show some hair and confront the pimps and the mess they drag in. I tacked a few posters in the lobby threatening to evict the girls if they kept it up, but by the next morning some clown had turned my signs into confetti. So, Kitty decided to take care of the problem herself and called her friends in the vice squad. Rumor has it the cops have a special relationship with the strippers in the Normandy Lounge, the club on Washington Street where Kitty works as a dancer. I really don't know the details behind any of these claims; all I know is when Kitty calls the vice squad, they seem to listen.

Panic has now taken over. News of the impending raid has flashed through the building like a fire in the stairwell. A bunch of cops marching down the hallways and banging on doors is the last thing my tenants want to see. All borderline felons and social deviants residing within these walls see themselves as targets. Mixed-race couples shacking up have begun to nervously doubt their freedom. Bits and pieces of drug life squirreled away in the recesses of cupboards and dressers are being wiped clean. Anxious expressions can be overheard concerning outstanding warrants matched with names on mailboxes. Guys who love to strut like they're marching in Mardi Gras are stooped behind their doorjambs; girlfriends at their side smelling the hot sweat of men trying hard to be cool.

This latest pain in the ass adds to a long line of grief I've had since coming here. My normal reaction is to take it easy and not let this mess get into my head, and that's just what I intend to do. It's Saturday night and I, for one, have better things to do than worry about my tenants.

Still, I can't help thinking about some of them. Particularly Kitty Boudreaux, a black beauty from Montreal, breathtaking in the art of exotic dance. She looks spectacular walking along Washington Street under the lights of the marquee. But, like most things offered to those who patronize the Combat Zone, Kitty is more fantasy than reality. One night I watched her drive a packed house into sexual frenzy after slipping down to nothing but pasties and a pencil-thin G-string. She purred into the crowd asking if they wanted her to take off more, and they begged with hands stretched-out like starving men grabbing for a morsel of meat. Standing tall beneath the spotlights, she spread her long legs and placed both hands on the side of her head, elbows out akimbo to the stage. "More?" she asked. "Are you sure?" Kitty yanked off her five-pound wig, a long curly black mane, and tossed it behind her back. The crowd went bananas! The slap of their hands on the tables echoed like gunfire. "Some more?" she asked one final time. A lustful, masculine roar surrounded her performance, "YES! YES! YES!" Kitty opened her mouth wide. Long, sinuous fingers reached inside her throat, appearing to be swallowed, and pulled out a full set of false teeth. She licked her naked gums with her tongue and threw her head back in a shameless laugh.

And then there's Julie, Apartment 3C, a shapely, bottle-hair strawberry blonde (more straw than berry), who never makes an appearance on the street without throwing on a pound of makeup and a mountainous blond wig to accompany her skintight satin pantsuit, and a pair of 5-inch stiletto heels so sharp you could use them to cut open cans. Julie and her old man, John Taylor, arrived here a couple of months ago. John, a disagreeable drunk, is fiercely jealous of any guy eyeballing Julie for longer than two seconds, an unfortunate trait for the boyfriend of a stripper.

John and his brother, Ed, Apartment 4C, are both musicians. They moved into the building with another band member, Jasper, Apartment 5B. When I first met these guys, I twitched whenever they came near me for no other reason than their appearance, especially Jasper, the flashiest sonofabitch on the block. My lily-white suburban upbringing hadn't prepared me for such social engagements. I first caught sight of Jasper standing in front of the Saxon Theater, decked out in an iridescent scarlet suit with matching shirt and shoes, capped off with a plump, floppy black bow-tie, enormous rings glittering on several fingers. I was certain his pimp attire, Little Richard mustache and wavy, lacquered hair concealed murderous intentions. But in fact, I never met anyone mellower, or more colorful. This soft-spoken dude has a silky suit ensemble in every shade imaginable: Leprecon green, Klondike gold, Florida orange, Vatican purple. I once had the opportunity to sneak a peek inside his closet, I opened the door to a rainbow; if Doctor Seuss was asked to draw a pimp, he'd draw Jasper.

Marvin Jones, Apartment 5C, believes the world has shown him little gratitude for the twenty-five hard years he's put into it. I don't buy it, considering the good fortune that came his way in the form of Winky Perez. Winky, a tall, lissome nineteen-year-old beauty, possessing the grace of a Nubian princess, will do anything for her man, whatever it takes. I like her a lot. I dig Marvin, too, and forgive his transgressions, since he watches out for me like a guardian angel. I welcome the attention, but find it pretty strange, considering he doesn't much like white folks. This fellowship, however, does not extend to Marvin's little brother, Benny, Apartment 4A, an ingratiating weasel who's always fast-talking and smiling his way into his next scam. Benny's old lady, Jackie, makes her bread performing girl-on-girl sex acts at stag parties, and it's rumored she occasionally dips into prostitution whenever times get hard, which seems to be more often than not.

Sam Dumont, next door in Apartment 6B, is too hip to own up to her christened name, Sheila, and keeps it hidden from most everyone. She honors me by sharing this secret. My friends all but genuflect before her, calling her slick, good-looking and wise. At twenty-one, Sam is three years older than me, but her mind works a generation above my experience. On weekday afternoons, she dances across the street in the Four Corners Lounge for tips and walking-around money, but the better part of her income flows discreetly from selling grass to band members and other dancers.

I love Saturday night. It's the highest-flying time of the week in our building. My neighbors dress up as bright as peacocks, their common goal to look hot; girls aiming to be desired by the men and admired by the women, guys often times look more colorful than the girls. The whole affair is one, big primeval mating game.

Kitty and Julie glide into my apartment like two regal swans, one black, one white. Following in their wake like subordinate ducklings, John Taylor and his mates, Ed and Jasper, and their girlfriends, cluster in silence in the center of my room. Seconds later, Marvin and Winky hustle through the door, very business-like. Marvin takes up residence in our easy-chair; Winky perches beside him with her ass over the cushy arm. Benny shuffles in with his head down and stands beside his brother. His old lady, Jackie, moseys up to a chair with a cigarette gripped tight between her fingers, and she lifts a skinny leg and steps down hard on the seat, resting an elbow to her knee. A sour look makes her skanky features nastier than usual. Sam walks in last, alone, seemingly perturbed, hands-on-hips, chewing gum with her mouth open, surveying the other characters gathered about as if they have lice. She sits down on my bed and crosses her legs, looking a bit anxious, waiting for someone to make the next move. This is the largest gathering of sober tenants ever assembled in one spot. Confused, I look over at Van Helden and shrug, "I didn't know we were throwing a party." His dumb look matches the one I'm wearing.

Benny and his brother Marvin appear to have

some kind of shit brewing between them. Marvin studiously folds his hands in his lap. "She's gone!" he says, motioning in Jackie's direction with his chin. "These boys," he points at Robert and me, our faces blank, "run her ass out with the rest of them whores. Evict them. That's it. No whores, no cops. End of story." Marvin brushes his palms together like he is wiping off dirt.

Jackie approaches, takes a healthy drag from her cig and breathes a line of smoke into his eyes, a dragon's weapon of choice.

"Are you gonna do this?" asks Benny, spinning in a circle. "She not doin' her business here." He exhorts the congregation, "What we gotta do to prove it?"

The atmosphere in the room has the peculiar formality of a tribal council sitting to decide the banishment of a disloyal clan member.

"What the hell's goin' on?" I ask.

A room full of agitated voices erupts in a chorus of recriminations. "The police be here tonight to close this place!" John Taylor's slight frame bounces up and down on his rear end when he speaks, like a Mexican jumping bean. "Because this dumb-ass bitch is talkin'!" He sticks a finger out at Kitty, who has been reclining lazily on my bed next to Sam. At his words, she springs from the bed as if she has been doused with a bucket of ice water, advancing towards him. Julie jumps up and pushes between them.

"STOP IT!" Her cry silences the room. "They talked to me, too! If Kitty hadn't helped them, I woulda done it myself! The police won't bother nobody who ain't got somethin' to worry about." John Taylor shoots her a homicidal look that she stares back down defiantly.

"The police can't shut down the building," I say. "That's ridiculous."

"See," says Ed Taylor, turning to his band mate, "I told you we don't have to move."

Jasper sits still, his face a study of misgivings. "I don't get in nobody's business," he says, quietly. "It's easy livin' here. But I worry some nights, coming home with my old lady. I see those white dudes in the hall watchin' me." He hesitates for a second and closes his eyes. "They lookin' like they wanna kill me." Jasper shakes his head from side to side, "Things gonna be bad some night… I just know it."

John Taylor turns to face Van Helden and me, replacing the cold look on his face with one of satisfied contrivance. "We don't have to have no trouble. These boys give Lykos a call on the phone," he smiles, "get him to tell the police to back off."

"What makes you think that?" asks Van Helden.

"You work for the man. You should be the one to call him. We all know how Lykos make his money. Shit, that man *own* the police. If he say keep away from my building, they do it!"

"Are you drunk?" I ask. "That's the dumbest shit I've ever heard."

Instantly, John stabs at me with his eyes. I fend him off with a glare of my own, and neither of us blinks. Sam rises from the edge of my bed, crossing between us.

"I walk in the front door at night and there isn't a guy standing out there on the sidewalk who doesn't think I'm a hooker," says Sam. "Frankly, it's starting to get on my nerves, especially if I'm with a guy I want to bring up to my room," she snickers. "He starts looking at me strange... like the trip up's gonna cost him twenty bucks." She walks over to the window and scans the street scene below. "Look at where we're living, people. It's all around us, and it ain't going nowhere. Want to change your life?" she sniffs, "Change your address."

Winky throws her head back laughing. Julie smiles and nods in agreement.

"What are you saying?" asks Marvin. "Don't do nothin'?"

Sam turns back and gives us a crooked smile, "That's right."

"It's a little too late for that," says Marvin. He rises from his seat and tracks a worried pace in the center of the room. "You don't know the police the way I do. You give them a reason to bust your head," Marvin wallops his right fist into his left hand, "and they do it! And here we are, opening the goddamn door for them."

"The police will come," says Sam, "but not because we invited them; they're coming because it's no secret where the hookers are in this neighborhood." Sam turns from the window and approaches Benny and Jackie, looking them both hard in the eye, "Any girl here taking in tricks tonight is a fool. There'll be someone knocking on her door and it won't be a John." Sam makes her way towards the door, passing along advice on her way out, "Leave the girls and the police alone... Step aside, let whatever happens happen."

In the end, tonight turns out to be just another Saturday night, except for the way it began. We hit the bars for laughs and drinks, strengthen alliances, extend connections, eye potential bed mates, the world we step into is full of promise, we taste life the way it's supposed to be, by 2:30 wander back home, and nothing has changed. The vice squad doesn't visit us, and our hookers continue to attract Johns with impunity. On the way to my room I pass several flitting through the hallways, like moths in the night banging into your back-porch light.

PART ONE
UNHINGED

1

Hartford – End of Summer, 1968

A bus terminal is always the saddest place you find in the city, a way station for terminal losers. It smells pretty bad too, especially on rainy days; the place has all the charm of an ashtray in a public toilet. It's no big deal, but I'm leaving home for the first time. My family didn't gather to see me off.

The bus to Boston idles by the curb with its engine running. The smell of diesel lifts my spirits, reminding me of the Good Humor truck that visited my street in the late summer afternoons. An old black porter takes the bag from my hand and pitches it into the belly of the bus. Stepping out of the rain, I get on board and drop into an open seat, lean my face against the glass, peering through a veil of drizzle at the filmy broken windows and sooty brownstone walls of the once muscular Union Station, its strength now worn-down along with the rest of this part of town. A wino convention hugs up against the entrance, squeezing a bit of shelter beneath a shallow stone cornice. So much of Hartford, once the most prosperous city in America, is now a no-man's land dominated by hard crime and bitter people. This city scares me, and I won't miss it a bit. I tilt back in my seat to relax, thinking of the ride ahead.

Up to this point in my life, I have not yet had any bona fide eye-popping experiences that come with approaching adulthood. I have never been on an airplane... never owned a car... never gotten drunk in a bar... never been high ... never gotten into a fist fight... never held a hand gun.... never seen a hundred-dollar bill... never been laid... indeed, never seen a naked lady. The fact that I haven't experienced anything exceptional in my life is not abnormal. I tell myself I'm progressing rather nicely; I just don't have any trumpets blasting in the background.

Whenever I board a bus alone I always hold out thin hope that Miss America will climb aboard and share the ride beside me. Without a shred of propriety, I do what I can to discourage others from taking her seat. My left hand rests rigidly on the open space next to mine as I fix each passenger filing past with a glare, unless of course *she* steps on board. I'll smile at her affectionately to draw her in, she'll settle down comfortably beside me, and throughout the trip I'll make her laugh, and she'll flirt with me and touch my knee with her fingertips. Before the ride is over we'll make plans to meet again, stay in touch. She'll slip me her number and I'll promise to call.

"Hey, buddy, move your hand!" A fat guy with a face like Porky Pig pushes me out of my dream and plops down in Miss America's seat. He slips his smelly stocking feet free from his Hush Puppies and lights a cigarette.

"Ugh... would you mind not smoking?" I ask. "It sort of bothers me."

"Yeah? Would you mind minding your own fucking business?"

Wentworth Institute of Technology, an all-male technical college in Boston's Back Bay, has the distinction of accepting anyone into their ranks with a high school diploma and a pulse, both of which I possess. Thanks to my low-income status, I was able to grab a part-time gig in the school's library for twenty bucks a week. Another helpful convenience is my relatives who share a duplex just outside the city; Uncle Arthur and his sister-in-law, Aunt Phyllis. Accommodations were arranged for me to move in with Uncle Art, sparing my people the necessity of shelling out dorm fees. The deal also provides a grounded connection flowing from my uncle and aunt back through to my parents. I've been set free to swing from the family tree, but deep down inside, I still feel hinged.

Having been raised in a crucifix-above-every-bed solid Catholic family, catechism, confession, and communion consumed my childhood. Every Sunday my folks packed the station wagon with my older brother, four little sisters and me, dragging us into Saint Gertrude's church, where the holy water always smelled like something from an old fish bowl.

Since I was a little kid I've dreamed of becoming an architect. Standing still on the sidewalk, I feel a sting of apprehension gazing up at the grimy brick façade as I face my dream. Perhaps it's the dark morning sky, but Wentworth seems to have taken on a foreboding appearance that was missing last spring when I made my sunny introductory tour. I march ahead, following the make-shift cardboard signs that direct me to the architecture department, Class AET 1-C, Architectural Engineering Technology, for first year students with last names beginning with the letters N through Z.

This morning's planned activity is student orientation. About forty of us assemble in the hallway waiting to enter a room that will serve as our drafting studio. We're all cut the same; a fresh crop of teenage boys harvested from white, straight-laced America, except for the one guy leaning in the corner. He looks around my age, but that's the only similarity we share. I'm wearing my brown corduroy sport jacket over a sunny-yellow polo shirt tucked neatly into pressed chinos, with a spit-shine glossing the toes of my penny loafers. My look is topped off with a slick, Peter Gunn haircut. This guy, on the other-hand, could be a rock star, easily fitting in with the crowd I've seen in magazines strolling along London's Carnaby Street. His pageboy cropped dark hair reminds me of the Sunday comics' adventure hero, Prince Valiant. He's sporting deep purple velvet bell-bottoms with a creamy silk shirt. His glasses are large gold framed wire-rim affairs usually seen on the faces adorning album covers. A dark complexion complements the gold-rim of his specs.

A young man, who I assume is our instructor, appears from inside the room, waves and directs us to be seated. I discover that our seating assignments have been prearranged; cards with our names written in bold block letters standing on each desk, an army of little pup tents. I find my seat, placed next to the rock star. After settling in I notice, standing next to the guy who greeted us, an older dude facing the class. The younger man seems ready to take a back seat to this tall humorless guy dressed in a drab gray business suit, completely bald save for a ring of thick black hair that loops around big ears like a dead mink, Buddy Holly glasses sitting on top of his fat nose. A commanding glare brings the room to quick attention. His expressionless, lipless mouth opens a fraction, like he is about to let out some air. Jesus, who's this stooge?

"My name is Calvin Plummer, and I want to welcome all you fine young men to Wentworth Institute of Technology. I am the Dean of the Architecture Department. Standing beside me is Mr. Leon Clemensky. Mr. Clemensky will be your drafting instructor." Plummer pauses a few seconds for us to take notes, if we so desire. He continues, "Today, you are about to embark upon your career as technical experts in the built environment. This college was founded in 1904 on a commitment to excellence, and since that time we have sustained a worthy reputation as..." Blah blah blah blah blah.... The stooge drones on like this for fifteen solid minutes, finally summing up his pep talk with words that I think were meant to inspire, but instead sound as canned as corn.

"Consequently, we graduate only the best of the best. Take a look at the man sitting next to you..." I eye the rock star, who returns my look with a wry smile... "Because he'll probably be gone before the year is out. You may have found it easy getting into this program, but by God, I promise you we are going to make it very difficult for you to leave here with that degree."

Following the Dean Plummer soliloquy, Leon jumps up and fills in the details of what is expected of us, how our classes will be scheduled, plus a brief dissertation on school policies for non-academic behavior. He lays out a few shockers vis-à-vis the school's dress code, attendance policy and classroom manners. I get a sneaking suspicion; that trip about making it hard to leave here with a degree, I wouldn't bet against it.

At noon, I commandeer an empty 4-top inside the Student Union cafeteria and spread out the contents of my lunch tray. Within a few minutes, three others, all of whom I recognize as members of my class, take up seats around the table. One tall, Goofy-Gus seems to be enjoying himself immensely, since the idiot smile he's had plastered on all morning never left his handsome face. The second dude who pulls up reminds me of the jocks I knew in high school; built like a varsity wrestler, short cropped hair, thick neck squeezed tight inside his white button-down shirt. All that's missing is the letter sweater. Last to join us is the rock star.

"Well, fuck a duck, guys. Welcome to Wentworth," I say to no one in particular.

A hand shoots fast across the table for me to shake, "My name is Andreus Theodokis. I am pleased to meet you, my fine friend," Goofy's voice chimes with a heavy, stilted accent. I extend my hand, which he pumps heartedly as a peasant cranking water from a well.

"Where you from?" I ask, freeing my hand.

"My home is Lemnos, a village in Greece, you must all come and visit. We have many many beeyooteeful women," he says, giving off a daffy salacious grin, his eyes dancing around the table like Zorba the Greek.

"Well, I am pleased to meet you, too, Andreus. I'm Jonny from Connecticut."

"Hi! Larry Portman," the jock offers his hand to shake as well. "I moved down here from Bangor with my wife, Paula, and little girl, Sally. She's one year old… my little girl, not my wife," he laughs at himself. "And who are you?" Larry turns to the rock star and extends his hand, which is grabbed without hesitation.

"Ahhhh… a very good question. Who am I? I guess whoever I want to be."

"Mystery-man," I say, detecting another European accent. "I think you're John Lennon."

"I'm Robert Van Helden."

2

And Whooooo Are Yoooou?

Classes are through for the day. I step off the trolley, drawing my coat in tight as I head for home. The bitter night air makes the distance from Mattapan Square to Uncle Arthur's seem so much greater. I approach the door of the duplex in silence and ascend the stairs to my section of the house, walking directly to my room, closing the door behind me, squirreling myself away.

"Jonny, is that you!?"

I open my door to answer my uncle, "Yeah, hi... I'm home. I'm gonna do a little homework before dinner."

"Can you come out here a minute? I need a little help," he asks, beckoning from his bedroom.

I walk into the room and find Uncle Art lying flat on top of the covers in his pajama bottoms; holding a plastic bottle out towards my face.

"Jonny, would you mind rubbing lotion on my back? My skin is so itchy. This cream's the only thing that helps."

Damn right I mind... would you mind if I go into the kitchen and grab a pair of oven mitts for this procedure? I take the bottle from his hand as my uncle flips like an egg-over-easy. "Sure, Uncle Art... let me see." I pretend to scan the label reading the product's medicinal applications, but I'm really just stalling. His flesh has the color and consistency of Silly Putty. I cover every square inch of skin in three-seconds flat and make a bee-line back to my room. Dinner doesn't seem appealing to me at the moment; I think I'll just knock out some homework and crash.

"In the name of the Father, the Son and the Holy Ghost," I whisper into my folded hands, knees planted on the oak floor beside my bed. "Dear God, thank you for watching over me and my family…" I say a few prayers and petition His forgiveness for any venial acts I may have enjoyed over the past twenty-four hours before climbing into bed.

Another weekday morning, I hurriedly take the stairs down to the street while chomping on a piece of dry toast, passing my Aunt Phyllis standing in her bathrobe and slippers beside her open door, arms folded across her chest, a Kent dangling from her lips with one-inch of ash precariously bending from the tip. My clomping down the stairs must have disturbed her; she is casting a grimacing look my way.

"What's all that thumping going on in your room at night?"

"Huh," I reply, a bit confounded.

"My bed is right below you. Every night I hear these two thumps on my ceiling, bah-boom! It wakes me up. Whatever it is you're doing, stop it."

Too embarrassed to confess those sounds are my knees hitting the hardwood when I kneel to pray, I shrug, "Maybe it's me doin' push-ups."

"Well, cut it out. You're waking me up."

On my walk to the trolley I decide it's time to quit praying. I'm a good kid. I don't need to keep doing this; Jesus will understand. Anyway, I'm in college now, and praying is for kids.

This past month has been one long drag. Living with my uncle, I'm cut off from anything decent to do in this town, as if I'm staring at Boston through a window with my nose pressed up against the glass. Using my palm as a visor, I lean my face into Senior Pizza's storefront window and examine the clientele, a society of Campus Radical Mod British Rocker Jesus Apostles enjoying an atmosphere of hippie camaraderie. Tilting back, I catch my reflection in the glass and let out a heavy sigh. Give me a silver badge and a white bandolier and I would make a dazzling high school hall monitor. Feeling more than a little intimidated, I venture inside and begin hunting for refuge in the form of my buddy, Charlie.

I can't tell you how jazzed I was to get a call from an old friend inviting me to join him for a night in the city. Charlie arrived in Boston a year ago and enrolled as a psych major at Northeastern. Psychology departments have bloated ever since Timothy Leary turned psychologists into celebrity gurus. Charlie became part of that glut, confessing to me last Christmas, "It's a great place to meet chicks." I respect that decision, given we have zero females within the confines of my chosen path of higher learning.

It's been nearly a year since Charlie and I last connected. A cigarette is dangling from his lips; I'm immediately envious over how hip and poetic

Charlie looks with his Doc Holiday gunslinger goatee and black turtleneck, sitting alone at one of the back tables nursing a Coke, legs stretched out, his eyes absorbed in a newspaper. I walk up and kick his foot, triggering a hearty salutation.

"Jonny!" Charlie beams, jumping out of his chair and wrapping me up in a bear hug. I hug him back, and we stand here grinning like a couple of clowns, letting a few seconds pass in silence, soaking up the satisfaction that comes with the warm reunion of old friends.

"How you like Northeastern… you gettin' laid?"

"I wish." Charlie gives me a disappointing nod as he reaches for a smoke to replace the one he extinguished seconds ago. He slips out a butt and tilts the box my way.

"No thanks," I say, shaking him off. I tried cigarettes in junior high and they made me gag. Looking around the room, I notice every table in the place is smoking up a storm. Charlie lights up, leaning back to blow a lazy cloud that folds into the haze hanging above our heads.

I pull one from the pack, "Gimme a light, Charlie." A short cautious drag later, I exhale. By the third puff, I start to relax a bit with it. "So, what do you want to do tonight?" I ask, curling smoke out my nose and mouth like a juvenile dragon-in-training, my head light with dizzy loops.

"I know this guy, Nathan Rhiner. He has an apartment on Marlborough. Nathan's having a few friends over. We're gonna kick back, do a little wine."

"Far out."

Actually, I am so starved for companionship I would have said the same thing if he had told me we were headed for the park to pick up litter.

During the walk, Charlie clues me in on Nathan. He has the sweetest living arrangement you could ever imagine. Nathan is a building superintendent. They give him an apartment and a telephone, and all he has to do for it is collect rent from a few tenants and sweep up once in awhile. What an inspiration! If I could land something like this I could say goodbye to Uncle Arthur and move into the city, have my own place, and it wouldn't cost me a dime!

We squeeze through a tight vestibule and meander our way up two flights of winding stairs into a dark corridor. Stopping at the last door on the right, Charlie knocks three times. I smell something pungent coming from within the apartment. Charlie picks up on the scent too, looking over at me with raised eyebrows, smiling like he just found a twenty-dollar bill. The door opens a crack.

"Charlie?" asks the low voice directly below the eyeball peering at us.

"Yeah, Nate... open up."

"Who's that?" he asks, pointing at me with his nose.

"An old buddy from high school, he's cool."

I'm cool? It feels good being labeled cool.

A guy with a head of hair like Bozo the Clown pops through the opening. He scans beyond us for a second, scrutinizing the corridor, perhaps checking to see his tenants are safely tucked away in their rooms.

The door swings open into a cloud of smoke, revealing a peculiar scene. The room is large and devoid of light and furniture, aside from a pair of stereo speakers, a skinny lamp table holding an amp and turntable, and a couple of folding chairs propped against the far wall. Records lie disheveled beneath the table. A streetlamp outside a prodigious bay window throws a shaft of light across a frayed oriental rug, dimly illuminating four guys sitting cross-legged in a circle, smoking from an exotic bubble pipe perched between them. A brass bowl the size of a small flower vase is positioned on the floor in the center of the ring. Rising from the bowl is a six-inch stem supporting a shot-glass cup filled with what I assume to be marijuana. Connected to the bowl is a long thin hose with a brass tip on the end you stick in your mouth. I saw a pipe like this in the caterpillar scene from Alice and Wonderland, *"And Whoooo Are Yoooou?"*

It's fascinating watching these guys pass the stem between them with tribal serenity, drawing smoke into their lungs and holding it in for several long seconds before releasing it with a long sigh in a haze of ghostly silver blue. With each inhalation, they make the embers in the shot glass burn red while watery-bubble sounds gurgle from inside the bowl.

Reluctant apprehension gives way to nervous enthusiasm as I wait for my turn at the pipe. No one but me knows the truth of the matter; I am about to be baptized in smoke. I can do this… I'm cool. The hose from the bowl is passed to me, and I close my eyes and raise the tip of the stem to my lips like a seasoned opium smoker. But instead of drawing fire into my lungs, I inadvertently blow hard into the pipe. Water bubbles from inside the bowl and shoots up the stem and into the shot-glass cup, extinguishing the embers and overflowing the contents onto the rug in a messy pool of soggy shit.

"Hey, fuck face!"
"Jesus Christ! What the hell did you do that for?"

Recapping the night's journey in my head during the trolley ride back to Uncle Arthur's house I feel anything but jazzed, in fact, I feel like an idiot. But on the plus side, I picked up a little insight into how I could manage living on my own.

3
The Offer

Robert Van Helden emigrated from Holland with his family when he was twelve, bringing along his dark, good looks and mysterious accent, bestowed to him by his Dutch father and Indonesian mother. There's some kind of fusion happening between us; our musical tastes travel in the same rock and roll world, we laugh at the same jokes, marvel together at the stupidity of purpose shown by the clowns running our country, and speak the same Neolithic hip-talk. We even look alike; or should I say, I'm beginning to look more like him. It's been nearly two months since my last haircut. The bellbottoms and a dungaree jacket I bought at an Army-Navy surplus store look perfect with the buckskin moccasins and cowhide vest with antelope-horn buttons I scored from a leather shop on Charles Street. Robert and I parade around campus with old army ammo satchels used as book bags, festooned with peace signs and graffiti, T-squares strapped to the back of our bags like battle lances.

My hair can hardly be considered long, but its hippy enough to give Dean Plummer a hard-on for me. He makes a surprise visit to our class this morning, performing an impromptu dress code inspection. Plummer marches up and down the aisles of desks like Adolph Eichmann, singling out victims on the basis of appearance. Van Helden and I are tapped on the shoulder, our hairlines precipitously below the top of the collar. It is also argued our sideburns present too close a resemblance to Elvis, vintage '56'. Along with a couple other mangy rebels, we trot off to pay Dean Boeller a visit.

Boeller, the Dean of Students, measures sideburn infractions by placing a pencil parallel to the ground with the eraser strategically planted in your ear canal. If the sideburn drops below the pencil line, you are instructed to have them trimmed. A short dude in our class from East Boston, Danny Roncioli, is Boeller's first target. Danny is a little scruffy, but not in a hippy sort of way, more like a pocket-sized James Dean. Boeller sizes up Danny with his eyes and pulls a pencil from his top shirt pocket. To get the proper perspective, he squats laboriously on his beefy haunches like a gorilla taking a crap and inserts his gauge into Danny's ear. The point of Boeller's tongue protrudes sideways between his fat lips like the tip of a Pink Pearl eraser. Danny's sideburns flunk the pencil test.

Van Helden and I refuse to be subjected to this idiotic procedure. I grudgingly volunteer to clean up my act, but Robert surprises everyone in the room by telling Boeller he will think about it.

"Think about it? They got us by the short-hairs, Robert! What's to think about?" I say to Van Helden on our way back to class.

"Nobody's gonna tell me how I should look."

Besides Van Helden, the other classmates I hang out with at Wentworth are Larry and Andreus, connections I made on opening day. But that clique ends when classes are through for the afternoon. Larry's got his hands full with his wife and kid, and Andreus spends all his spare time running odd jobs for his older brother, Lykos. According to Andreus, his brother is some kind of real estate tycoon on a stove-hot path to becoming a Boston Big Shot. At lunch today we learn Lykos is looking for a manager to run one of his investments, an apartment house someplace downtown.

"Larry, this would be a good job for you. You must come with me to see this building. It's beeyooteeful."

"Why me?" asks Larry, surprised by the offer.

"You are married, you have a family… you are a very very grown-up person, very very trustworthy. Tomorrow, I pick you up and show you this building."

Before class, I join everyone in the Student Union for coffee, anxious to hear the details of Larry's arrangement with Andreus' brother.

"Andreus picked us up in his Camero," Larry begins, holding an anxious grin. "We pulled up to the curb on the corner of Tremont and LaGrange. When I opened the door, Paula jumped over the front seat and grabbed me. Her hands were shaking… she wouldn't let go… Christ, she was nearly bawling! I said, 'Honey, I'll be right back. I wanna go inside and check it out.' Paula begged me not to leave her and Sally alone in the car."

Larry continues, now laughing. "Andreus wanted to bring me back later without the family. Paula was screaming, 'Don't bother! Take us home!'"

I glance over at Andreus, impassively munching his chocolate doughnut.

"Andreus, you fucker!" says Larry. "You held back one very important detail about your *beeyooteeful* building, didn't ya?"

Andreus shrugs.

"You never said it's in the goddamn Combat Zone!"

"What's the Combat Zone?" I ask. It doesn't sound like a nice place for Paula to be pushing around a baby carriage.

"Mondo Bizarro, 42nd Street, nothing but bars, strip clubs, pimps, hookers. Next door to this place, both sides… bars and strip joints, across the street, another one… around the corner, both directions, more strip joints. The neighborhood is a friggen freak show. It scared the shit out of Paula!"

"I'll do it!" I say to Andreus.

Robert has a quizzical look on his face, "You'll do what?"

"I'll take the job."

Andreus puts on a broad grin, doughnut crumbs sticking to his teeth. He turns to face Larry, "You don't want the job? Good! I give it to Jonny."

A second later, my brain catches up with my mouth. I slow down and consider the implications of my impulsiveness, realizing I don't have a clue what I'm getting into. "I don't have to do this thing alone, do I?" I ask Andreus, softening my tone of voice a couple of notches.

"What do you mean?"

I look over at Van Helden with a positive smile. "Robert, let's do this! The semester is almost over. Get your ass out of the dorm. This is perfect timing."

"Actually, I'm thinking of dropping out," Van Helden dumps his news in the middle of the table with a thud.

"You're kidding me?" I ask, my smile taking a nose-dive. "You're leaving Wentworth?"

"They treat us like shit here. Come on, you know what I'm saying. This place is a joke... it's worse than high school."

"Whoa... you're really leaving? Well, that's cool... I guess," I say under my breath, without meaning it.

After a moment of silence, I spring back, hit with an epiphany. "So what if you drop out! You don't have to leave Boston, do you? Stay in town! Get a job! We move into Lycos' building and run the place together. Robert, this is such a sweet deal, we can't pass this up. Live rent-free!"

"And free telephone," adds smiley-face Andreus.

"Hey, Robert, you might have a little fun being around all those naked women. Maybe you can add them to other free shit you'll be scoring." Larry laughs, "If I didn't have Paula and Sally, I just might think twice about it."

"Come on, Robert, why not?"

The table becomes quiet, waiting for an answer. Van Helden strokes his chin and narrows his eyes, "Okay, Jonny," he gives his head a halfhearted nod, "Why not."

4
POOOFFF!

On the night of the move, Lykos instructs Andreus to bring Van Helden and me to the building early, since it is Monday evening he is fairly certain his tenants will be home, and this way Andreus can make the essential introductions, but more importantly, we will witness the rent collection business first hand. Robert and I are to tag along with Andreus and check out his style for hitting on the deadbeats.

Neither Van Helden nor I have any possessions to speak of other than clothes, toilet accessories, and my schoolbooks, which makes moving a simple affair. We rendezvous with Andreus, bags in hand, in Park Square, jumping into his red Camero for a quick ride to Tremont Street. Andreus pulls up to the curb in front of our new home. I find the street scene not nearly as insane as Larry made it out to be, either because Monday night means few people are out, or it is too early for anything crazy to be happening. One fact Larry didn't exaggerate is the number and proximity of bars, although I can't tell if any of them are strip joints. I suppose you have to stick your head inside the door and see for yourself.

We stand on the sidewalk holding our bags while Andreus grabs a flashlight from the trunk of his car. "This is it," he says happily, waving the flashlight in an arc above his head, taking in the building above us. I study the featureless, yellow brick façade and fire escape that hangs over the street like a rusty cage, hoping the inside isn't as grubby as the outside. The street level houses a greasy-spoon diner with tables and stools for about twenty-five customers. I look over at Robert, swallowing hard, "Welcome home, my man."

A tiny foyer opens to the street. To gain access to the apartments you enter through a locked storefront and pass down a skinny hallway with soiled yellow walls the color of old bananas. A single fluorescent tube hangs low from the ceiling, buzzing in my ear like an angry bee. There is no stairway; the hallway dead-ends at the elevator. We are informed a staircase found at the back of the building is our alternate route to the upper floors. Recessed on the foyer wall are fifteen locked mailboxes, and next to them, an intercom panel. Andreus acquaints Robert and me with the protocol for guests. The automatic door opening function is on the fritz along with the audio system, but the buzzers sort-of work.

"When a tenant hears their buzzer they must come down the elevator and open the door."

Sounds like a major pain in the ass, especially if you live on the 6th floor where Lykos plans to stick us. "What we got here is essentially a door bell," I say to Andreus. "You guys plan to fix this thing?"

"Of course! Anything broken, we fix."

The three of us squeeze our way into an elevator the size of a phone booth and ascend to the

6th floor to drop off our bags and wait for Lykos. Andreus opens the door to Apartment 6C, snapping on a dull ceiling light, and we all walk inside. The empty room has a scummy film that inhabits the surface of everything; cabinets, walls, ceiling. I can't tell if the color of the linoleum floor is white or gray. Robert and I share the same indifferent look, a counterpoint to the big smile across Andreus's face. Our breath surrounds us in a wreath of fog. "Jesus Christ, you can hang meat in here," I say, blowing into my hands.

"We will go to some of the vacant apartments and find you furniture," Andreus offers. He bends over the radiator and turns the knob until steam begins to hiss into the pipes.

Earlier, we learned that all of the units in the building are furnished studio apartments that rent on a weekly basis. The larger studios, like the one we are standing in, go for thirty five dollars. The smaller units cost five bucks less. Our studio consists of one room, about twenty-five feet deep and fifteen feet wide. A small kitchenette is squirreled off in the corner. Robert walks up to the sink and works the faucets, brown water spills from the spout. A fusty bathroom designed for midgets and smelling like rotten fruit sits behind the wall of the kitchenette.

I survey the room while waiting for Lykos. One window faces into an airshaft about ten feet square. Turning the window crank, I peek into a dark abyss; the stench of garbage juice blows across my face. A fire escape descending to the bottom actually leads to nowhere; it's like dropping a staircase into a hole in the ground. I walk over to the apartment's other window across the room; this one looks out over a parking lot that could be mistaken for an auto-wrecking yard. The lot borders a dark section of LaGrange Street, a site ripe for a felony to strike.

It isn't long before this oily gentleman in a dark pinstripe suit strides into the room. With one hand in his pant pocket jingling change, he paces back and forth impatiently, as if looking for a way out. I immediately dislike him. Andreus makes the introductions.

"How do you like your apartment?" asks Lykos, without a hint of concern. "It's nice, isn't it? I'm giving you the nicest room in the building. It's the most quiet. You'll see." Lycos continues, "Only half of my units are occupied. The others we'll rent after you get in there and clean up. Don't worry about scrubbing them too good, just sweep the floors and wipe down the kitchen and bathroom."

Lykos pauses for a second and gives Robert and me a stern look of disapproval, like we screwed up already. "Let me tell you about the people here. They like to play tricks with us; sometimes they won't answer the door when you come to collect." He pulls out a golden key of polished brass, turning it between his thumb and forefinger as if he is about to show us a magic trick. "This is your master-key. It opens all the doors in the building. Never, ever misplace it. Never drop it on the floor. Never lend it to anyone. Never leave it out where someone will take it. This key will cost me five thousand dollars to replace if you ever lose it. Guard it with your life. Do you understand me?" Lykos fixes a glare on Van Helden.

"Yessir," Robert pledges obediently.

"Yessir," I echo, as Lykos jumps his eyes into mine.

"If you go to collect the rent and the tenants are playing hide and seek, open up the door and look inside. You'll probably catch them lying in bed. They will always tell you they have no money… come back tomorrow. They'll pretend to cry, hope you'll feel sorry for them. You have to know when they're lying. You guys are college boys. You're smart; you can figure things out. If they start to play games with you, use psychology. Do you understand me?"

"Yessir."

"Yessir."

Lykos says goodbye to his younger brother, and tells us he'll be calling with more instructions as soon as our phone is installed.

"Let's go see about some furniture," Andreus says brightly, slapping his hands together.

We scavenge a few vacant units and drag stuff into our room with no regard for placement, figuring we will decorate later. I do a quick inventory: a mustard-yellow vinyl couch with a pull-out mattress (Robert's bed), a twin bed with a mismatched mattress and box-spring (mine), a black and white pebble Formica table edged with cigarette burns and three beat-up wooden chairs (our dining set), two orange plastic end tables that look as if they came from George Jetson's yard sale, two porcelain lamps etched with a Chinese dragon motif, and a wooden dresser painted baby-blue (the completion of our bedroom ensemble).

Moving in essentially complete, Andreus motions us to follow him down to the basement to begin our orientation. We go out to the street and walk back into the building through the diner. After a brief intro to the cook and the monkeys washing pots and pans in the back room we descend a wooden staircase into a dank dungeon; the building's cellar. Andreus flicks on his flashlight to light our path. A veil of cobwebs snags my face. At the bottom of the stairs our tour guide pulls a string hanging from a single bare bulb fastened to an open beam. We continue into the bowels of the building, the light behind my back cast our silhouettes across a sooty concrete floor and onto a forged-iron boiler that bathes my face in glowing heat.

"You should never have to come down here, but it's important you know how everything works," says Andreus, seriously. "This switch is for the boiler. This panel controls all the electricity. This valve turns off the water."… and so on, and so on.

Climbing out of the basement, we dust off our hair and soon find ourselves upstairs meeting our new neighbors. Our first stop is Apartment 2A, inhabited by a dumpy, affable character named Raymond who, we learn, works as a waiter at the Park Plaza Hotel, and never misses a rent payment. We exchange pleasantries and are having a nice chat when a very large black man enters the corridor from the elevator and walks straight up to Andreus like he is gunning for him.

"Where's my fuckin' heat, man!?" He presses his nose up against the Greek's.

"It's not working?" Andreus acts surprised. Not backing away an inch or blinking an eye, he says, "You owe me for last week. Last week you had heat."

I feel uneasy watching these two big men square off, each holding their ground.

"Listen, man! You don't get a dime until I get my heat."

"Tomorrow, I will send over a mechanic. Turn

your oven on tonight and open the door. That will warm things up till he gets here. Barry, I want you to meet the new building superintendents, Jonny and Robert. They moved in to Apartment 6C." Andreus speaks amiably, trying to steer the conversation in a more friendly direction. Robert and I both have pathetic smiles on our faces.

"My oven? Warm things up!? What the fuck do you think I'm doing up there…baking motherfuck'n muffins?" He snaps his eyes over at Robert and me, "Hi!" Barry extends a large hand for us to shake. "I'll be looking for that mechanic tomorrow, Andreus. Make sure he comes!" He points at us and backpedals towards the elevator.

We say goodbye to Raymond and walk to the end of the hall to 2C.

"The guy who lives here drives a taxi all night. It's hard to catch him home. His name's John Delmonti. He owes me for three weeks." Andreus knocks twice, waits half a second, takes out the master-key and opens the door. We stick our heads inside and scan the dark room. No cab driver. Andreus shuts the door and we head up to the next floor. "Mr. Delmonti must pay this week. You will have to speak with him."

The next door we knock on, Apartment 3A, opens to reveal a bizarre family of sorts; two sisters in their late teens, introduced as Robin and Penny, purr lasciviously at me and Robert as a couple of snappy dressers in their early twenties, look on apparently amused. I'm immediately puzzled by the dynamics of this arrangement. One of them, Byron, presented as Penny's husband, has a black tuxedo jacket draped open to reveal his naked chest. A long saffron scarf wrapped loose around his neck hides little of his pink flesh. The other guy, a willowy character with a funny chimpanzee face and ears that protrude out from his head like large clam shells, is rocking back and forth on the balls of his feet. He's wearing leather pants as tight as stove pipe. "Hi, I'm Jamie," he says, greeting us warmly, holding out a boney hand, his monkey eyes glued on Van Helden. "So, you're our new supers… *Super.*"

Robin giggles.

Andreus approaches Byron and discusses payment. Byron, obviously the patriarch of the group, forks over the rent while Andreus scratches out a receipt. Penny complains about their toilet backing up. Andreus says they mustn't be throwing things into the pot that don't belong there.

Robin giggles some more.

Working our way back up to the sixth floor, we stop here and there for dollars and introductions before finally making it back to our door. Andreus hands over his receipt book and directs us to keep records of all transactions. Never take money without giving a receipt, he admonishes. He says goodbye and wishes us good luck before disappearing into the elevator, and in a few seconds he's gone, instantly the place becomes eerily quiet. Robert and I face each other and smile wanly. We turn to our room and confront our collection of junk yard furniture. My feelings are bouncing between panic and fortitude. This could be a bad ride, but I plan to make the best of it.

Robert sets his radio on the kitchen counter and dials up the cream de la cream of the airwaves, WBCN. Andreus provided cleansers, rags, a mop and a broom for keeping the building squeaky clean. We get busy putting the products to use, spending the next couple of hours rocking out, cleaning house and organizing our stuff.

After a long, exhausting night, we flop down on the couch, thoroughly spent. Van Helden pulls out a smoke and tips the pack towards me.

"Sure," I say, lighting up and stretching out my legs. "You know what we need here?" I point to the air in front of us, "A coffee table. Where the hell are we supposed to put our feet? They belong up on a coffee table."

Ferocious pounding comes from our door sounding as if a large fist is about to punch its way through. I look into Robert's startled face, "What the fuck?" Van Helden and I approach the door like it is about to explode. I open it cautiously. Confronting us are the tenants we met over the past few hours, now a riotous crowd. The large black man, Barry, is standing in front of the pack; obviously the one who "knocked". A cacophony of loud complaints come raining down on us at once, "Fix my heat, man!" "My toilet's backed up, do somethin'! Get me a plumber!" "Fix the intercom!" "The elevator door sticks... fix it!" "My window won't shut... fix it!" "Where's that mechanic!?" "FIXIT FIXIT FIXIT!!!"

I spread my arms out straight like Merlin from Fantasia stopping the onrushing flood and wave an imaginary wand in the air over the crowd as if casting a spell.

"POOOFFF! It's all okay! Nothing is broken... everything is working again! Go back to your rooms!"

Six pairs of confused eyes stare back at me in silence. I send them away with a sweeping gesture of my hand and close the door.

"What'd you just do, man?"
"Psychology," I smile.

The lights snap off a few minutes before 1:00.
"How's your bed, Robert?" I ask through the darkness.
"It ain't too bad… it smells a little, though. How's yours?"
"I don't know… I'm so beat, I could sleep on rocks."
"I'm hip. You think we did the right thing, man?"
"What do you mean?"
"You know… coming here. I'm a little freaked."
"Yeah… me, too."

It's been a while since the last time I prayed before climbing into bed. Tonight, before drifting off to sleep, I ask God to keep an eye on us.

5

The Mod Squad

The Saxon Theater sits across the street from our building. Some art-flick about a dancing hooker and her dumb boyfriend is playing tonight. I thought I would check it out. A few feet into the street, I slow my step and pause to consider the intentions of a shadowy, black man standing in front of the theater's entrance. He's wearing a spectacular outfit in a striking shade of red, as clean and shiny as a licked cherry lollypop. Marquee spotlights beaming above his head bounce off his suit like light striking a faceted ruby. I nervously approach the foyer praying he won't kill me, pausing just outside his range.

Blackcherry Man turns to his right, grabs the handle, and swings open the door.

"Thank you," I nod.

"You're welcome."

During the day I feel safe in our little section of Boston. It seems no different from most areas of the city. But evenings are another matter. The occasional women I encounter look like walking pornography, as distant and untouchable as pictures in a men's magazine. Police cruisers roll by every few minutes staring at us like we're convicts in a prison yard, and the Navy's Shore Patrol march up and down the sidewalks on a regular basis, traveling in pairs, slapping nightsticks into their hands. Even with all this heat, trouble still finds a way to creep into the scene. Last week a college student was stabbed in the chest less than one hundred feet from my front door. I don't wander much.

We spruced up several of the vacant apartments, making them decent enough to rent. Lykos advertises whenever one becomes available. He called to remind Van Helden and me we still have the business of our delinquent cabbie, John Delmonti, to deal with. We seem to run in different time zones. Since moving into the building we continually fail to make his acquaintance. Delmonti is now over five weeks past due. We've been down to his room several times leaving notes pinned to his door, but he just blows us off. Lykos suggested using 'psychology' on the guy.

"You're college boys. You're smarter than he is... Use your heads." Lykos is looking at us like we completely missed the boat. "If you can't get in touch with him, let him get in touch with you. Do your job. Go inside Delmonti's room, remove something valuable he's sure to miss. Write a note; tell him he's seriously behind in the rent and he must come to see you. When he shows up, tell him you'll return his things after he pays." Lykos makes it all sound so simple, but I'm not too sure about this shit.

A few days have passed since he instructed us to squeeze Delmonti. "Maybe we boost something small... you know, just get his attention," I cautiously propose.

"It's not like we're stealing... is it?" Robert surmises.

Reluctantly, we make our way down to the cabbie's room. Knocking a couple of times and getting no response, I pull out our passkey and open the door.

"Mr. Delmonti?"

No answer.

We flip on the light and walk inside, shutting the door behind us. Van Helden plops down into a big, cozy La-Z-boy chair that Delmonti has parked in front of a portable TV, as if he was getting ready to watch a show.

"I know what I want," he says, smiling at the blank screen.

I yank the cord from the wall and lift the set off the small table it shares with a few books and magazines. "Here's our new coffee table!" I say, staring at the spot where the TV had been.

Van Helden jumps up from the La-Z-boy, knocks the literature to the floor and grabs it.

I examine more of the cabbie's stuff placed around the room and spot a tinted-glass water bottle in the corner by the bed. It looks as if it could hold five gallons, but it isn't full of water. Instead, it contains about fifty pounds of jing… mostly copper, but a healthy share of silver and nickel as well.

"This must be John's stash from all the cheap tips he brings home. Let's grab it."

Van Helden sits back down and lights a cigarette, waiting as I draft a note to Mr. Delmonti. I simply state we are holding a few things until he can arrange payment. I sign it, "Building Managers – Apt. 6C."

"Let's get out of here," I say, picking up the TV and heading for the door. Van Helden hasn't moved. "Come on, man… let's split!" I say, feeling a bit anxious.

"Jonny, I really love this chair. Check it out." He rises up and motions me to take it for a spin. I slump into the spot and immediately agree, "This is one helluva chair."

We had to make two trips to carry all this loot back to our apartment. The chair couldn't fit into the elevator, so we hauled it up four flights.

Robert and I are lying in our beds with the lights off, catching a little Carson on our new tube. Johnny's guest tonight is that gawky English chick Twiggy, who's yakking about her career in fashion; all the exotic places she's been to and all the bread she makes.

I don't get it, "How the hell did that Bony Maroni ever make it as a model?"

"I wanna do that," says Van Helden.

"You wanna do Twiggy?"

"No… model, you know, be a model. I need a job, right. Why not that?"

"No shit? Where'd this come from?"

"I don't know… I just think I can do it. I got the names of a few places in town that hire models. I'm gonna check it out."

"You know… that sounds pretty cool. You're gonna meet a ton of chicks."

At one o'clock we say goodnight to each other and snap off the TV. I have an early class in the morning and have to be out the door by seven. Van Helden plans to hit the street early, too, giving all the model agencies in town a crack at signing him up.

I'm disoriented, not sure if I should cover my head or jump from my bed. Someone is trying hard to kick down our door, slamming against it with vicious blows. My alarm clock shows 2:15. We step out of bed into the dark. Van Helden yells at whatever evil thing is on the other side, "All right, quit it!" He swings open the door and I squeeze beside him, adjusting my eyes to the blinding glare of the corridor's fluorescent light and the hazy figure of the man.

"LISTEN UP, ASSHOLES!! PUT MY THINGS BACK IN MY ROOM!! PICK UP EVERYTHING YOU TOOK FROM ME AND RETURN IT NOW!! AND NEVER COME INTO MY ROOM AGAIN!!" His big, round crinkled face is inches away from mine; wafting foul breath that reeks of alcohol, and when he yells spittle flies from his mouth into my face. God played a trick on this man and gave him the head of a pit bull. My eyes fight to adjust to the white light of the hallway shining behind the edges of his moon face like the penumbra of a solar eclipse. Never before in my life have I come face to face with such fuming, white-hot rage. But for some odd reason I can't explain, I feel calm. Maybe it's because I'm so tired. I ask in a monotone voice one simple question, "What about the rent?"

"FUCK THE RENT!!!"

"Mr. Delmonti, its 2 a.m. ... we're not going to deal with this now. We'll bring your things back in the morning, and you can give us a check... if that's all right with you?"

"Okay. You put everything back." The cabbie is huffing and puffing through his open mouth. He loosens his fists and turns slowly on his heels, heading for the elevator.

It isn't until we close the door and return to our beds when the adrenaline begins pumping through my veins like a fire hose working a burning building. I feel like we had just diffused a ticking bomb.

"Jesus, he was pretty pissed-off," Van Helden says after a minute of silence.

"Yeah, what an asshole."

Before heading off to class this morning I stop by Apartment 2C to talk with Delmonti. My intentions are to get the money he owes, and after I get home from class we'll give him back his stuff. I knock a few times and wait, figuring he must be one of those guys who are slow crawling out of bed. Maybe he's a heavy sleeper? I give the door a few good whacks. Standing with my hands in my pockets far longer than necessary, I decide to use my passkey and poke my head inside the room.

He ain't home. A note is spread out on his kitchen table addressed to Van Helden and me:

> Building Managers:
> Thank you for returning all my things.
> I will bring you the rent money later tomorrow.

Damn. This is not the arrangement we agreed to last night. I take my Bic from my ammo bag and pen a response:

> Your things will be returned to you immediately upon our receipt of your rental fee.

Sincerely,
The Building Managers

Once a week Andreus and I sit down together in the student union for an official business breakfast; the subject of money is consistently our opening topic. Information concerning new tenants and the condition of the building is passed along as well. This morning's routine is no different. I hand Andreus thirty dollars in cash.

"We rented 3B to this exotic black chick. Her name's Kitty. She's about twenty-five, or maybe thirty; has a French accent. She's pretty fancy looking."

"Does she have a job?"

"I guess… said she dances in some club, acts like she's some kind of big star. I saw some clippings from the newspaper with her picture."

"She's a stripper," Andreus curiously notes, more a statement than a question.

"She's real friendly."

"You got Delmonti's rent?"

"We're working on that. We got the fucker cornered. He's gonna cough up his dough tonight." I feel confident Robert and I have begun to master the management business. We won't have any trouble from our cabbie.

A guest bed has been added to our domain, a smelly, beaten-up army cot Van Helden found inside an empty apartment. I doused it with a cocktail of bleach and Old Spice, punched the stuffing inside the pair of pillows that came with it and propped the ensemble tidy-like up against the wall.

Barry manages to stop by every night filling our little room like a bus backing into a tight parking space. The big dope gets his jollies off freaking us out… like the funny way he knocks. He gives our door a couple of hard whacks, bolts to the opposite end of the corridor and crouches down like Rosey Grier lining up on defense. The moment we swing open the door he explodes off the line tearing head-on into us, not hitting the brakes until he's halfway into our room. So far our reflexes have allowed us to clear out of his way to avoid being knocked comatose. I've asked him to cut this shit out; it's getting on my nerves.

"What happened to my little keychain thingy?" asks Van Helden.

"Barry probably lifted it." I'm quick to charge our obnoxious guest with petty theft whenever something comes up missing. I saw him finger my jackknife from the top of our dresser and fiddle with it during one of his stupid visits about nothing in particular. Jackknife's gone. It either developed legs or it left the room hiding in Barry's pants.

Van Helden and I invited a few tenants and some old friends over for a little house warming party. Robert is dressing for the event, tying a sapphire silk bandana around his neck to accent his creamy-white shirt, tucked in tight. A black leather belt with a silver buckle the size of a license plate holds up his striped bell bottom pants.

Robert had struck up a conversation with a lady he met while waiting inside the lobby at one of the model agencies he was scoping. The girl had said she needed a place to live and he offered the apartment next door to us.

"You're gonna dig this chick, Jonny, she's kinda special. Her name's Sam. I asked her to come tonight."

"She done any modeling?"

"Naa.. she's just checking it out, like me."

"How did that go today?"

"They wanted to see my portfolio."

"What the hell's that?"

"It's a kind of photo album… shows you posing in different moods. I got the names of a few photographers to get it done. I think this thing is gonna cost me like two-hundred bucks."

"Jesus… You don't have to get naked, do you?"

"Naa… I don't think so." Van Helden gets busy hanging a veil of wooden beads in the bathroom doorway. "How's it look?" he asks, combing his fingers through the beaded curtain, making it sway and click musically.

"Nice touch."

Robert steps back to admire the new décor. "Should we invite Barry?"

"Ugh uh, I don't want that thief anywhere near here."

We are interrupted by a hard, lazy knock coming from our door. I walk over and open up, surprised to find Barry paying us a visit like a normal person. He stares down at me with his hands on his hips, like I have done something wrong. The big dope probably had his fat ear pressed against our door listening to me bad mouth him.

"What's up?" I ask, not really caring.

"We need to talk."

I turn and he follows me into the room. We sit down at our table facing each other. I smirk to let him know he has my half-ass attention. "What do you want to talk about?"

He folds his hands together and looks at me with hardened eyes. "You're having a party tonight," he says, more a statement than a question.

"So, what of it?" You're not invited, if that's what this is all about.

He lets out a heavy sigh and continues, "I just left John Delmonti. He knows about your little party, too. John says he's planning on coming. He said it would be a real shame if some of your friends get hurt, because he only wants to mess with you. He showed me the gun he's gonna use to put a bullet in your head."

Robert and I fly through our room grabbing all of John's shit, dragging it back down to his apartment. I thought we might bump into him, but as usual the guy isn't anywhere to be seen. We still have only met him once; the time he made his late-night call. I don't want him to get the wrong idea that we are letting him off the hook just because he plans to shoot us, so I leave behind another note:

> Mr. Delmonti:
> You will find everything back in its proper place. We expect full payment no later than noon tomorrow.
> Sincerely,
> The Building Managers

Our buzzer announces the arrival of out first guest.

"That's Omar!"

Van Helden runs down to the foyer and returns a few minutes later with his hometown buddy at his side. Omar's carrying a small duffel bag over his shoulder, steadying it by the strap with one hand. His other hand holds a guitar case. A handsome smile beams beneath his Poncho Villa mustache; dark, animated eyes scan across the room.

"Nice pit, Robert. You've really come up in the world."

Van Helden hands his friend a pair of long candles, and retrieves two empty wine bottles from the top shelf of our closet. "You can help us set up… Get to work."

The buzzer signals again, one long buzzzzzz followed by a series of short blasts, as if someone is sending out a S.O.S. I jump to the rescue, taking the elevator to the street. Looking as virtuous as Mousketeers, my old high school friends, Jillian, Trisha and Mandy, are frozen together in a tight ball inside my foyer. A pane of glass separates them from two black men standing outside the door, dressed in gold suits brighter than King Tut. The colorful guys appear disinterested in the girls, focused instead on the flashing lights from a pair of police cruisers parked in front of the strip club across the street. A white chick with a troubled face is being escorted into one of the cruisers by two middle-age men in windbreakers, each holding an arm of her fluffy jacket that covers everything but her well-formed legs; blonde curls bounce on her shoulders as she walks. A crowd begins spilling out from the club as a third cruiser rolls by the scene.

The three girls melt apart by the time they reach my room, but before I have the chance to get them comfy our buzzer sounds once more and I beat it back to the street. Charlie is standing in the entry holding a grin, his eyes opened as wide as tennis balls, as if needing an extra large oculus to take it all in.

"Woofa! The trip in the street is right out of Caligula, man!"

Candle light does wonders for our room; the shadows offer intimacy while dimming out the grime. No one bothers with chairs, selecting the floor to get easy. A bottle of wine is being passed around. The three Mousketeers, having dropped their inhibitions, drink like champions. Robert and I have been answering the door every few minutes, ushering tenants into our party. A light knock gets me up off the floor again and I open the door to a mysterious female, her slender frame cocked at a slight angle, placing her weight on one leg, counterbalanced by the hand on her hip. A dark beret fits snug above her forehead, pulling back auburn, short-cropped hair, accentuating oval chestnut eyes which seem to summon a response.

"Yes?" I say.

"Yes?" the lady smirks, giving me a superior look. "Are you sure? I didn't ask my question yet… Maybe the answer is, no."

"I say, yes, a lot" I smile. It's worked for me before. I thought I'd use it again."

"Well… déjà vu, sweetheart."

"Sam!" Van Helden jumps into the doorway between me and our guest. He proudly escorts the pretty lady into the room, introducing the new neighbor to everyone before spreading out beside her on the floor.

The party drifts into the night with Omar and his guitar painting romantic tones inside our dimly lit space. The calming trio of smoke, wine, and music has taken effect. Robin, the daffy chick from downstairs, slides in close to Charlie, her mouth intimate inches away whispering silly giggles into his ear. He puts on a dopey smile as the tip of her tongue rolls into his ear. Robert is swaying lightly to the music as the girl from next door kisses his neck and tenderly rubs her hand over the top of his thigh. Mandy's eyes have taken on that wistful look of too much to drink. I nuzzle up tight beside her and she laces her fingers into my hand.

"We've got to get going," Jillian signals Mandy, patting her leg.

"That's right," Trisha says, standing. Jillian and Trisha grab their coats and head for the door, Mandy slides away from me to join her friends.

I guess you can say our party was a success, since nobody came by to shoot up the place. I volunteer to stand guard as the three girls cross Tremont and head for the trolley. Halfway up the block Mandy parts from her friends and comes back in my direction. She approaches me, I see that wistful look hasn't left her eyes, and places her hands on my shoulders. I open my mouth, thinking I should say something, but before any words come out she plants a warm kiss on my lips.

"I would love to see you again," she whispers into my breath. "Why don't we do it in a couple of weeks?"

The sanctuary of the doughnut shop greets us with a warm, sugary scent. I am thankful for the reprieve from the cold January morning air. After picking up our order we drop into a booth beside the door. Outside our window an old man hobbles beneath a dozen layers of ratty threads, pushing a shopping cart that contains all his worldly possessions, his mouth snapping angrily at an invisible adversary. Perhaps he's arguing with himself, or maybe with God.

"You and Sam were looking pretty tight last night," Omar says to Van Helden. "You gonna see her again?"

"I don't know… Dig it… She dances in that club across the street."

"Yeah?" I blow on my coffee.

Robert takes a slow drag off his butt, the smoke rolls from his mouth, "Sam's a go-go girl. She just turned twenty-two."

"Whoa." I'm mightily impressed by Robert hitting on a chick of her caliber.

High Noon, we have a duel with Delmonti. Omar, Robert and I stand impassively in the lobby waiting for the elevator to drop.

"It's time," Robert taps his watch, nudging my shoulder,

"Yeah," I say, wishing this crap would go away. "Let's get this over with."

We step onto the second floor and warily approach Delmonti's door. Robert knocks a few times. Not getting an answer, he pulls out the passkey and holds it up to my face looking for affirmation. I nod my head for him to proceed. Robert slips the key into the lock and turns the knob, opening the door cautiously.

"Mr. Delmonti? John? Hello?" We inch forward into the cabbie's life, quietly stepping into the middle of the room, shocked to find the place utterly devoid of any sign of life. The only things he left behind are a few coat hangers and some loose trash alongside dust on the floor. He not only split with all his stuff, he took all of Lykos' crap too. This is the ultimate "Fuck You!"

I kick around the trash with the toe of my shoe.

"Shit!" Van Helden spits out. "Jonny, I'll flip you for who makes the call to Lykos."

Folding my arms across my chest I blow out a lungful of air while walking a tight circle in the middle of the room before spinning off toward the corner and kneeling down to sift through the trash. I pick up a crumpled wad of paper and spread it open, discovering a receipt for a pricey sales transaction. Written on it is the name and address of a woman I've never heard of, a Miss Margo Sweeney, listing a street I recognize in the South End. The receipt recorded the sale of a fur coat from Filenes Department Store for four hundred eighty bucks.

"I think I know where to find our cabbie."

I make a call to Lykos and brief him on the situation. He gets all hot when I reach the part about finding the receipt. Lykos is not the least bit interested in reporting the incident to the police… saying something about never seeing a dime taking that route.

"I want my money… and you have to get him to return my furniture. I want this settled," he says in a very business-like manner. Lykos encourages us to beat the bushes for our guy. "You might get lucky and find him with his girlfriend. If not, well… maybe then we'll bring in the police."

Robert and I could care less about collecting this debt; we don't take kindly being lied to. "Let's show that asshole he can't mess with us."

"I'm hip," Robert agrees. "Delmonti's a fat-ass lying snake. I say we get him."

I tuck the receipt inside my shirt pocket and we button up our coats and head off into the cold afternoon walking south in the direction of Miss Sweeney. Omar comes along with us, sharing a little of the excitement felt by Van Helden and me. It takes us thirty minutes to reach Margo's house, an old triple-decker in need of a paint job and new shingles. A trash can is tipped over beside the front walk, dinner pickings for the neighborhood dogs. We strategize on the way up to the front door that it might be wise if Omar makes the initial contact; just in case Delmonti is lurking behind the curtains. He pushes the buzzer, as Robert and I stand discreetly in his shadow.

Two fairly attractive ladies dressed in shorts and tank tops answer the door, one about our age; the other woman looks thirtyish.

"Hello," the older one says politely. "What can I do for you?"

"Hi, we're here to see Margo Sweeney."

"I'm Margo… and who might you be?"

"My name's Omar. These are my partners, Jonny and Robert." Robert and I put on proper smiles and give a little wave. "We would like to speak to you about a friend of yours. Can we come in?"

Margo let us enter, perhaps because we look innocent, or maybe the temperature outside, nearly freezing, is a little hard for her to handle, standing here with the door wide open dressed the way she is.

The living room is warm and homey, bric-a-brac overflowing every available table and shelf – colored glassware, bell jars, ceramic dolls. Flowery prints adorn the walls and needle-point embroidered pillows are scattered around sofas and armchairs draped with lacy white doilies. The room looks like somebody's grandmother went nuts decorating the place.

"We're looking for your friend, John Delmonti," I say, in a matter-of-fact tone of voice.

"I don't know the man," she replies, flatly.

"Miss Sweeny, are you sure you don't know Mr. Delmonti? A crazy looking dude about my height… face like a pit bull, kind of smells, goes bat-shit when he's pissed-off. Think again. Do you know this man?"

"No, I don't. I never heard of the person you described."

"Did you recently receive a gift of a fur coat?" I ask.

"Who are you guys?"

I pull the ace of spades out of my pocket and slip it in front of her face. "How do you explain your name and address on this receipt found in Mr. Delmonti's apartment?"

"Are you with the police?" the younger woman asks after standing on the sidelines quiet the whole time.

"We're the Mod Squad, Mam," I reply in a dead-pan voice, sounding like Joe Friday.

"The what?"

"Just kidding, we're rent collectors. Delmonti skipped out on a bill he owes us."

"Yeah?… All right, I know who he is," Margo fesses up. "But I wouldn't call him a friend. He never comes around here, and to be honest, I don't expect to ever see him again."

"Why's that?" asks Robert.

"Listen boys, that's none of your business. I'm not going to say anything else to you about that guy. But let me give you some sound advice you should take very serious. Stay away from him. Drop it. Go home."

On our retreat to Tremont Street we talk only about the two attractive women we just met.
"What do you think they do for a living?" I wonder out loud.
"I think they're whores," says Van Helden.
"Maybe they're sisters, or lovers?" Omar speculates, "Or maybe mother and daughter."
"I think Robert's right," I say. "They're hookers, no doubt about it. They just happen to be living in Grandma's house. I wonder if Grandma knows what they do for bread."

6

Home, Home on LaGrange

The elevator is dead. It had been acting funky since the first day we arrived so we aren't surprised it finally bought it. Of course, the tenants hold Van Helden and me accountable for the disruption. A mechanic I phoned made a house call and pronounced the thing unfixable without a new whatamajigger. He says he has to order the part from Kalamazoo, or Timbuktu, or some goddamn place.

"I really don't care where the hell it comes from, just get it here fast."

"It might be quicker just to replace the damn elevator. This fucker's pretty old… heh, heh."

I hate this guy.

Now, the only way into the building, other than scaling the fire escape, is through the back door reached from La Grange Street, passing colonies of rats and trash bins that line the dimly lit parking lot behind our building. This route is particularly risky at night, given the obstacle course of parked cars and garbage cans we have to negotiate, arranged like the blocks inside a crossword puzzle. No telling what kind of nasty characters creep in the shadows waiting to pounce. The back door leads to a dark and narrow flight of stairs that ascend to the second floor. Living on the sixth floor of our building makes going in and out a personal hell. It's gonna get old mighty fast.

I walk into our room and find Van Helden dozing on the couch, stretched out like a corpse. I resurrect him, smacking my books hard on the kitchen table with a metallic thwack.

"Jonny?" Robert slowly folds his frame into a seated position and reaches for a cigarette. "I didn't hear you come in. What time is it?"

I sit down beside Robert and pull a smoke from his pack, sharing his match. "Hard day, man?"

"I've been dragging my ass in and out of buildings all day… I only got in to see two people. This modeling shit is a lot harder than I thought." Van Helden's tone is dragged and tired.

"Did they ask to see your portfolio?" I question him, knowing he lacks this important detail.

"Yeah… I had some pictures made, but when I showed them, they looked at me and laughed." Robert walks over to the dresser and opens the bottom drawer, retrieving a small envelope. He returns to the couch slapping the envelope in his hand, extracting its contents; two small one inch wide strips of black and white photos about six inches long. Each strip contains four distinct portraits of Van Helden; various side and front profiles, some smiling, a few with indifferent expressions, one smoking a cigarette. The photos come from a department store picture-booth where you drop in a quarter and close the curtain. Van Helden's entire portfolio cost him a grand total of fifty cents.

"Hey, these look pretty good!" I have to admit. "But maybe they want to see what the bottom of you looks like."

"I'm hungry... let's go do some chow." I'm not feeling up to frying something on the stove.

Van Helden opens his wallet, spreads the billfold and peeks inside. "I only got a buck," he says, smiling wanly.

"I got a few dollars. Let's hit Dirty John's; my treat."

Two weeks ago, Van Helden and I discovered a hotdog shop around the corner from our building, a crummy little grease hole with counter-seating for about ten. It is called 'John's', named after the slob that owns the place. John looks like a guy who just suffered a beating; filthy apron, mussed-up hair on top of a puffy face in need of a shave. He could be the poster-boy for the Hepatitis-A campaign. We nicknamed his place Dirty John's. Robert and I consider eating there when we're low on jing. A typical selection of two gnarly dogs chased down with a cup of orange colored sugar-water sets us each back 65 cents.

Ambling into John's little hotdog hovel, we find two open spots at the counter. I look around at the clientele and figure this must be the place where junkies go for fine dining, slap a buck-thirty down and order four franks and two orange sodas. Dirty John pokes our dogs off the grille with a fork and drops them into buns he pulls out of a drawer. We smear on an assortment of condiments and munch through our meal in silence.

Two junkies at the end of the counter are confronting John over his failure to intervene in an attack inside his establishment. It seems a friend of theirs recently was seated at the counter enjoying a meal when a scrappy looking alien stepped into the shop and pulled a longshoreman's hook out from under his jacket. He flung the hook into the gut of their buddy who dropped to the floor in a pool of blood.

"You coulda warned him, Ace. You knew it was coming, why didn't you open your stupid mouth? You're a real peach of a guy."

"I taught he came in ta talk. How was I suppose ta know he was gonna do somethin' like dat?" John shrugs his shoulders.

"Fuck you, Ace! Screw you!" they say in unison, spitting the words in Dirty John's face as they turn to leave.

We eat a little faster and leave without dropping a tip. On the sidewalk headed home I look over at Robert, "I don't know what I like more about that place; the gourmet chow or the stimulating conversation."

"It's a toss up," Robert says, picking a bit of dog out of his teeth with his little finger. "I'm not ready to head back. I think I need a walk around the park to clear my head. I gotta lot of shit on my mind."

"You wanna talk about it?"

"Naa, I'm okay. I just need to think about what I'm doing here… that's all."

"I got some studying to do," I say, not knowing how to respond. "Hey, here's thirty-five cents… could you pick up some smokes?"

I thank Robert as he takes my change and watch him head off in the direction of the Common.

Engineering books spill out across the kitchen table as disorganized as my mind. I'm having trouble focusing, worrying about the possibility of Robert leaving. His fashion bubble has burst in his good-looking face. I guess that must be pretty hard to take. Maybe he's thinks living here is not such a sweet deal after all. I hope he doesn't cash out, I can't see myself running this place alone.

Van Helden had been out for less than an hour when he walks into the apartment and slams the door hard behind him causing me to snap my head up from my books.

"I was robbed!"

"You're shit'n me'!?" This is stunning news; given the fact he has nothing for a thief to take.

"I was coming around the corner on La Grange and out of nowhere this guy walks up, pulls a knife and pushes me up against the wall. I opened my wallet and laughed… He took my buck."

"Shit, Robert, you all right?"

"Yeah, I'm okay." Van Helden is acting as if it's no big deal to be mugged at the point of a knife.

"Ya got the cigarettes?"

For the remainder of the night we roam around our room saying very little to each other. I try to keep everything positive, best not to give his troubles any juice.

Earsplitting sirens are wailing outside our window. Robert and I jump out of bed and run to investigate. In the alley across LaGrange Street an automobile is completely engulfed in a ball of flames, the bonfire topping out at our neighbor's second story window. We climb out on our fire escape to watch it burn, staring through the dark winter night at a distance far enough not to feel threatened, but close enough to feel the heat. The car is toast, fire engines arrive too late to do any good.

"Weird, I didn't know steel could burn that fast," says Robert.

"Maybe someone doused it with gasoline."

On my way out this morning, I examine the contents of last night's lightshow, walking by the scene, sniffing the charred remains of the gutted metal carcass. My nostrils fill with a dank, sharp mixture of carbon and caramelized rubber.

I meet up with Andreus inside the Student Union and tell him about Van Helden getting mugged and the burnt car.

"That neighborhood can be dangerous," says Andreus.

"Thanks for pointing that out." I hand him a pile of cash. "We had a good weekend… rented two apartments. A pretty white chick took Delmonti's old room. Her name is Karen… very quiet, nicely dressed, mid twenties. Apartment 5A went to a chick named Pamela… she's white, too, tall, good-looking, seems real street-wise."

"What's that, street-wise?" asks Andreus.

"She looks capable of handling herself… you know? Tough, as opposed to the girl in 2C, who looks like she could use a body guard."

"What do these girls do?"

"I don't know. Am I supposed to ask? Karen looks like she could be a schoolteacher, or maybe a secretary. Pamela, who knows? She said she likes the building's location… says she works in the neighborhood. Maybe she's a bartender, but that's only a guess.

Andreus taps his watch in my face; English Literature starts in ten minutes. I have one last piece of serious business to discuss. "You gotta move faster on our elevator. It's a real drag coming in through the back door."

Andreus waves me off. "It will be fixed."

"Where's Robin?" asks Charlie. He shuffles in from the hallway and drops his frame on our couch. "She's not in her apartment."

"How would I know? She's probably out wandering Neptune."

"I'm thinking about asking her over to my place," Charlie announces, sounding rather tentative.

"Why you wanna do that?" I ask. "That chick's a Looney Tune."

Our conversation is interrupted when Van Helden marches in with a pleasurable beam in his eyes. "I got a job!" His voice rings out through the room like a church bell.

I whistle a cheer!

"Where you working?" asks Charlie.

"Robert is going to be a model," I answer proudly for him.

"I gave up on that shit, Jonny. That business is full of fags. I got a job at Filenes. They're making me an assistant designer for their store windows."

"Woofa!" howls Charlie. "Department store windows, man, that trip is crawling with queers."

"You kidding me?"

"Robbieboy," Charlie laughs, "you just jumped from the frying pan into the fire!"

There is a knock at our door. Byron from Apartment 3A marches into the room, heading directly for our back window that overlooks the parking lot. He leans over huffing, placing both hands flat on the windowsill.

"Christ Almighty! All these stairs I have to climb to see you boys! I feel like Hannibal. When are you ever going to fix that elevator?" he asks, gulping exaggerated breaths while gazing out at the parking lot below. "I *love* your view."

"What can we do you for, Byron?" I ask, trying hard to be polite.

"I don't need anything from you, thank you very much. I'm here to inform you boys we're leaving next week, so our marvelous little home will be available for Lykos to peddle to some other gullible chump, or chumpette, be that as it may," he says, still gazing out the window.

"Robin leaving, too?" asks Charlie.

"*Yesss… and Toto, too*."

"Thanks for telling us. Clean up your shit before ya leave."

"We'll make it sparkle." He turns on his heels to face us. "Jamie saw you straightening up inside 5B. The last tenant who lived there died in that bathroom. I bet you didn't know that. It was simply *horrid*," he makes a face like he just ate a worm.

"I never heard that," I confess.

"Me neither," Robert says, sounding interested.

"It was a heart attack. His name was Humphrey… I don't know if that was his first name or his last." Byron goes on, "Humphrey was as big as an elephant, and he smoked like a saloon full of sailors. I wasn't surprised when he dropped dead. He probably ate all the wrong foods. He was *such* a mess."

"When did this happen?" I ask.

"Three or four months ago… Does it still reek in there?"

"We didn't notice anything different from what most of the rooms here smell like," says Robert.

"He was in there for days before the stink started leaking into the hallway. It was *putrid*. Someone called the police to complain…it *wasn't* me," says Byron, placing one hand on his chest and fanning his face with the other. "I never went near that stinky man. They couldn't swing the door open to get him out," he continues, chuckling. "It seems he fell off the toilet, and his fat ass got stuck between the bowl and the door. They had to use a chainsaw to cut open the door to drag him out. It was *such* a spectacle."

"I'm sorry we missed it," I say.

He turns to leave. "Oh, don't get up, please. I'll see myself out."

"Me too," says Charlie. "Maybe I'll say goodbye to Robin."

"What's that?" I lift my face and spit toothpaste into the bathroom sink. A loud crackle is coming from outside. I hear it again, sounds like somebody's playing with back yard fireworks. Van Helden is busy metamorphosizing the pull-out couch. He drops his mattress frame to the floor with a loud bang and races to the window.

"Jonny, get over here!

Van Helden is pointing to a guy on La Grange Street, firing a gun, using a Buick as a screen. We stand side-by-side in our underwear peering into a dark scene of sparsely illuminated pockets of sidewalk and cars, the view limited by the few functioning streetlights. More shots fill the air, but the guy we have our eyes glued on didn't fire them.

"Look up there!" I say, aiming my toothbrush at flashes of light in the direction of Washington Street. Another gun, perhaps two, began shooting further up the block; apparently blasting away at our boy behind the car. He is bobbing his head up and down above the hood; snapping off shots the way I did as a kid, hiding behind the living room sofa playing cowboys and Indians with my brother. The guns up the street return fire, raining bullets down on the car.

All is quiet for several seconds; nobody's moving. It seems our guy behind the car has vanished.

"You see anything?"

"There he goes!" Van Helden points to the figure of a man sprinting in the opposite direction of the fight; his retreat followed by the crack of a gun. The impact of the bullet to the back buckles the runner's knees and drops him face down in the middle of the street.

"Holy shit," Van Helden breathes out the words, soft as a prayer.

Two figures emerge guardedly from the shadows, white guys in windbreakers, guns in hand fixed on their lifeless target. Within minutes, a crowd materializes through the dark edges of light surrounding the body; I recognize a few of my tenants. Police cruisers and ambulances converge on the scene, lighting up our little street like a Saturday Night carnival.

I can't sleep. I've been lying in bed all night stirred by the sounds of the city. Van Helden is tossing under his covers like laundry in a dryer.

"Robert?"

"Yeah?"

"We gotta get that elevator fixed."

7
Flick my Zippo

Before leaving home last summer I had walked into Ellsworth Drugstore to buy a few provisions. My mother thought it wise to make myself a first aid kit for college. I remember the conversation with my pal Paul Peters who works behind the counter as a part-time clerk. He was decked out like a junior pharmacist, wearing one of those white high-collar shirts worn by druggists, barbers, and the Dave Clark Five.

"Paulie, where you keep your band-aids?"

"Straight down on your right."

"Where's your aspirin, Paulie? I also need mercurochrome, a bottle of pHisoHex and some Vicks."

Paul dropped my medicinal gear into a paper bag and wished me well. "Stay in touch, Jonny. Let me know if there's ever anything I can ever do for you down here."

"Actually, there is something else I can use," I whispered, looking over my shoulder. I leaned forward to cut off any eavesdroppers. "Could you get me a box of rubbers?"

"I think I can take care of that for you, brother," Paulie magnanimously smiled, "What kind you looking for?"

Jesus, I nervously calculated my size in relation to the rest of mankind. "Oh, I don't know… large, I guess?"

"No asshole, I don't want to know how big your dick is… what brand you want? You know, Trojans, Sheik?"

"Trojans… that's what I normally use," I said, not fooling him for a second.

"All right big guy, but I can't deal with it now. After you get settled in Boston, drop me a line and let me know where to send them."

The package arrived today. I am immediately surprised by its size, easily as big as a shoebox. Paulie must have sent me a lifetime supply! I run with the box up the stairs to my room, sit on the edge of my bed and rip off the butcher-paper wrapping, which did indeed conceal a shoebox, from Tom McCann's, flip off the lid and grab hold of the contents, again more wrapping, this time with tissue paper, which I rip off and toss to the floor. I stare down at Paulie's joke, a pair of black rubbers; rainwear that your father slips over his wingtips to protect the shine. I feel like a kid holding on to a popped balloon.

Paulie, you bastard, you're one funny fuck. I throw the rubbers to the floor, pissed off I didn't get my Trojans, but at the same time appreciate his sense of humor. Looking down at the black rubber slip-ons, I pick one up to try it on for size. Slipping it over my shoe, I feel an obstruction in the toe and pull it off my foot for closer inspection. There, wedged deep down in the recess of the rubber toe is my box of Trojans along with a note, "Wear them in good health!"

Boston's February disposition has been a balmy breeze, and I'm counting on it to stay this way while Mandy is visiting this weekend. The notion of putting Paulie's gift into service has dominated my thoughts since she agreed to sleep with me. At least I think we'll be sleeping together; why else would she want to spend the night? We're not in high school any more. When a college girl asks a college boy if she can sleep over it can only mean one thing, right? But, maybe I'm reading this all wrong. Maybe she's thinking something else entirely, completely innocent, like she's coming here to shop. After all, Mandy Carpino is a proper young lady, entangled by the same Catholic roots that got me by the balls.

    We arranged to meet at the fountain outside the Park Street subway station at eight o'clock this evening. I'm across the street from her, waiting for a breech in the traffic; she looks helpless standing alone with her tiny suitcase at her feet. Mandy spots me and waves. After a tender welcoming kiss, we walk the few blocks down to my apartment. On our approach to the rear entrance we bump into a pair of glamorous ladies on their way out for the evening, dressed provocatively in white faux-fur jackets with nothing else showing but their shiny vinyl calf-high boots cut tight to their long, shapely legs. I immediately recognize Kitty from Apartment 3B. She and her girlfriend share look-alike Barbie Doll bodies. They both have on luminescent scarlet lipstick, deep blue eye shadow, and thick, piled-high hairdos with big Shirley Temple curls. Other than the fact one girl has ebony skin and raven hair, and the other being pasty-white and platinum blonde… they look identical.

Kitty grabs me by my arm and pulls me close to her and her friend, "Come here, Child!" She exclaims with unabashed pleasure, "Julie, this is our Super. Didn't I tell you he was cute," she coos with a lilt of French in her speech. Bright sunbeam eyes and a killer smile blend with her animated voice like a recipe for sweet sugar pie.

"Hi, I... um, pleased to meet you."

"Julie needs an apartment. You go find her a nice room in our building. You can do that, can't you Child?" asks Kitty, hugging me close.

"We, ugh, have one next to yours available, um, next week. I probably can show it to you sooner than that, uh, if you'd like to see it," I stammer, staring into Julie's long, dark lashes, gripped tight to Kitty's fur jacket, miserably feigning attentiveness to Mandy. Julie smiles at me radiantly, "Next week would be just fine."

I step back to rejoin Mandy. She appears painfully incongruent standing beside these two tall beauties in her plaid skirt, dark knee-high socks and navy-blue P-coat.

"This is Mandy," I say, addressing the two women. "She's a friend of mine from high school."

The girls all smile hello to one another.

"I'll come up to see you next week," Julie winks as she turns away with Kitty. The Barbie twins go on their way off to work, I assume, in the direction of Washington Street.

"Nice friends you have here," Mandy says good-naturedly, laughing as she turns into my building. I stand still, suddenly lost in thought. "Are you okay?" Mandy asks.

"What?" I can't admit it, but I feel a power-rush creeping up inside me, radiating from knowing I am part of the life of those two women. For the first time since moving into this neighborhood I feel exclusive, unique, and I love it!

"You look a little funny. Are you okay?"

"Sure… I'm cool."

Rounding the first flight of stairs, we pass Raymond in Apartment 2A. My dumpy little tenant's job as a waiter is weeknights only; he's home alone most days and weekends. He likes to leave his door wide open as a friendly invitation for his neighbors to stop and chat. Nothing and nobody can pass by Raymond's door without him knowing about it. He considers the hallway his domain, his equivalent to a front porch. Aside from Robert and me, Raymond's the only person in the building with a telephone, and he has no problem letting his neighbors use it; considering it an honor to be of service. It gives him the opportunity to act as host, thinking the callers have come to visit him, not his stupid phone. He installed a lock on the dialer and wears the key around his neck. Anyone making a call places it under the annoyance of Raymond's snoopy nose. He makes it a point not only to know where the call is going, but also why you're making it. One important phone-rule agreed to by all is Raymond never takes messages. He's leaning against his doorjamb smoking. "Hi, Jonny! How are you tonight?"

"Pretty damn okay, what's shakin', Ray?"

"I think I'll be going out for a walk later. I need to stretch my legs."

"Raymond, this is Mandy."

Raymond flashes a salacious smile, bowing his head slightly, gently shaking her hand, "I'm very pleased to meet you. Care to join me for a little drink?" he asks, his voice buttery, directing us to follow his fat ass, like a head waiter leading guests to their table.

"We're gonna pass."

"Well… please stop by again when you have more time to visit."

At the third floor I notice Barry's apartment door is wide open. I try to speed on by but Barry catches sight of us turning the corner.

"Come in here!" he shouts out, flagging me down. I reach over and take Mandy by the hand and walk into his room. Barry is not a big advocate of light. His place never has more than 20 watts burning at once. The room is as dark as a cave.

"What's up?"

"You know that girl you rented to last week in 2C, what's her name… Kathy? Karen?

"Karen."

"Yeah… Karen. She's turning tricks in her room."

"No shit? I don't believe it." Karen is much too sweet-looking to do anything like that.

"Believe it. And that other chick in 5A you just rented to, she's a whore too."

"How do you know this?"

"I just know it. I see them bringing in Johns. It's all business-like. Old fuckers. Ain't no way these guys are boyfriends."

"Jonny, this sounds exciting," says Mandy, squeezing my hand.

"Who are you?" asks Barry, looking down suspiciously at my girlfriend.

We leave Barry and continue to the top floor. I told him we will keep an eye on the girls and try to catch them in the act, although I'm not sure what we'll do about it if we did. Reaching my floor, we pass Sam leaving her apartment.

"Hey, Jon, want to do a little smoke," Sam smiles wickedly.

"You bet! Come on in."

The two women check each other out, exchanging curt hellos. They had met before at the party Robert and I threw a couple of weeks ago. I motion for them to sit down on the couch while I flip on the radio and pull up a chair. Sam reaches inside the small velvet bag she carries around… it's more of a pouch than a purse, and pulls out a joint. She holds it to her lips and looks my way. Pausing for a second, I get the hint, reach over and flick my Zippo, steadying it beneath the number while she breathes in the smoke. Sam holds it out for Mandy to sample, which she kindly refuses. I take a few hits and hand it back, coughing out my words, "That's enough for me."

Sam pats my leg and laughs, dropping the roach in the ashtray beside the radio along with another fresh number. She stands up and lets herself out, walking from the room with a dizzy smile on her face.

"Sit here, Jonny," says Mandy. Eyeing the spot beside her on the couch, I eagerly slide into a make-out position. I want to jump on top of her, but keep my cool and move in casually.

"You like Sam, don't you?"

"Of course! What's not to like?" Mandy looks down into her lap. Maybe my answer sounded a little too personal. Quickly correcting course, I add, "I think she likes Robert."

"You're smoking a lot of marijuana now, huh, Jonny?"

Sometimes I do, sometimes I don't. I can take it or leave it," I lie, feeling a little intimidated by the question. I need to change the course of this conversation. As I'm about to put my arm around Mandy the door swings open and in pops Van Helden with his arms wrapped around two bags of groceries. Robert amiably chats with us on his way toward the kitchen. He drops provisions on the counter, pulls out a bag of Hershey's Kisses and makes himself comfortable beside us on the couch.

"Kiss?" asks Robert, motioning his open bag of chocolate into Mandy's face.

"Maybe later," she smiles.

"Where did we get the grass?" Robert eyes the numbers in the ashtray and plops a chocolate into his mouth.

"Sam left us a present."

"Far out!" Grinning, he lifts my Zippo and pokes the joint between his lips, "I love that lady," says Robert, holding his breath, sputtering out terse, smoky words. "She's decent."

"That's just what I said to Mandy a minute ago. Robert, I heard some shit tonight about Pam and Karen. Barry says they're whores, bringing in guys off the street."

"He's an asshole."

"Maybe so, but he sounded pretty convincing. I told him we would keep an eye on 'em."

"I'll tell you what…" Robert extinguishes the roach and drops it into his shirt pocket, "You eyeball Karen and I'll check out Pam." Van Helden jumps up, grabs the rent receipt book and heads for the door.

"Where you going?"

"Down to 5A to see Pam. I'm gonna collect some rent," he laughs on his way out the door.

The music from the radio plays on softly. Mandy is talking about some nonsense she's studying at school. I'm finding it hopeless to follow what she's saying. There's a gang of devils inside my head challenging me to make a move on her. The image of us sleeping together has dominated my thoughts since that kiss two weeks ago. I glance over at my bed a few steps away. So close... so far away. Does she even want to do it? Mandy isn't acting like a girl eager to jump into bed, although how would I know what that looks like? She must want to make love to me, right... otherwise, why did she come? Maybe I misread her; she came not as a lover but as a friend. Besides that little kiss we shared at the fountain this evening has not exactly been passionate. I wonder if she's a virgin. I wonder if she knows I'm one. Maybe she's scared? She certainly doesn't look it. I wonder what I look like to her. *OH, SHUT THE FUCK UP!*

I tell my mind to sit down and relax, take a deep breath, trust my instincts to do whatever comes natural. I rise from the couch and turn the music down low, shut off the lights and walk over to the window to lower the blinds, but decide better of it. The blessing of a perfect full moon lifts the darkness from the room and with it, my apprehensions. I step over to my bed and turn down the covers, walk to my closet and reach in and remove a white dress shirt. I return to the couch and lift Mandy up by her hand and escort her to my bed. She sits down on the edge, crosses each leg in turn to remove her knee socks. Mandy looks up at me; her face displays no emotion, as if she's deciding to try a new brand of chewing gum. She moves silently, pulling off her sweater, shaking her head while running fingers through her hair, untangling her wavy blonde locks, standing, unbuttoning her blouse, dropping it to the floor, unzipping her skirt, letting it fall, gently kicking it free. I hold my shirt out to her; an offer she wordlessly accepts, slipping it on. The shirt is much too large; her hands lost inside the sleeves, it looks perfect on her. Mandy reaches behind her back, unfastens the clasp from her bra, shifts her shoulders, little shrugs this way and that, and walks her fingers up through the shirt, pulling the bra free, I catch myself breathing too fast.

Mandy slips between the sheets, waiting for me. I remove my clothes and lay down close to her, easing her body into my arms.

"Hi," I say. I'm sure I am smiling, because I certainly feel happy.

"Hi," she smiles back.

Kissing her gently on the mouth, her eyes, circling her face with soft kisses, coming back to her mouth, kissing passionately, she holds me tighter with each kiss.

I made love to Mandy tonight, and before we fell asleep in each other's arms, I made love to her again. At least that's what I want to believe. When it was over, she crushed my libido with something she had said. I had remembered the Trojans Paulie had sent me; the box remains unopened inside my dresser. I had whispered to Mandy, "It's a little late now, but I should have worn protection."

"Why?' she asked.

"Why?" I repeated her question, confused. "You know why… to keep you from getting pregnant."

"What? Pregnant? How?"

I felt as if a lightning bolt flashed a shot through the window and hit me between the eyes, instantly recognizing the meaning to her question. I hadn't entered her, not once. The whole time I believed my manhood was doing its thing, it was actually stuck somewhere else, someplace safe. But where, I'm not sure? My guess is I landed somewhere below her vagina and above the sheet.

"Oh, forget it… I don't know what I was thinking." I squirmed out a stupid reply.

The morning sun pours into the room. Mandy is lying on her side, turned away from me. I get up from the bed without disturbing her, slip on my pants and walk over to the window. Her head pokes out from under the covers, "Hi handsome, what'cha doing over there?" she asks in a sleepy voice. "Come back to bed."

"Let's get out of here; go get breakfast… I'm starving." I feel squirrelly about last night and feign hunger to get away from the scene of my incompetence. Mandy crawls out of bed in my dress shirt and scoops up her clothes, making a beeline to the bathroom. She looks pretty damn adorable.

Van Helden came back to our room in the middle of the night. He is fast asleep, blowing breezy noises through his mouth. I imagine he spent most of the evening "collecting rent" from Pamela. Robert rolls over in his bed and begins to show signs of life. I walk up to him and quietly ask how he made out last night.

Robert pops open one eye, "I balled her."

"I sort of guessed that. Did you find out if she's turning tricks?"

"It's true. She said it's all very civilized; by appointment only, very careful about who she lets in. I asked if she knew anything about other girls in the building doing it."

"Yeah? What'd she say?"

"She wouldn't say."

"Wouldn't… or couldn't?"

"More like, wouldn't. I think she's bound to some hooker code of honor. Hey! I see you two got it on last night. All right, Jonny!"

"Ssshhh, not so loud. Yeah, we had a nice time together," I say, with a phony smile across my face. "We're headed out for breakfast after I shower up. She's making it back to her dorm this morning."

I'm a dishonest schmuck, stuck in a lie. I want Robert to believe Mandy and I are lovers. Hell, that's what *I* want to believe! Mandy walks out of the bathroom and finds Robert and me yakking together.

"You boys talking about me?"

"Yep," I say, and dart past her into the bathroom. I catch my reflection in the mirror (What are you looking at?) and step inside the shower. The spray of hot water forever feels luxurious to me, no matter what mood I've sunk to. I place my hands against the wall and lean into the hot stream, letting it wrap me in a mist. The meditative effect of the shower brings me back into bed with Mandy. What exactly did happen last night? How could my dick miss the target, is it that difficult to hit? What the fuck's wrong with me?

After breakfast at Ken's in Copley Plaza, I walk Mandy to the trolley and wait beside her until she boards. The goodbye kiss she leaves behind has about half the octane than the hello kiss she came here with. The intimacy we shared last night has vanished; I have this empty feeling inside of me. Mandy had said over breakfast, "Jonny, don't ever change. Promise me?" At first I took this as a compliment, a charming way of saying she likes me. But later this afternoon, back in my room, lying down on my bed recalling the moment, I think she was saying something else entirely. I think she was saying goodbye.

8

Mister Eyeballs

"We rented out a few rooms this weekend." I provide Andreus the details over breakfast in the Student Union while discreetly slipping one hundred dollars in cash into the palm of his hand. Three couples from Baltimore had moved into Apartments 3A, 4C and 5B; one pair dragged along a three-year old girl.

"Are they nice people?"

"I don't know…The guys are in a band; black dudes, flashy. They're playing tonight at the Downtown Lounge."

"What do you mean, flashy?"

"They wear these crazy colored outfits. Have you ever seen Sly and the Family Stone?"

"No."

"Well, anywho, they look like those dudes, only without the Afros. Two guys are brothers, John and Ed Taylor, the third guy is this cool looking dude named Jasper. They're all shacking up with white chicks. One of them, the one with the kid, she's a dancer, well… a stripper, actually. Her name's Julie, she's a friend of Kitty's. She dances at the Normandy. I don't know what the other girls do; they seem kind of quiet."

Andreus leans into me with a salacious grin, "The stripper... nice body, eh?"

"Killer."

"How old?"

"Probably twenty-one, or so."

"Woooouuu." Andreus rubs his hands together like he is about to perform some heavy lifting. "What do the other girls look like?"

"They're okay... nothing special."

I fail to mention Julie's boyfriend, John Taylor, has taken an immediate dislike of me. When moving in Julie said something to him about us being "old friends" and wiggled her fingers at me in a flirty little wave. She was smiling and being nice, so I smiled back and asked the couple if they needed any help. John Taylor stuck his face in mine; it was as cold and hard as frozen meat, except for his upper lip that kind of twisted when he spoke. "We don't need no help from you."

Occasionally, I walk into the building's storefront diner on official Lykos business. Tonight, for the first time, I came as a paying customer. The diner's graying plaster ceiling gives the appearance of a sooty, overcast sky. I chose a seat at the counter. A thin line of an aisle separates me from tables arranged in a single row against a wall covered with travel posters featuring the Grand Canyon, Miami Beach, the Golden Gate Bridge and Yellowstone Park. I guess the owner imagines America the Beautiful might rub off on this place.

Three men work the grille, zipping beside each other like Moe, Larry and Curly, wearing identical dirty white aprons strung over worn out T-shirts. The same barber must attend to their dark, wild clumps of hair. They have matching olive complexions with serious expressions in need of a shave. The three bark at each other like dogs in a fight. I select the "Dollar Ninety-nine Special", meat loaf and gravy over mashed potatoes, tastes like they dumped it out of a can.

A walk around the block might be a good way to work off the lard I ingested. Exiting the diner at a clip, turning the corner onto Stuart Street I bump into a heavy-set black man with a round head like a cannon ball with fuzz on top. I've never seen anything like this guy. By the expression on his face he appears to be suffering some kind of excruciating pain. His hands flail out in front of him, and he's taking pathetic little steps like a man lost in total darkness. His pupils are rolled back into their sockets; eyes bulging out like a pair of ping pong balls. I shove my hand into my pants for some change, pull out two quarters, and place them gently into his open palm.
"Here you go, man… Take care of yourself."
"Thank you, sah," says Mr. Eyeballs, clutching my charity in his fist. I watch the poor man struggle his way down the sidewalk, hands flailing about.
On my return trip around the block, I pass Mr. Eyeballs again. Only this time his eyes look as natural as my own. He has them opened wide; the pain on his face vanished. He appears to be pretty pleased with himself, leaning casually beside the doorway of a liquor store, counting coins he pulled from his pockets with an attentive digit.
My after-dinner walk complete, I retreat to my room and slog through a pile of homework I

should have completed days ago. Distracted by thoughts of Robert and Sam, I close my book and light a Marlboro. They started sleeping together a few days ago, and I'm a little jealous; not so much over Robert seeing Sam... it's more like he's banging all the chicks in the building and I'm still a friggin' virgin! I begin to fantasize about the new girl in 2C. Maybe she really is a hooker... I wonder if she takes her clothes off when she screws? I would love to get to know her. A knock on my door interrupts my reverie.

A clean-cut, well-dressed guy is standing before me with his hands in his pockets; seeming kind of lost, a wary look on his young face.

"What can I do for you?"

"Are you the building manager?"

"Yeah... well, half of one, anyway."

"Excuse me?"

"I'm just joking. My buddy and I run this place. Whaddaya need?"

"I'm looking to rent an apartment. I heard you have a vacancy," he says, nervously.

I wonder how he got inside the building. Who told him we had a vacancy? This kid looks like he doesn't belong here, too vulnerable to be walking alone in this neighborhood at night. Maybe he's running away from something. He's acting a touch desperate. "Do you work around here?" I ask.

"I'm in school," he answers weakly, sounding not too sure of himself. "My name is Aaron Nichols."

Without further qualification, I escort Aaron down to Apartment 5B and introduce him to his new home.

"Is this my bed?" he asks, pointing to the soiled

mattress, sheetless and pillowless. "Is this the only window?" Aaron points to the darkened airshaft. He sticks his head inside the windowless bathroom then quickly closes the door without comment. Aaron makes the place seem more depressing than it actually is, if that's possible. I ask him if he has a blanket for his bed. He doesn't. I offer to lend him one of mine, along with some sheets, until he can buy some. As far as a pillow goes, he is on his own.

"The room is thirty dollars a week, in advance," I say. He follows me back to my apartment, pays in cash, I rip him off a receipt, and he walks off carrying my extra blanket and sheets. I shout to his back going down the stairs, "Come up and see me if you need anything!" and wish him good luck before closing my door. What a lonely son of a bitch. I better check on him later, make sure he's okay.

This hour goes by agonizingly slow as I wade ankle-deep in a murky sea of math. Dismally lost, I decide to give up the struggle, close my books and stretch out on my bed for a little break.

Van Helden pops into the room, "You got any smokes?" he asks, twisting his head around the place in search of cigarettes.

"Over there." I point to the pack on the table. Robert grabs a couple and heads back out the door. "Where you going?"

"I'm sleeping with Sam tonight," he answers, matter-of-factly.

"It's pretty creepy how some folks make a buck around here." I begin to tell Robert about Mr. Eyeballs, but he doesn't hear me, darting from the room on a mission too important to be delayed by idle conversation.

Midnight is fast approaching and I need to get to sleep. I look hopelessly at the pile of homework abandoned on the kitchen table as I walk around the apartment snapping off lights. I'm in bed for what seems less than a minute when a knock at my door stirs me from my drowsy state. I flip on a lamp and grab my pants, stepping into them as I stumble my way to the door, swinging it open. Aaron is standing in front of me with an anxious look in his eyes, cradling my extra blanket and sheets in his arms.

"Hello," I say, surprised to see him. I flash on my earlier thought of checking up on him. "Everything okay?"

"I met a couple of guys downstairs, Jamie and Byron. They told me the last guy to live in my apartment was found dead in the bathroom. Is that true?"

"They said that?" I ask, shaking my head.

"Yes. They said he lay dead in there for days before somebody found him. Was that for real?"

"Well, yeah…sort a. It wasn't nothin' freaky. He was a fat guy who keeled over. He died of natural causes. It's not like somebody whacked him, or something."

Aaron's voice begs, "Can I have my money back, please? I can't stay here."

"Sure," I say, without hesitation. He follows me into the room and I give him back his cash; he gives me back my extra blanket and sheets.

I shut the light and climb back into bed, thinking about how scared Aaron looked. I hope he makes out okay, I sort of like that guy. Shit, he kind of reminds me of me.

9
Karen

Over the past couple of weeks it has become obvious to me Karen is indeed a hooker. I've seen a few of the skuzball clowns she services coming and going from the building, all wearing suits and ties, old enough to be her father; none of them could be under forty. Raymond, across the hall, indirectly provided confirmation when asked who these guys were.

"I know nothing. I see nothing. I hear nothing."

I've been told Raymond plays that line whenever he witnesses felonious activity.

"Hi, Jonny." Karen opens her door wide, greeting me with a magnetic smile.

"How ya doing, Karen?" I return her smile. "Rent time."

She signals with her finger for me to come inside. Karen is wearing a sleeveless ruby-red top tucked into a black miniskirt. My eyes lock on her as she walks over to the bed and lifts her pocketbook off the mattress.

"Let me see," she says, fishing her hand inside the open bag, "thirty-five... right?"

"Ah, yeah." I quietly reply. I am staring at her bare bracelet-bangled arm, exposed above the top of her purse.

I have trouble keeping my cool around Karen; I

get all tongue-tied and nervous whenever I'm near her; for several reasons: Every part of her is physically perfect; soft, brunette curls frame her lovely features. Her full, gorgeous mouth and round saucer blue eyes have just the right touch of makeup… never overdone. The snug fitting skirts she always wears complement her valentine ass. Her beauty is delightfully accentuated by a subtle, dreamy scent… maybe it's her perfume; perhaps her body lotion, she smells like warm honey. Mix this luscious potion with the graceful manner Karen conducts herself, her delicate conversational voice, and the titillating fact that she's a prostitute, and I'm lost in an unbearable struggle to keep my heart from heaving out of my chest. I want her so bad, I don't know what to do with myself.

She hands me three tens and a five.

"Thanks… um, let me write you a receipt." I stumble around my pants and shirt pockets searching for a pen.

Karen places her fingertips gently on my arm. "Forget it. I trust you."

I look up from my pockets, caught in the clutch of her gaze. She smiles into my eyes and I melt on the spot.

After leaving Karen's room, I walk up to the top floor and pace back and forth in the hallway outside my apartment, mumbling to myself, "I'll go down there and talk to her… About what? I don't know… I'll ask her out. What! Like on a date? Sure, why not? Where you gonna take her, to the movies!? That would be stupid. I don't know… maybe we can go for a walk, or how about the Museum? I know! I can take her to hear some jazz! Oh yeah? How you gonna pay for that? You can't even afford the taxi to get you there. Forget it, yoyo, it ain't gonna happen."

Sam's apartment door opens, she pokes her head into the hall. "What are you doing out there? Get in here… you look like you need to relax."

"What?" I ask, a little embarrassed, wondering if she heard my muttering.

"I said… get in here. I won't hurt you."

I walk into the room and sit down beside her at the table. Sam is working a small pile of grass into several smaller piles, tiny manila folders sit nearby; awaiting packaging. She pulls a pack of Zig-Zags from inside her pouch, peels off a sheet and expertly fashions two joints, sticks one behind her ear, the other she lights and passes over.

Before taking a hit, I blurt out, "I think I like Karen."

Sam, trying hard to hold down her smoke, sputters out a raspy cough; little puffs of clouds escape from her lungs. The coughing subsides only to be replaced with a cackley laugh. "What'd you say?"

"Okay, so maybe it's a dumb idea… me and her, but why not? Why can't we make it together?"

She draws another hit, "Several reasons." Sam closes her eyes and holds her breath.

"Name one."

"All right, she's a junkie."

"Okay, that could be a problem… I didn't know that. What else?"

"Two… she's turning tricks to support her old man; he's a junkie, too."

"Is that it?"

"What?" Sam starts to laugh again. "You need more? Okay, her old man also happens to be her pimp. He's a bad dude, Jon… he would fuck the both of you sideways if he ever caught you messin' around."

Sam and I sit chatting for the next hour; talking about our families, friends, and past loves. On the last subject I had little to contribute. She confessed she had had a slight crush on Van Helden, but now simply sees him as a friend.

"Your buddy, Robert, isn't much interested in relationships, is he?"

"I can't answer that. You know, guys don't discuss their personal shit. You chicks love to yak all the time about that shit, don't ya?"

"Yeah, right," Sam sneers, taking a drag from her Camel, blowing smoke into the space between us. "It's all we ever talk about."

As I get up to leave Sam pulls the other joint from behind her ear. "Here you go, for the road." I thank her for the smoke, and the advice.

Sam has a tough way about her, operates like she needs no one but herself, but I think that's only an act. She likes to flash around a sharp edgy side, but I bet that comes from having been dumped on one too many times. I know more about Van Helden's relationship with her than I let on. He told me Sam wanted one, and he made it clear to her he didn't. Sam was hurt, and she's faking it like it was no big deal.

Sam's probably right about keeping away from Karen. I shouldn't get any closer to her than what my fantasies offer. Still, the least I can do is be Karen's friend. She certainly is good to look at… maybe she's fun to be around. I bet she'd jump at the chance to spend a little time together, share some smoke… get to know each other better. Sure she would!

I decide to toss the dice, go downstairs and invite Karen up to my room for a visit. Bolting down four flights to her apartment I round the landing onto the second floor corridor and spot two figures standing in front of the door to 2C, grab the steel banister and freeze. Karen is leading a dark suited middle-aged man into her room. She has a hand on the door, stops and glances up in my direction, catching me standing in the shadows. A blank expression has taken over her face… the smile is gone. Karen looks away, enters her room, closing the door behind her as I back out of the picture.

10

College Boys

Coming home from class I am delightfully surprised to find Van Helden sprawled out on the couch in front of a portable TV.

"Where'd you get this?"

Robert sits up motioning me to park beside him. "My sister brought it from home. Pretty cool, huh."

That's an understatement. With this new acquisition Robert and I, Princes of Privilege, have the singular honor of owning the building's sole television set. We face the black and white screen with sublime expressions, fully engrossed in the exploits of Rocky and Bullwinkle.

"I rented 4B," Van Helden announces during a commercial break. "An old dude moved in with his girlfriend. He looks like a steelworker. His name's Frankie Barlow."

"How old?"

"I don't know… thirty… forty maybe."

"Ecchhum!" Barry is straddling our threshold clearing his thick throat to get our attention. I left our door opened when I arrived earlier, a newfound habit saving us the trouble of getting up every time company stops by, which happens more often than not these days now that most of our rooms are rented. We ignore him. He rolls into the room and leans on the tube.

"Ooouuu, nice," Barry's voice a near whisper, rubbing his big hand across the top of the box.

"Back off! We're trying to watch a program here," I bark.

He moves away slowly, but not before brushing my Zippo off the top of the set. "I love these guys!" Barry laughs, pointing a finger at Peabody and Sherman.

"What's up, Barry?" asks Robert.

"What are you doing about them whores?"

"Whatsamatter… they bothering you?"

"We like those chicks… and they pay the rent."

"All right, so let em stay… it can't hurt. I won't have to leave the building anymore to get balled. You guys want to go for pizza?"

I'm startled by his offer to socialize. We never hang together and this would be a first. Robert passes, but I decide to take him up on it. Maybe I'll get to see another side of this guy I might actually like. I keep an eye on him while I grab my coat; he slips my Zippo into his pants. I hold my hand out in front of his face, "My lighter."

"Oh?" feigning surprise, Barry fishes it out from his pocket, "I spaced out. It looks like mine," he shrugs off his perjury.

We make our way down two flights of stairs, rounding the third floor, Barry points to his door and says he has to grab something important. I follow him into his room. It's so dark in here I wouldn't be surprised if he has bats hanging from the ceiling. Barry sweeps something off the counter into his hand; it makes a tinny clink when he accidentally drops it to the linoleum floor. Picking it up, he opens his wallet and places whatever it is inside.

"Let's go," he says, shoving his billfold into his pants, big white eyes looking at me in the dark.

In the corridor I ask Barry what he had stuck in his pants. He stops, reaches behind his back, and smiling from ear to ear, flips open the billfold.

"Check it out, my man."

"Jesus, where'd you steal that?" My eyes lock on what appears to be a bona-fide Boston Police Department detective's gold shield.

"It's all about who you know," he says.

"No, really, where'd you steal it?"

Barry said he couldn't give up his sources, saying only it cost him fifty bucks. He's lying, but what the fuck. I don't really care where it came from. I know he's a thief… I just want him to admit it.

We round the stair down to the second floor. "You got any grass, Barry?" I'm thinking it won't hurt to get loaded and take the edge off.

"Smoked my last joint a little while ago," he grins back in my face. "Sure is convenient having a pusher in the building."

"A pusher… who's that?" I honestly have no idea who he is talking about.

"Your pretty little neighbor, Sam. Brother, don't you know how she makes her bread?"

I knew Sam sold a little grass from time to time, but I see her as more of a dabbler than a dealer. "Sam's a dancer," I answer flatly.

"Yeah… and I'm a cop," Barry laughs. "I scored twice with her this week; once when I bought some grass, and again last night when I balled her."

"You *balled* Sam! I don't believe you."

"Man, you believe what you want… I don't give a shit."

Senior Pizza is blowing supersonic rock from the jukebox. The place is covered with wall-to-wall freaks and college kids. We get in line and each score a slice and a coke. I tag behind Barry as he searches for a decent table. He finds two chicks sitting alone and asks if we can share the pleasure of their company. They smile and shift their paper plates around to accommodate us. Barry introduces himself and wraps his beefy arm around my shoulder telling everyone in a ten-table radius, "This is Jonny! He's studying architecture at MIT!"

"Really?" the girls both sound very impressed.

"No, not MIT…Wentworth," I screw my face into Barry's in an admonishing glare.

Barry brags on my behalf about what a top student I am. He then volunteers his own academic credentials, telling the girls he's studying psychology at Harvard. He is lying, of course. Barry does indeed commute to Harvard on a daily basis, and he spends a good deal of time in the psych department's laboratories. He cleans rat cages and sweeps and mops the floors. Barry works in the custodial field; but tonight, inside Senior Pizza, he's a psych major attending a prestigious university, proudly wearing his school colors; a sweatshirt with the words HARVARD emblazoned across the chest.

"My name is Leslie," says one… "Hi, I'm Brenda," says the other.

Leslie and Brenda both look to be enjoying themselves. Brenda's dark chocolate hair is cut in long bangs that draw a straight line above the top of her eyes. The rest is pulled back from the crown of her head and braided in a thick, knotty ponytail wrapped in a leather string, dropping in a line that runs halfway down her spine. Leslie has on a wide-brimmed black wool hat with two multi-colored feathers that protrude out sideways from a colorfully beaded hatband; like ears from some psychedelic donkey.

"So… What do you girls do?" asks Barry.

"We work for a medicinal supply company."

"Medicinal supplies? What's that, drug paraphernalia? Jonny, these chicks probably work in a head shop. HA HA HA!" Barry drums his hands on the table, thinking he's quite the comedian. Leslie and Brenda think he is funny, too, and laugh along with him.

"You wouldn't happen to be carrying any of those medicinal supplies with you tonight, would you?" he asks under his breath, stretching his bulky chest across the table to make himself heard.

"If you're wondering if we have anything to smoke, this is your lucky night," Brenda smiles and opens her leather purse wide enough for us to cop a peek; two skinny joints are wedged within the cellophane of her cigarette pack. She closes the purse tight with the drawstring; bright, satisfied smiles shoot across the faces of both girls.

"Sorry to disappoint you ladies, but this is *definitely* not your lucky night," Barry says in a dark tone of deep seriousness. "You're busted!" With an overhand tennis swing, Barry brings his wallet down hard in the center of the table, flips it open to reveal the gold shield.

I choke on my pizza. Barry's stupid act slaps the smiles right off of their stunned faces. Leslie drops her arms straight down tight to her side. She is shivering like she's standing naked in ice water. Brenda buries her face in her hands and starts crying, sadly whispering to herself, "No, no, no."

What's this asshole doing!? "Barry! Tell them you're kidding! He's not a cop!" I reach over and close the wallet.

"Okay, okay" Barry smiles, "I'm just fucking with ya. Nobody's getting busted. I'm joking!"

Leslie voices the general consensus of the table, "YOU FUCKING ASSHOLE!!"

"That was stupid, man. I want to apologize for this idiot," I cock my thumb in the direction of Barry's face.

Leslie and Brenda stare at us with hateful eyes. The vibe coming off the girls' signals it is time to go, so I throw my slice of pizza down onto my plate.

"I'm gonna sky, I lost my appetite. Sorry, again." I slide my chair back and stand beside the table. "It was a pleasure. Maybe we can do this again sometime." My lame attempt at a joke fails to soften the mood.

Barry jumps up, "Yeah, we gotta be going. Nice meeting ya."

I'm not sure if it was Leslie or Brenda that said, "Fuck you," as we head for the exit.

Out on the sidewalk I am moving double-time back up Boylston trying to keep a few lengths ahead of Barry. I can hear him yelling behind me, "Hey! Slow down, dude!"

I keep moving.

"SLOW DOWN!" shouts Barry.

I stop and turn to face him. "What do you want from me, Barry?"

He places his hands on his hips and inhales a lungful of air, "We were on our way to getting balled tonight, and you had to fuck it up."

"What?! Is that what you think?"

"You blew it, man." Barry says, pointing a finger at me. "We had them eating out of our hands, and you had to go and spoil it with all that, 'I'm so sorry' bullshit."

I can't believe what I'm hearing. Barry is not only an idiot; he's also a dangerous idiot. "You like to get your jollies off scaring the shit out of people, don't you? You actually think you could have scored after that shit you pulled back there? You're fucking nuts! Those two girls would rather eat dog puke than spend time with you."

"Fuck you, college boy."

"Fine. Think what you want… I don't give a shit. I'm goin' home… alone." I turn and head back, not waiting to see if Barry is following me.

11

Vietnam Pot Luck Blues

"Hey, Jon-nee, man... what's happening?" the drawl of his words pour out slowly from the phone, as if being emptied from a pot of glue. I recognize the dull, narcoleptic cadence of my old friend's voice. I'm both troubled and elated to hear from him; how long has it been, one year... eighteen months? My ambivalence is to be expected; after all, Donnie is the worst best friend I ever had.

"Where you calling from, Donnie?

"I'm back in the world. I got airmailed here a few days ago. I'm in the hospital, man... dig it... I'm right here in your backyard."

"Did you get shot, or something?"

"I guess you can say that. I picked up a little shrapnel."

I hang up the phone after committing myself to a trip tomorrow morning to the Chelsea Navy Yard a few miles north of Boston.

My old friend, Donnie Pyle, and I grew up on the same street a few houses apart. We've been as tight as brothers since we were five, but as we passed into our senior year of high school the relationship began to unravel. While I looked ahead to college Donnie looked forward to only one thing, shooting up. Donnie's a certified junkie; He will beg, borrow, steal, lie, cheat, crawl, or claw his way to his next hit. After his addiction kicked a hole in his soul it spelled the end of his chances to finish high school with the rest of us. Rather than face the ignoble consequence of repeating his senior year, in January, 1968, Donnie marched into the Marine recruiting station in Hartford, signed on the dotted line, and quicker than you can say "Di di mau" he found himself walking point in rice paddies along the Mekong Delta.

I received two letters from Donnie since he's been gone. The first one came from Boot Camp, Paris Island, North Carolina, telling me how hard it is to be a Marine, "but the good news is, I'm learning to kick ass". The second letter was addressed from Saigon; it said nothing about kicking ass. "Today is day 260. I count backward from 365 until the day I can come home." I knew he wanted to be anywhere but there. I almost felt sorry for him.

I remember when Donnie and I were fourteen; he got himself a .22. I followed him and his rifle into the woods in search of targets; a branch dangling from a tree limb, a tin can perched beside a log, a bee's nest wedged high in the fork of an old pine.

"What do ya want me to hit next?" Donnie grinned.

"Aim at that bird over there, but don't hit it," I pointed to a tiny sparrow about two hundred feet away. "Fire at the ground next to it just to scare it, you know, make it jump."

"How close should I get?"

"Aim right at it, you're bound to miss."

Donnie raised his rifle, drew a bead on his target and pulled the trigger, blowing a hole in the bird, killing it instantly. He threw down his rifle and ran up to the lifeless thing. Falling to his knees he gently lifted the dead bird, caressing it in the palm of his hand. Donnie looked up at me, crying, "Why did you tell me to aim right at it, why?" he sobbed. "Look what you made me do!"

The bus drops me a few yards away from the entrance to the Chelsea Navy Yard. The guards at the gate point in the general direction of where I might find Donnie. I look up through the beating rain and face the base hospital; a bulky, red brick edifice with carbon stained limestone trim around its openings. Black clouds surround the building, giving it a haunted look. I dart inside feeling thankful to be out of the rain. After a round of further instructions from nurse details located at end points of the corridor I stand beyond the double doors to Ward B, Donnie's new home. The air smells yellow… like burning piss and rubbing alcohol.

Wading through the room slowly taking it all in, I find the space almost as large as my old high school cafeteria, but instead of lunch tables, there are rows of hospital beds, dozens of them, each containing the life of a fighting man, fighting to be whole again. Pendant fluorescent fixtures are all turned off, tall window bays provide the ward's only source of light and since today's offering outside is nothing but dismal gray the murkiness inside is only magnified. The room is oddly quiet, as if filled with nothing but strangers wanting to be left alone.

Donnie is sitting up, smoking, and wearing pajama bottoms and a T-shirt. He looks different, thinner than I remember, definitely less hair; but there is something else that's not quite the same.

"Hi, Donnie... how you doing, man?"

"Jon-nee," he nods hello, and goes back to his cigarette, regarding it as if checking to see if it's burning properly.

I stand beside his bed, feeling awkward. Should I shake his hand? Are we supposed to hug? Donnie won't look me in the eye.

"Are you okay?" I ask. "Where'd you get hurt?"

"Ah... it's nothin', man... really," he says, sounding hesitant. Donnie reaches down and removes his white sock, revealing a few puffy sores about the size of quarters across the top of his right foot. "They got infected... gave me a case of trench foot."

"Did you get hit there with shrapnel?"

"Yeah."

I don't know a damn thing about wounds, but I've gotten worst scraps from falling off my bike. They sent him home for this? I keep my thoughts to myself. While staring at Donnie's foot I notice something peculiar. There is a line of red puncture points above the soft fold of skin between his first and second toe. Tracks? Is he shooting up between his toes?

"Donnie, what's this?" I ask, pointing.

"What?" he slips the sock back in place.

"What are those red dots?"

"Oh... I had stitches taken out. That's just a scar."

I understand Donnie well enough to know when he's lying, and he's lying to me now. I let it pass. "How long you got to stay here?" I ask. "Are they gonna send you back, or what?"

"I think they'll keep me here for a little while. Then I'm gonna see about getting discharged." Donnie gazes off to the side continually as he speaks. His voice distant, he seems unsure of himself.

"Well, if they let you out to get some air, come on into Boston. I'll show you around."

"Can I crash with you?"

"I can put you up for a weekend." I'm not willing to commit to anything greater. "Oh, here! I brought you something." I hand Donnie a copy of *Playboy* I picked up at a newsstand on the way over. "Anything else you need just let me know."

"Send me some tail, man. I can't remember the last time I had a white piece of ass."

"I'll tell those chicks down the hall to take care of you," I laugh. The combined age of the two nurses I passed easily exceeds one-hundred.

I return home from Chelsea and fill Van Helden in on Donnie Pyle's condition.

"He looks to be all in one piece, physically anyway. I can't see any reason why they need to keep him there."

"Let's go get something to eat," says Van Helden, throwing on a sport jacket. I follow Robert out of the room and down the stairs.

"You know, Robert, I don't know if he's all there."

"Who… your friend?"

"Yeah… I think his head's fucked up, maybe that's why they sent him home."

"Did he kill anybody?"

"I don't know. I didn't ask. Do you think I shoulda asked him if he killed anyone?"

"Maybe… why not?"

"Next time we talk I'll see if he has any war stories."

We leave the building and head towards La Grange Street. "He's still shooting smack, Robert. I saw tracks on his foot. I wonder how he managed that."

"Yeah, where's he gonna get drugs in a hospital?" laughs Robert.

"Jonny, your pal Donnie's on the phone!" Van Helden yells into the hallway. It's been a week since my trip to the hospital. I am standing outside my doorway leaning on a broom, in conversation with Sam about the nightlife in our neighborhood. She is telling me what it's like to be a dancer in the bars down here.

"Who's Donnie?" asks Sam.

"I'll tell you later," I say, running into my room and grabbing the phone out of Robert's hand.

"Donnie? How you doing?"

"Jon-nee, man, the ladies here told me to go out and get'some. I'm thinking of doing Boston for a couple of days."

"Are you getting any medical treatments?"

"Naw… they gave me some easy duty. I report in the morning and work a few hours. I lay around my rack the rest of the time, doing nothin.'"

"What's your job?"

Donnie chuckles into the phone, "Dig it, they got me working in the base pharmacy."

I return to Sam's door and take up where we

left off a few minutes ago. "Donnie and I have been friends for as long as I can remember," I tell Sam. "He wants to come visit… stay a few days," I shrug.

"You seem really excited," says Sam. She takes a drag from her Camel, tipping the ash into a coffee cup looped to her finger.

"It's hard to stay friends with a guy you can't trust. He steals anything that makes him feel good: my girlfriends, my money, booze from my old man's liquor cabinet. I've gotten beaten over the head by Donnie so many times I lost count, and every time I blow it off and go on like nothing's happened. I don't wanna do it anymore."

"But you will."

"Yeah, I guess so. He'll be here tomorrow."

The bus from Chelsea rolls into Park Square, I stand by the curb waiting as Donnie steps off carrying a green duffel bag in one hand and waving to me with the other. After a quick hello I head off in the direction of my building with Donnie by my side. We skirt the edge of Chinatown on the way.

"Gooks," says Donnie, under his breath, as we pass by a few local Asians strolling along the sidewalk.

On the way up the stairs to my room, Donnie asks, "So, Jon-nee, what kind of deal you got going here?"

"Me and Van Helden, my room mate, manage the building. For that we get free rent and a phone. I also got a little side job at Wentworth. I help out in the library for a few bucks a day."

"This neighborhood's pretty freaky, man. What kind of people ya got living here?"

"Entertainers, mostly musicians and dancers," I say, as we reach the landing to my floor. "Oh, and you might bump into a prostitute, now and then," I smile and slip my key into the door.

"Sounds decent." Donnie looks around, surveying my room. "Nice digs... this my rack?" he points to our skinny cot.

"That's it, man."

"Outstanding."

"Any questions?"

"Where do I stash my diddy bag?"

"Throw your shit on the floor under the cot."

Donnie sits on the edge of the cot and reaches inside his bag, pulling out shaving supplies, tooth brush, and a pint-size bottle of pink capsules.

"My survival kit," he says, shaking the bottle of pills up near his ear, making a rattling sound.

"What are those?"

"Valium, ten milligrams... two hundred of 'em, courtesy of the U.S. Government, actually, as of this morning, more like one hundred and ninety." Donnie tosses the bottle over to me.

"What do they do? They speed or somethin'?" I ask, flipping off the cap and peeking inside.

"They're downers, man. They mellow you out."

I inspect a pill up to the light, pinched between my fingers, "How many you take?"

"You only need to drop a few to maintain a nice edge, but if you take six or seven, they'll knock your dick in the dirt."

I put the pink pill back into the bottle and snap home the plastic lid. "Listen, man, I got some homework to do. You can hang here, or you can go out and sight-see... it's up to you."

"Oh? I thought maybe we could get loose, hear some music, go to one of those strip clubs you got down here."

"I can't… but that doesn't mean you can't. Go out, man. Knock yourself out."

"Naw, I think I'll just crash. Maybe later you'll change your mind."

The past two hours Donnie hasn't moved from the cot. I finish studying and put my books away. Donnie is out cold, flat on his back with a green fatigue jacket covering his entire face. He must have covered up earlier to shut the light from his eyes.

"Hey, Donnie! You up?"

"Yeah," he groans without moving an inch.

"What's with the coat over your head?"

"Mosquitoes… they'll eat your flesh right down to the bone." His muffled voice filters through a face full of cloth.

Mosquitoes? I haven't seen a mosquito since coming to Boston. "We don't got any mosquitoes here."

Donnie slowly pulls his jacket from his face. "You wanna go out and do somethin'?" he asks, sitting up and dropping his feet to the floor.

"The only thing I want to do is grab a bite. We got a hotdog stand right around the corner."

"Fucking A! Let's get some chow."

Donnie and I nestle up to Dirty John's counter for dinner.

"Pass the mustard." I butter up a pair of dogs and begin to chomp away. "How much longer will you be staying at that base?" I ask between bites.

"I've applied for a discharge. I hope to be out

in a week, but I can't say for sure. The Green Machine might want to hold on to me a little longer," he says, with a mouthful of dog.

"Will you get a medical discharge?"

"I've asked for a General under Honorable Conditions."

"What's that?"

"A clean way out."

"What was it like over there, Donnie? Was it as bad as they say it is?"

"No... worse."

"Were you scared?"

"Fuckin' right I was scared. Everybody's scared... except the psychos."

"Did you kill anybody?"

Donnie swallows hard and put his dog down on the paper plate, stares ahead at the blank wall, regarding my question. "I saw this figure running through the bush," he begins slowly, "I didn't think, I just aimed and shot. Turns out he was this old man... the village grandfather or some damn thing. He was holding on to a shovel, I thought it was a rifle. Everyone in the fuckin' place came running out of their hooch... old women, kids and shit... they all started bawling and wailing. My lieutenant told me he's gonna write me up on charges, said I murdered the guy. I had to go in front of these shit-bird officers, they eye-fucked every inch of me, threatened to throw my ass in the brig. Finally, my Colonel stepped in and saved me, told everyone to back off, said it was an honest shot." Donnie picks up his hotdog and takes another bite, "An honest shot," his voice echoes softly.

"What are we doing tonight? A little poontang is in order, don't you think?"

"Well, we can check out Senior Pizza's, there's usually a lot college chicks hanging there. They got a jukebox."

"Jon-nee, man, fuck that jukebox pizza shit. You got a strip club right across the street and a shit load more around the corner. Why not do that?"

"Donnie, we're underage. You can't walk in those places if you're not twenty-one," I say this as a matter of fact, although I never tried to enter any of the clubs.

"They wouldn't card a Marine," he says confidently.

"Let's go back to my room, just kick back… maybe I can rustle us up a joint."

"You wanna rustle something… rope me a piece of ass."

I left Donnie sitting alone in my apartment while I reconnoiter the building, looking into the possibility of bumming weed from one of my good neighbors. I try next door first.

"Sorry, Jon," says Sam. "I'm down to seeds and stems. Try Barry… I know he has something."

I walk down to the big man's room, pause flat-footed in front of his door, wince, and give it a couple of knocks.

"Hello, Barry. How are you doing tonight?"

"What do you want?" he snarls.

"Is that Jonny?" Robin calls out from beyond the door.

"You gonna invite me in, or what?"

Barry flicks his thick head in a 'follow me' gesture. I track after him, the sweet smell of pot wafting in the air.

"Hi, Robin," I sit down beside her on Barry's couch. "What are you doing here?" I ask, slapping her on the knee. I haven't seen her since she moved out weeks ago.

"Hello, big boy," Robin giggles, slapping me back. "I'm just visiting."

"What do you want?" Barry repeats his snarl.

"I need a favor, man. I'm gonna ask you to do your patriotic duty and help out one of our brave servicemen by rolling a joint and allowing me to deliver it to the front on your behalf."

"Whut the fuck you talkin' bout?"

"You got any grass?"

"Yeah… why should I give you any?"

"I got an old buddy sitting up in my room. He's a Marine, just came back from Nam. He got wounded… they sent him to the navy hospital in Chelsea. Now, I'm asking you kindly, do your part in supporting our fighting men by rolling him a little joint."

"Roll him a joint, Barry," Robin smiles, "I'll take it up to the Marine Man."

Van Helden has come home from a date and he and Donnie are sitting down watching television. Robin follows me into the room and approaches Donnie. She has a goofy smile on her face. "Is this the Marine Man?" she asks, breathlessly.

Donnie stands up facing her with an equally goofy smile. I look at the two lovebirds, checking each other out so overtly sexual I nearly bend over laughing.

"Hi, Robin," Van Helden breaks in. "Where you been hiding?"

"Hi, Robert," she says in return, not taking her

eyes off Donnie. "I've been nowhere," she adds, nearly whispering.

"Robin, this is my friend Donnie."

"I'm pleased to meet you." Robin's silky voice sounds like Marilyn Monroe.

After sharing a joint and twenty minutes of courtship, Donnie and Robin look as if they are ready to elope. Donnie takes me aside into the corridor to talk privately, "You got any empty rooms in this place we can use?"

I think for a second before answering, "There's one on the fifth floor, but it's got no furniture."

"Who gives a shit, we ain't gonna play house."

"Wait a minute," I say, snapping my fingers. "I think there's a mattress in there on the floor."

"Lock and load," smiles Donnie. "Gimme the key."

"No… I'll open it up for you."

"All right, wait right here." Donnie ducks back into my room, seconds later reappears with Robin behind his back. This is too easy. She is going to put out for a guy I don't respect, and I'm the one who made it happen.

I flip on the vacant apartment's wall switch beside the door, but the ceiling light blows out like a spent flashbulb leaving the space in darkness. A curtainless window at the rear of the empty room casts borrowed light from the street lamp bordering La Grange and the parking lot behind our building. A soiled twin-size mattress lays naked on the floor in shadow and light beneath the window. There is no color in the room, only black and grays.

"Well, I'll leave you two alone," I say to the quiet couple standing beside me as I back out into the hallway, closing the door. "Don't mess up the place."

The night had already ended for me when Donnie returns, alone. Robert and I crashed a few minutes before he knocks on our door. I get up to let him in.

"How was you date?" I ask.

Donnie grunts an indecipherable reply and disappears into the bathroom. I climb back into bed. After a while I hear him drop his boots to the floor and fumble into his cot. I look over his way; he has his green fatigue jacket pulled up over his face.

Donnie had gone back to the navy base to arrange for his 'Honorable under General Conditions' discharge. The day they release him, before heading back to Connecticut, he returns to Boston to spend the night at my apartment. I say goodbye to him in the morning while he lay in his cot, wishing him luck before heading out the door for class.

On the trolley ride home at the end of the day I'm thinking about cutting my old friend a little slack. His visit has turned out to be okay. Maybe I've been a little too hard on him? What's past is past. From now on I'm going to give Donnie the benefit of the doubt instead of mistrusting everything he says. I grab a newspaper before walking into my building, Vietnam is on the front page, staring me in the face. Nearly three-hundred Americans killed this week... Jesus Christ, I shake my head hopelessly. Stepping inside my room, I drop my books on top of the dresser and empty my pockets of coins and gum, sprinkling them into the top drawer. In the corner, hiding beneath a pile of papers, I stashed two twenty-dollar bills to see me through the month. The twenties are gone. In their place, a small strip of white paper folded in half. I open it and read:

Jonny,
Needed cash to see my people.
I.O.U.
Donnie

12

Social Intercourse

My friends who visit have been instructed to use a code to let me know they're downstairs. After hitting the buzzer inside the foyer to the beat of *"Shave and a haircut... two bits"*, they book-it around the corner to the back of the building and run up to the rear door. I speed down five flights, and if my timing is right, open the door just as they arrive.

The silence in my room is broken by the buzzer code, I crush out my smoke and hustle downstairs with perfect timing, arriving just as Charlie and Nathan Rhiner approach the door.

"I scored a couple of six-packs," says Charlie, hefting a bulky paper bag in the air like a trophy. "When's Lykos going to fix your conveyance?"

I shrug.

The door closes behind us and we sprint up the back stairs. Raymond sticks his big nose into the hallway, "Jonny! You didn't get my rent. Come in here!" Raymond has on his usual goofy smile, waving us into his room, "Who are these young men?"

Charlie and Nathan introduce themselves. Charlie spots a funny shaped drum resting on the floor near Raymond's bed. "What's this?" he lifts it up for closer inspection.

"Oh!" Raymond jealously snatches the drum away from Charlie's fingers and cradles it to his chest like a baby. "It's my Doumbek." Raymond paints us a quick picture of the drum's eminence in his Lebanese ancestry. "Let me show you." His hands begin thumping a rich base beat from the goat-skinned silver chalice. Raymond skip-dances a few short steps towards his stereo. He turns the knob and a record robotically drops to the turntable, belly dancing music fills the room. Raymond begins banging away and whirling around his apartment like he is performing tent-side at some desert oasis.

"Ray... your money?" I remind him.

My two friends are enjoying the show; laughing and clapping along with the beat. He puts down his drum and prances over to his dresser, pulls cash from the top drawer, and musically counts out the rent.

"Listen, Ray, we gotta take off. Maybe you wanna come up to my place later on? I'll write you a receipt, and you can hang out with us."

"Really? That would be wonderful! When should I come?"

"How about around eight... by the way, do you smoke grass?"

"Marijuana? Never," he makes a sour face, "But it won't bother me if you do."

The three of us lumber upstairs to my apartment. I flip on the lights and the radio. Mose Allison is singing a song about city life. My guests drop their coats and grab chairs at the kitchen table. Charlie extracts a joint from a pack of cigarettes and pops open a beer. "Who's got a light?"

"Jonny... Charlie tells me you rent to hookers and strippers," says Nathan, flinging Charlie a book of matches from his shirt pocket. "Do you ever hang with any of these ladies?"

"Sure," I lie. "I see them all the time. They're nice girls," I smile, knowingly.

"Nice? ... In what way? Nathan presses.

I sift through my brain pan searching for a cool comeback, "They don't cause no trouble," I bumble out.

"Why don't you invite a few over for a beer?"

I slump down into a chair and face my smiling, eager friends lamely promising, "I'll see what I can do."

The apartment door swings open and Van Helden and Omar blow into the room like a gust of wind. "What's shakin', guys!?"

"Jonny is going downstairs to invite a few of your exotic neighbors to join us," says a grinning Charlie.

"All right!" Robert slaps his hands together, "Let's get it on! If we're gonna entertain ladies we need to improve the atmosphere!" Van Helden dives into our closet and resurfaces holding a paper bag. He circles the room unscrewing 100-watt bulbs, replacing them with 20-watt blue lights, instantly transforming our dreary apartment, casting us in a misty glow of vaporous blue shadows. I oblige him by placing a blue light inside our scummy bathroom; an excellent alternative to cleaning.

"You really gonna ask some of the girls to come up?" Robert confronts me as I exit the toilet.

"What do you think?" I smirk. "Those guys are dreaming."

"I'll go out and find somethin'." Robert throws his coat back on and leaves the apartment.

"Where's he going?" asks Omar.
"I don't know... He didn't say."

"Ssshhh," I signal Nathan to hit the radio. A faint tapping is coming from the other side of my apartment's door. He leans over and turns down the music. The tapping continues, sounding tentative. Slightly paranoid from the pot smoke drifting through the air, I walk over and face the sound, "Who is it?"

"It's me, Raymond."

I open the door and find my sheepishly pathetic, freshly showered tenant in a white dress shirt, dark pants, and a neatly combed Howdy Doody haircut, holding his drumbaby in his hands.

"Raymond! You crazy fuck... get in here!" I hustle him inside. "Take a load off Ray, relax... Can I get you a beer?"

"Yes, that would be nice. I hope I'm not interrupting. I brought my drum."

"I can see that," I smile.

After a thirty minute absence Van Helden reenters the room, arriving with a cool, satisfied expression across his face, leading a pack of females. Five starched, preppy girls wade into the room in a tight line behind his back, looking as if they are tethered together at the waist by a short rope, their eyes cautious and alert. I check out the guys... all smiling fiercely, a lair of lounging wolves delightfully surprised by the sight of lost lambs wandering into their midst.

"Woofa," mutters Charlie.

"This is it, Ladies!" Robert leads them into the center of the room, "These are my amigos... Omar,

Jonny, Charlie, Nathan." He spots Raymond sitting in the corner of the room, his white face and shirt glowing an eerie blue. "Raymond! When'd you get here? That's Raymond, hiding over there!" Robert points to the only guy in the room who appears uncomfortable. "I'm sorry, but I forgot your names." Van Helden addresses the first girl in line, "And you are…?"

"Debbie." "Alison." "Marilyn." "Barbara." "Meg."

For several minutes the girls remain stuck together mumbling girlie-talk under their breath. They seem about a second away from bolting. I stare at them from the couch, wedged in between the other guys. Somebody say something. I stand and walk beside the girls, park myself by the back window. Moving seems to stir things up, Omar reaches for his guitar and begins finger picking a melody, Raymond lifts his silly drum and thumps along with him. Two of the girls break from the pack and bury themselves inside the bathroom. A joint circulates through the crowd; Charlie passes it over to one of the girls, which she accepts without comment. One chick, I think she said her name is Debbie, comes and stands beside me, gazing out through the dark panes of glass.

"When you look out your window, what do you see?" she asks.

"So many strange faces staring back at me."

"Oh," she blandly mutters, and turns back into the room to rejoin her friends.

I think my comeback deserved greater appreciation than just a simple 'oh'.

"What college do you chicks go to?" asks Charlie.

"Simmons College," one girl replies.

"We're not chicks," admonishes another, staring Charlie down.

"How do respectable *females* like you end up wandering into this part of town?" asks Charlie, grinning into the face that criticized his colloquialism, the joint burning between his teeth.

"We didn't know we would end up *here*," she sneers at Charlie. "We met Robert in Copley Square… he asked us to this party… he said it was right around the corner. We were walking *forever*. *I* wanted to turn around," she stabs her finger at Robert, "but *he* kept saying it's not far, *we're almost there*."

I grab Van Helden by the shirt and lead him off to the side.

"How the hell did you manage to pick up five chicks?"

"Pretty simple… I saw them standing on a street corner. I walked behind them and dropped my key on the sidewalk. I picked it up and asked, 'Anybody lose a key?' They all started digging inside their pocketbooks. We talked for a little bit, and just like that," he snaps his fingers, "they followed me here."

As much as I appreciate the artistry of Van Helden's ability to score, the chicks that followed him home are bummers. There has been no attempt at mixing in with us. I've had better social intercourse inside my dentist's waiting room. After Raymond, considerably tipsy, jumps up to perform solo and dance about the room, our female guests decide it is time to call it quits, exiting like they're on a fire drill. Nobody exchanges numbers or makes any plans to reconnect. They just leave… fast.

13

Chinese Fireworks

They call what I'm seeing snow clouds. The morning sky is packed with dirty fiber, one-hundred square miles of muslin stretching over the city to hold back the snow. The radio reports a major winter storm is rolling towards us.

By the end of the afternoon, the clouds continue to form into an even heavier mass, the temperature is dropping yet not a single flake has landed. The last class of the day concludes sooner than scheduled. My drafting instructor wants to beat it home in his Chevy before those unforeseen flakes become moguls on the turnpike.

I return to my apartment surprised to find Van Helden has taken the afternoon off. The start of another week means Robert and I have cleaning duties and rent collecting to perform. We switch off chores to keep things from getting too dull. It's Robert's turn to get the rent. "This is a good time to catch'em," he says, lifting the receipt book off the counter on his way out the door.

"I'm gonna turn on the tube." I kneel in front of the box, spinning the dial. "Maybe I can find out when this storm's supposed to get here. Hey!" I yell into the hallway, "Raymond paid already! Write him a receipt!" I lean over and fiddle with the channels, adjusting the fuzzy black and white picture.

Robert reappears in the doorway. "Jonny, there's somethin' strange going on down there."

"Down where?"

"The fourth floor… This Chinese chick is hanging out in front of the apartment we rented to that steelworker, Frankie. She's acting really freaky."

"Like how?"

The force from the explosion spins Robert like a top, reeling him back into the room and slamming his body against the wall. Shielding my head from the blast, I plunge my face in the cross of my arms. Coming through the shock after a disoriented second, Van Helden and I rush into the hallway and are met by a wall of smoke billowing up the stairwell. Sprinkler pipes activate, spraying water everywhere. At the fifth floor, visibility less than an arms length, we hear our tenants yelling from the floors below, their voices lost in the excruciating clanging of the fire alarm bell mixing with the sound of water showering down from the overhead pipes. In an instant we are soaked to the skin, cutting our way through the smoke to the source of the blast on the fourth floor. Flames cover the wall surrounding the door to Apartment 4B; the sprinkler pipes fighting to contain the blaze. Robert runs down to the third floor, banging on all the doors he passes as I run back to the upper floors and do the same, both of us shouting, directing everyone to leave the building any way they can. Spinning the crank on the casement window leading to the fire escape, placing my foot on the sill, I take one quick look back into the hallway and see the smoke beginning to clear.

Returning to the point of the explosion, I discover the fire extinguished. The sprinklers continue to beat it to death as the alarm bell bangs away and sheets of water cascade down the stairwell to the floors below. Dazed by the sight of the damage, I continue walking through the shower and rejoin Robert on the third floor. Five men from the Boston Fire Department enter the building from the back door, running up the stairs in full gear, some carrying axes. Van Helden and I wave them on, directing them to follow us.

One fireman steps forward, "What the hell happened here?"

"A bomb, I think," says Robert. "We're the Supers."

Van Helden looks pitiful; standing here soaking wet; hair matted down flat to his skull like a black bathing cap, face covered in soot.

"I'm Lieutenant O'Malley," the fireman says, shouting over the cacophony of bells and spraying water, "Where's the power and water service located?"

I guide O'Malley and a second fireman into the basement. A police officer we meet outside tags along. A fireman steps over to a gang of black pipes and quickly begins turning a large red wheel, O'Malley spends about a minute inspecting the boiler and electrical system.

We slosh our way back up to the fourth floor. The sprinklers and clanging have mercifully ended, but puddles of dirty water are everywhere. Black soot covers the corridor walls and ceilings, making the space feel more confined than it already is. Linoleum tiles are charred and curled; the paint burned off the blackened walls. Our firemen find what caused the blast; an unsophisticated bomb fashioned out of a metal can of gasoline, sort of a high-octane Molotov cocktail. Frankie Barlow and his girlfriend emerge cautiously from inside their room and nervously posture themselves beside the tattered hole blown in their door.

The police officer steps beside Lieutenant O'Malley, produces a pad and pencil from his pocket and starts asking questions, he writes down my name, Van Helden's name, information we give him about Lykos, the names of Frankie Barlow and his girlfriend. Frankie uneasily admits knowing the Chinese woman, "We had a little fling together. I guess you could say she still has the hots for me, heh heh." Nobody finds Frankie's joke funny but Frankie.

"There's going to be an investigation into the events that transpired here this afternoon," Lieutenant O'Malley informs us. "The power to the building will be shut down until we're satisfied all conditions are safe and operational."

"What! You're not shutting off our electricity."

"It will be down for about a day."

I shout into his face, "What are we supposed to do for heat?"

The officer gives me a nasty glare, "There will be no argument on this point. Are we clear?"

"Yessir… What do we tell our tenants?"

"Tell them its standard procedure."

After the uniforms leave the building, Van Helden goes upstairs to check on the condition of our apartment while I circulate the hallways giving everyone the news we will be without power later today, and this uncomfortable state of affairs will likely continue for the next twenty-four hours.

I walk into the apartment and find Robert sitting quietly at the table surrounded by a thin pond of dirty water, a cigarette burning in the ashtray. "You look like shit, man," I laugh at the sight of him.

"Me? Go dig yourself."

Inside the bathroom I face myself in the mirror. Robert and I look like a pair of coal miners pulled from a tunnel disaster. While staring at my reflection the light over the sink flickers out. I turn on the hot water tap to wash my face, within seconds the water turns ice cold. Van Helden and I smell smoky-bad and need to change out of our soggy clothes and somehow clean up. A hot shower is out of the question. The building is now without electricity and heat; I realize the room will be getting colder and darker by the minute. A thin slice of dusk is coming in through the bathroom window, I look outside; snow has begun to fall.

14

Appeal to the Great Spirit

Monday
8:00 pm

Van Helden and I watch the phone ring. Sooner or later we have to talk to Lykos. He's sure to blame us for this trouble. I pick up on the seventh ring.

"Yessir?"

"Where the hell have you two been? What the hell happened over there? Why didn't you call me immediately? Why did I have to get the news from the police? Who is this guy you rented to that has girlfriends planting bombs in my building?"

Lykos is hysterical. I picture him at home on the other end of the line pacing back and forth in a bathrobe over his underwear and shirt and tie. He is firing questions at me like shots popping from a pistol. I want to slam the phone in his face.

"Lykos, did the police tell you they cut off our power? We don't have any heat or electricity."

"What! Why the hell did you let them do that? Are you crazy!?"

"Routine business. They want to make sure none of the electrical wires were fried in the fire. It's getting nasty cold in here, Lykos, and its wicked dark. We got a couple of candles going. The batteries you gave us for the flashlight are dead."

"Watch out with them candles. I don't want

you to start another fire. Have you collected any rent?"

I'm amazed by this son-of-a-bitch.

9:05 pm

Staring outside my window, the world is black beyond the incandescent glitter of snow descending within the glow of a pair of streetlamps. I feel helpless, trapped inside this dark room, encircled by the fog of my own breath. Van Helden and I had changed out of our wet clothes, but we still smell like soggy charcoal. My hair is stiff and stinky.

"I feel like a crusty booger. I don't know about you, but I can't sleep like this."

"Jonny, I got an idea." Robert's voice sounds confident. "I never returned my old dorm key. Let's take the T out to Wentworth. We'll use their showers."

Van Helden and I take our seats on the trolley and move outbound from the Boylston Street Station. I catch my reflection in the window, a strange face is staring back at me, my eyes dark pools encircled in ripples of soot. I turn my head towards Robert, his face vacant; lost in his own thoughts. We ride to our destination, the only sound the mechanical humming of the trolley and the clacking of its wheels. Stepping off at Huntington Avenue we trudge a path through the pelting snow towards Wentworth's dormitories. With Van Helden leading the way, we execute his plan without a hitch. After freshening up and making a clean get-away we track our way back for the return trip. Neither of us owns a winter hat or a pair of boots, and the miserable shoes we have on are useless tonight. Robert is chattering through his teeth about something or other; I am having trouble hearing him with my hands cupped over my ears.

"What did you say?"

"I said, I feel like Doctorfuckin' Zhivago."

We stand at the trolley stop, exposed for what seems like an eternity, rocking back and forth on frozen feet, I begin flapping my arms up and down like a penguin trying to fly.

The trolley's beaming headlight appears through the stormy haze. The car lumbers to a stop and we board with the joy of rescued trekkers, sitting down in heated comfort. I look around inside the empty car; Robert and I, its only passengers.

Moving ahead slowly, we come upon the commanding classical façade of the Museum of Fine Arts, metamorphosized tonight into a grand winter palace. Cast beyond the building's floodlights the falling snow sparkles like diamonds. Positioned at the entrance is a great equestrian statue of an American Indian, shirtless and riding bareback, wearing nothing but a headdress and a loincloth. This gallant man defying the storm with his face searching towards heaven, arms extended with palms drawn before the sky, beseeching God; his body sheathed white with snow.

We exit up the subway's staircase to a deserted city. The blanket of snow makes the line between street and sidewalk indistinguishable. This emptiness brings something I've never seen before in this part of town, serenity. It's so quiet I can almost hear the snow falling.

Inside our building we climb the staircase in impenetrable darkness. The worthless windows facing the airshaft have as much effect as portals into a black hole.

"You got your key?" asks Robert.

I fiddle through my pants.

Robert and I set up camp, laying out provisions we purchased at the drug store up the street: Arrange candles; reload flashlight; pack loose clothing over bedding for extra insulation; rip open candy bars; place smokes, matches and ashtrays at the ready. I drop a battery into our transistor radio.

11:36 pm
"Robert… you asleep?"
"Nope."
"You wanna hear somethin' funny? Barry told me he balled Sam."
"That skunk's a liar. Sam doesn't ball just anybody."
"That's what I thought."

11.38 pm
"Jonny?"
"Yeah."
"It's goddamn cold in here."
"Ssshh… I'm praying."

Tuesday
8:05 am
The view outside our window displays a world transformed. LaGrange Street has vanished. The snowfall buried the few automobiles that remain parked behind our building. No longer cars; misrepresented now as giant polar bears reclining in the midst of an arctic landscape, I stand at the window trapped by the view of sinuous soft forms both familiar and alien. The relentless snow con-

tinues to fall. The radio reports all schools, as well as every other human enterprise, except winter sports, are canceled.

10:10 am

The snowstorm has paralyzed all regional traffic. City services are performing battlefield triage. Lykos phones just to let us know we are on our own. "Don't expect any help from nobody," he counsels.

Van Helden and I think it wise to tour the building and check on our tenants. Our first stop is Sam's apartment. I tap on the door and enter with my passkey after she fails to answer. No Sam.

I look over at Robert and shrug, "She has a mother in Brockton… my guess is she's probably holed up there. Good for her."

Robert knocks on the door to 5B, Jasper's place. The door opens slowly with Jasper sticking out only his nose and eyes from the edge of the jamb.

"Good morning, Jasper," I say, with mock cheerfulness. "You doing okay in there?"

Recognizing his Supers, he opens the door and returns our greeting with a bright smile. Jasper, always the fashion plate, has on a fur coat that looks as if it was cut from the back of a woolly mammoth. His thin, dark, naked legs stick out from the bottom of his coat, like skinny logs chopped from a cedar tree. On his head he wears a silky black do-rag.

"My floor got pretty damn wet yesterday. I mopped it up with some towels. If I hadn't, I'd be ice skating in here this mornin.'" Jasper says this with a good-natured beam in his eyes. I think he is taking his circumstances rather nicely. "Smell smoky bad here, too… How we gonna get rid of that?"

"It won't happen till we can clean up the halls. And that won't happen till we get the power back on." I say, as if we have a plan in the works.

"When that gonna be?"

"They promised to have it turned back on sometime today. We just have to put up with this a little longer."

"Tell them to hurry up, we're freezin' in here!" The order came from Jasper's girlfriend, Dianne, who stuck her head up from under several piles of covers; their bed looks like a nest.

"I know you boys doin' what you can," says Jasper pleasantly. "You didn't get rent from me this week."

"Baby! Don't you be given them money without no heat in here!" the bird in the nest squawks.

"Ssshhhh!" he whips his head around to face her. "I'm talkin' to these boys!" Jasper turns back to us, "I apologize for my old lady. I pay my bills… I'm good for what I owe."

"Thank you, man… but that won't be necessary. Nobody's forking out any rent until we get things straightened out around here." I say, perhaps a little hastily; considering we never discussed this policy with Lykos.

We stick our noses into Apartment 5A, Pam's bed is made up, but her closet is empty.

"When was the last time you seen her?" I ask Robert. I hadn't spotted Pam in over a week.

"I don't know… maybe a few days ago. I think she splits her time between two places. She doesn't always sleep here. She uses this room more for business than a home." Robert discovered this fact from their limited relationship.

"Pam's a decent chick," I say, closing the door on the way out. I think it would be nice if I could get to know her better.

On the fourth floor the fire damage and the smell, mixed with the freezing temperature, gives the darkened space the impression of an abandoned building. Black soot covers the walls and ceiling. The damaged door to 4B is opened. Robert and I walk in and survey the room; except for the furniture, the place has emptied out. Frankie Barlow and his girlfriend have split.

"I guess things got a little too hot for them here," I say, trying to make a joke.

Van Helden scoops up the room key they left behind on the countertop, and snickers, "Lykos can start advertising again."

We canvass the remaining apartments and find at least half the occupants made temporary accommodations elsewhere. Those are the lucky ones. The tenants that remain likely have no other option. Their only alternative is to grin through chattering teeth and bear it. Most are dirty, cold and angry, but fortunately they are not taking their grief out on Robert and me. People here believe we are doing our best to return things to normal. They don't know the truth; Robert and I feel like we're holding onto the oars in a sinking boat.

Wednesday
<ins>2:45 pm</ins>

Snow continues to fall hard, petrifying all movement outside my window. Except for the incessant scraping growl of plow trucks and the occasional wail of a siren, the streets are deserted and silent. Inside my room I shuck my gloves, squint through the smoke from the cigarette in my lips and fumble with the phone book, skimming pages for a department or agency that can turn our electricity back on. My first call goes to the fire department's main headquarters. "I want to speak with Lieutenant O'Malley."

"O'Malley? What's his first name? We got a lot of O'Malleys in the Department," a gruff voice on the other end of the line asks.

"I don't know," I say, agitated. "How many of them can be lieutenants?"

"Three."

"Oh… well, ah, this one works the Combat Zone. We had an arsonist start a fire in our building on Tremont two days ago. You guys shut off our power and promised to have it back on in 24 hours. We'd like to know when you plan to get here. Lieutenant O'Malley was in charge."

"First, the fire department does not shut off power in the City of Boston. Boston Edison handles all utility power. Second, Lieutenant O'Malley is in Operations. If you had a suspicious fire in your building, you need to speak with someone in Investigations."

I dial several numbers, speak to numerous know-nothings, and get zilch. Investigations tell me they do not have the authority to touch the electrical box, "You need to contact Boston Edison."

My next call goes to the electric company. Some asshole explains without authorization from the fire department the utility company will not budge, "It's an open investigation and a fire department issue."

I go back on line with the fire department and

grumble, "Boston Edison needs some kind of a release from you guys before they'll come back to switch us on."

Investigations acknowledges their formal inquiry has not been scheduled due to the snowstorm, while reminding me, "Electrical service issues are under the utility company's jurisdiction."

This pretzel logic is getting me nowhere. "Can I speak to somebody who can cut through this crap!"

"I don't think the Governor's too busy. Why don't you give him a call?"

"Blow me!" I slam the phone down in disgust and sink my head into my hands.

Thursday
10:20 am

I feel like I'm marooned on some distant ice planet. Flakes are falling from the sky like snowballs. I walked behind the building this morning and stuck my 36 inch T-square straight down in the snow. It disappeared. The radio reports an interesting phenomenon; there are at least a quarter of a million people in eastern Massachusetts without power. So… we're not exactly alone.

11:15 am

Pam came back to her apartment with a suitcase in her hand, filled it with the tools of her trade; pillows, bedding and clean towels. She dropped her key on the counter and vanished, not bothering to say goodbye or leave a forwarding address. Raymond told me he spotted Pam marching down the stairs. He wished her good luck on her journey, wherever it may be. Raymond said Pam returned his farewell salutation by laughing out loud all the way out the door.

12:05 pm
No one from the fire department has been out to inspect the building. Dialing both Fire Investigations and Boston Edison, I'm given the same bullshit run-around as before. I place several useless phone calls to City Hall, "You need to get over here quick; the fire department, the utility department, public works, I don't care who… just send somebody!"

A tightly wound clerk from Mayor White's office snaps back, "Have ya bothered to look outside lately? We got a crisis on our hands. Deal with it!"

I hang up the phone, pissed off and hopelessly lost. *'Deal with it'…* his words roll around inside my head as I open the Yellow Pages, grab the phone and begin dialing electricians alphabetically. On my tenth call I find one outfit vaguely interested in sending someone over to take a look.

"Whatever you charge I'll triple it if you get the job done before 5:00."

"I'll send someone right over," the man promises.

1:35 pm
I greet Dolan Electric's service truck as it rolls up behind the building, festooned with tire chains, ladders, cables and a variety of tools and boxes.

"Are you Dolan?" I ask the thin, pale dude that dropped out of the front cab. He is wearing bib-coveralls beneath an opened winter parka, which he quickly zips up, and has about two days growth of itchy stubble on his face. The guy looks like he just busted out of prison.

"Are you fuckin' kiddin'? Dolan would neva come out on in weatha like this. My name's Jimmy Tuck." He shakes my hand, "What's the problem?"

I use my passkey to open up the back door to the diner and direct Jimmy Tuck to follow me down into the basement.

"You don't know how happy I am to get you out here. We haven't had heat since Monday."

Jimmy's powerful flashlight cuts a wide path of light through the pitch-black crypt. We reach the bottom of the stairs and stand in front of the electric panel.

"Christ, its cold down here… my nipples are harder than Japanese arithmetic," Jimmy says, as he blows breath onto his fingers and opens the panel door. "Uh huh… those bastids."

"What? Is there a problem? Can you fix it?"

"Piece a cake. I gotta go back to my truck and grab some fuses. I'll have ya runnin' in no time. While I'm down here, I'll get the boila going. It's not my trade, but I'll take care of ya."

Jimmy Tuck kept his word; and I kept mine. The bill for fifteen minutes work came to one hundred-five dollars, triple the normal rate. I pay him in cash, using rent money I'm holding for Lykos. The power, heat and lights return to the building without any fanfare, but to me, it is the Fourth of July, my birthday and Christmas morning rolled into one glorious event.

Friday
<u>9 pm</u>
   The snowfall ended this evening after coming down 101 consecutive hours; a record for Boston; the radio announces thirty-seven inches measured at City Hall Plaza.

15
Boston's Finest

Lykos paid some guys to repair the damage caused by the fire. After replacing the door and floor tiles they gave the halls a fresh coat of paint. The long-awaited fix for the elevator is underway. The weather in the month of March is turning out to be the flip side of the shit that came down in February. Abnormally warm temperatures dispatched the snow as quickly as it had arrived. I am astonished today seeing grass poking up amongst the pasture in the Boston Common.

"What you wanna watch?" Robert flips through a few stations and reviews our options. "We got Mickey Mouse and Ed Sullivan."

We do not hear her enter. Like most nights our door is left open. Julie, the tall blonde Barbie living in 3A, walks in unannounced and fixes her eyes on the portable TV without saying a word.

"Sit down, Julie. We're gonna watch Eddie Sullivan."

"I came up here to tell you what happened to my old man last night." Julie hasn't moved an eye muscle away from the screen as she speaks to us. "John fell down the back stairs coming into the building and broke his leg."

"Jesus... how'd that happen?"

"You boys got a television?" she asks.

"Yeah… join us," I say, happy to share our tube with Julie and maybe get to know her a little.

"I'd love to, but John is expecting me back soon."

"How did he fall… he slip or somethin'?"

"Yeah, I guess you could say that," she snickers. "He was blasted; he made it to the top step and keeled over backwards down the stairs on his butt. He didn't feel a thing," said Julie, waving it off. "Raymond called the ambulance. John's got his leg in a cast… he won't be playing in the band for a while."

"What does he play?" I ask.

"Drummer."

"Bummer."

"So," Julie continues, "When the hell is that elevator gonna be fixed? My old man ain't climbing those stairs with a broken leg. He'll be cooped up in our room all day, I already have one three-year old to deal with, and I don't need another one."

"We can only report what's told to us. The parts have arrived and the repairs are happening," says Robert, looking over at me for confirmation.

"That's right. That old thing will be working again before ya know it," I say, making the sign of the cross.

I meet Andreus after physics class for a business lunch in the Student Union and immediately begin ragging on about the repairman. "Our tenants are ready to beat the shit out of us. He better get this done fast. People are screaming they're gonna quit paying," I lie. I want the elevator working more than anyone. I'm tired of coming in the back way and climbing all those damn stairs.

"It will be fixed," says Andreus, clipping the words out in between bites. "My brother wants you to get in the airshaft and clean out the garbage. He says it's your job; you must do it, please." Andreus is speaking to me with a mouthful of mash potatoes; pointing his fork at my face. "Pass the salt and pepper, please." He stabs in their direction with his knife in his opposite hand. He reminds me of my Ukrainian grandparents, eating with both hands. This must be some kind of old world trait.

"I'm sorry Andreus, but I can't do that. I wouldn't go down there even if I had on scuba gear. The stink is horrendous; the rats are bigger than alley cats. That pile of garbage is three fucking feet deep. There could be dead bodies buried under there, for all you know. Last week, a tenant tossed a chicken out their window."

"A *live* chicken?"

"Not a *live* chicken, you goofball, one from the supermarket; a whole one, uncooked. It looks like someone placed a decapitated head on top of the heap. It's starting to turn purple, man. It's goddamn disgusting."

Andreus promises Lykos will foot the bill for cleaning the airshaft if I make the arrangements, "We will pay twenty-five dollars."

"I'll look around the neighborhood. I'm sure I can find some knucklehead who needs the money."

On my way into the building this evening, I cross paths with the elevator man leaving the basement. He looks as if he's through for the day, heading in the direction of his panel van.

"Is it runnin' yet?" I ask, crossing my fingers.

"I gotta come back tomorrow. That should do it." He opens the door to his van, hawks up a wad of spit and shoots it to the ground like a dart.

"Thanks." I give a slight wave goodbye and enter the building through the back door, hopefully for the last time. Raymond's door is wide open; he's standing by his window looking down into the street.

"How you doing, Raymond?"

He doesn't reply, turns his back and ducks beyond my line of sight. That's funny? Maybe he didn't hear me.

At the sixth floor I round the corner and can see down the end of the hall; the door to my apartment is open. This is a bit of a surprise; Robert isn't supposed to be home for at least another hour. I take a few steps closer and cross the threshold into my ransacked room, it looks as if hurricane Carla came in and did our decorating. My eyes spin in circles through a whirlwind of clutter, taking inventory of this miserable mess, clothes and personal belongings are scattered across every square foot of space, furniture knocked on its side. The mattresses are pulled apart; our drawers flung upside down in disarray; the contents strewn across the floor. I feel dizzy, want to sit down, but everything to sit on is piled in a mangled heap. Our closet has been rifled through; clothing dumped in disorganized clumps. The TV is gone, naturally, along with our clocks and radios. Lying on the floor next to Van Helden's photographs is the envelope where we keep the rent money. I pick it up and slap it across my open palm... I don't remember how much we had in it. One crowning, disconcerting detail caps this host of hard luck; blood is splattered everywhere.

The window into the airshaft is open, the thief's point of entry. Shards of shattered glass spread across a bloody windowsill and onto the floor below. Swirls of blood streak the windowpane, macabre finger painting rendered by a deranged hand, the blood trails the action of a frenzied junkie's hunt for loot. My shock from this discovery quickly evolves into anger. I want to find the guy that did this to us. I take some consolation knowing at least the slimeball hurt himself. The junkie likely sliced skin and muscle breaking through our window. I blow out a hard breath and look around for the phone, finding it tangled between a pair of my pants and the cushions from Robert's couch.

"I wanna report a B&E," I say to the police officer who answers my call.

Leaning against the back door, I look up surprised to see the policeman I pass everyday on the corner of Stuart and Tremont, Patrolman Bucky Johnson.

"Are you the one that called?"

"Yeah… I thought you guys would send a detective. Aren't you a traffic cop?"

"Listen, you want me to come in and take a look… or you gonna be a wise ass and make jokes? Choice is yours, kid."

"I'm sorry… don't you guys have special investigators for solving crimes."

"You've been watching too much TV. What happened here?"

"Well, the big thing is someone stole our television… and some money, a radio… shit like that."

"I think I can handle this," Patrolman Johnson smirks.

At the third floor landing, I turn the corner and look back at the lumbering officer walking heavy up the stairs.

"Hey, junior! What floor did you say you live on?" Bucky stops and leans his large frame into the steel banister, using it as a brace. I detect a slight wheeze to his breathing.

"Six... it's the top floor in the building."

"Where's your elevator?"

"We're working on that," I say, smiling. "We might have it running again tomorrow."

The cop turns his shoulder towards the exit and begins to walk out. "Call me tomorrow when you get it working."

"WAIT!" I run back down the stairs and stand between him and the door. "My apartment is a goddamn crime scene! There are tons of clues and shit all over the place... blood everywhere! Ya gotta see this now! We can't hold off and wait for the damn elevator. What if it don't get fixed? What then? No investigation? Come on up, please."

"You expect me to walk up six friggin' flights of stairs?"

"You're supposed to be 'Boston's Finest', remember?" I say, charming the cop to keep moving.

The hike to my room takes triple the time it normally does, brief respites at each landing slow us down. The officer takes out a pen and begins filling out a report. He laughs when I fail to answer the basic questions concerning our possessions. I don't know how much money was taken; the color, exact size, make or model of anything. He agrees with me that a junkie likely committed the crime, obviously entered from the fire escape, and most definitely cut a serious slice into his flesh as a result of his forced entry. Aside from that, the investigation is over. He closes his notebook and shares his thoughts on the possibility of ever seeing our things again, "Don't count on it."

"What should we do about all this blood?" I ask, wondering how the police treat major clues such as this.

"Try watering it down with some bleach, that's what my wife uses to get out stains."

Like a couple of seasoned sleuths, Van Helden and I examine the bloody fingerprints on the windowpane and surmise the thief is right handed. He cut his right arm when he reached in to release the latch. The bloody prints come from a right-handed man. We trace his movements in the room, piecing together bits of the puzzle he left behind.

"The bastard wouldn't have left the same way he came in," I conclude. "He would have bolted down the stairs and out the back door. And if he did it in one trip, he would have needed a bag like the one Santa carries."

"Maybe there was more than one guy," Robert speculates upon a different scenario. "One dude comes up the stairs, knocks on our door, 'Anybody home? No? I'll just hang here and wait.' His buddy enters the airshaft from a different floor, climbs up the fire escape, breaks our window, crawls in and opens the door for his pal. Then they both go wild inside our room and split with their arms wrapped around our stuff. How does that sound?"

"Possible… possible." I let this idea ferment a bit. "I think there's one sure way to find out."

Robert and I walk downstairs to drill Raymond. He gives us nothing to advance either theory. Raymond takes his usual stance when witnessing felonious activity in the building.

"I saw nothing, I heard nothing, I know nothing."

"You're lying, Raymond. You'd rather protect some junkie asshole than help your friends?" His attitude has me flipping between anger and disgust. "I know you saw this guy running down the stairs with our shit. What was it, Ray, one guy, two… three? Come on, man…what'd you see, what'd they look like?" Raymond's mute expression turns away to face the wall. He quietly mouths his empty reply, "I saw nothing."

"Fuck you, Ray."

Van Helden and I walk over to Dirty John's for a hot dog dinner and surreptitiously stake out the place, hopefully to nail a junkie with a bandaged right arm. John's place is a way station for scumbags and derelicts. Junkies gather at John's like flies around the city dump. After downing two dogs apiece and a watery caramel drink we unfortunately leave with nothing but indigestion.

I return on my own the next day and hang out by the front door, pacing the sidewalk for about thirty minutes before coming up dry and calling it quits. I did, however, obtain glaring looks from a pair of police officers who rolled slowly by in their squad car, plus two commercial offers; one from a beastly hooker and the other from a guy pushing a small taste of brown smack. I passed on both. I'm beginning to believe the cop was right, we can kiss our stuff goodbye.

On the lighter side, I want to report rent collecting is a pleasant chore. It gives me the opportunity to get better acquainted with my neighbors. Most of our tenants work Saturday nights till the bars close, when their shift ends the parties begin and the building rocks with soul music. This lifestyle translates into long, boozy nights, and the morning-after is as somber as a funeral. I discovered in the process of rent collecting you can't shake them out of bed until early Sunday afternoon. I wait till then to pay my respects.

    John, the older of the two Taylor boys, acts like a tough-guy, standing between me and Julie with a scowl on his face pulling rent money from her pocketbook while spying down on me with assassin eyes, making me feel I'm causing some kind of trouble just by being here.

    Ed Taylor, on the other hand, is reserved, soft-spoken and polite. My receipt book in hand, I knock on Ed's door. "Hello, rent's due." I say, stepping inside at his invitation. Standing tall and shirtless, Ed has a red, silk bandana wrapped tight to his forehead forcing his crop of hair up like a sprig of broccoli. His wife, Sherry, is several feet behind him leaning in the doorway to their bathroom, hidden from his view, but clearly in mine. She is barefoot, wearing a T-shirt and pink, skin-tight pants with slits that lace up from her thigh to her hip revealing a peek of rosy flesh between the laces. Ed opens his wallet and lazily thumbs through his cash, moving his lips, counting to himself. He doesn't seem to be just paying rent; I believe he's taking stock of his financial status, mumbling, "damn" in between his numbers. I peer over his shoulder at Sherry and smile; she catches my look and smiles back. Little by little, as if moving her hands in slow motion, she begins untying the laces in her pants. I quickly look away and put my attention back on Ed. His fingers pull a stack of cash from his wallet. I hold out my hand as he drops each bill into my palm, idly counting out loud as he goes along.

"Five, ten, fifteen, sixteen, seventeen…"

My eyes dart between Ed and Sherry… my attention drawn back to the bathroom doorway. She pulls open the slits, turns around to reveal the top of her bare ass.

"Eighteen, nineteen, twenty…"

Sherry silently, playfully slaps her bottom with both her hands; looks back over her shoulder, wordlessly mouthing something to me I can't quite understand.

"Thirty-three, thirty-four… thirty-five. There you go. It's all there."

"Yep, I can see that," I say, as I look Ed fast in the eye and step backward towards the corridor, tripping over the kitchen chair.

"Watch yourself!" he warns.

"You bet," I reply, hurrying out into the hallway.

Sam's door is open. I stick my head into her room, "Hello… it's me."

"Look who's here," says Sam, her voice sprinkled with pleasure particles. "Come in, Jonny, come in." She is fixing something to drink in her kitchen. A new girl about my age is sitting barefoot on the bed with her legs crossed, dressed casually in cream-colored shorts and a purple Angora sweater, spreading a line of grass into a leaf of cigarette paper, flicking out errant seeds with her index finger. A magazine opened across her lap is acting as a shield to catch the dregs.

"Hi, my name's Angel," says the fizzy blonde, looking up at me with shiny eyes. "I'm a friend of Sam's."

"Hi, my name's Jonny. I'm the wicked rent collector."

Sam let out a smoker's cackle, one part laugh to two parts cough. "Are you still looking for your 'one-armed man'?" Sam asks.

"Naw… What's the use? Our stuff is probably halfway to China by now."

Continuing on my rounds pleasantly stoned I knock on Kitty's door, announcing myself. Her faint reply directs me to enter. The door to her room is closed, but unlocked. I walk inside the darkened space, the solitary light a feeble bedside lamp in the corner of the room, dampened by a kerchief draped over the top of the shade. My eyes are drawn beneath the lamp. Something odd and fleshy sits inside a clear glass of water, illuminated by the slim cast of light no stronger than a candle. Curious, I approach the glass for closer inspection. Kitty's gleaming, polished white teeth are grinning at me from the bottom of the glass. I recoil, backing away quickly from the hideous thing. My eyes continue to roam through my neighbor's domain. I spy Kitty's signature head of poodle curls sitting alone on top of her dresser. Straddling the radiator, a ruby-red G-string with sequin glitter. Looking over my shoulder to make sure I'm unnoticed, I lift it up delicately to my face and give it a sniff. Ugh! My head jerks back; the thing smells so bad it hurts. It feels as if someone squeezed my nose with hot pliers. I put the thing back down where I found it.

"What are you doing out there, Boy?" Beyond the bathroom door a silky French accent asks playfully.

"Kitty?"

"In here, Child."

"I'm here to get your rent. I can come back later if this is a bad time."

"Come in, Baby."

I open the bathroom door and find a sea nymph lying in a bath of luxurious white bubbles, Kitty's ten red-polished toenails popping out at one end of the tub, her head resting on a bath pillow at the other end. My eyes zero down on her coffee brown breasts floating like undulating desert islands in a sea of snowy foam.

"Pick up that brush," she says, pointing with the tip of her red toe. "Scrub my back for me… will you, Lover?"

Kitty sits up straight, her hair is cut short, as thick as wool. I kneel down anxiously beside her and run the brush down the line of her spine and over the wings of her shoulders, desperately trying to act natural and unaffected, telling my nerves to calm down and take a seat in the corner.

"How come you never come by to see me dance?"

"I'm only eighteen, Kitty. They're not gonna let me in. You got to be twenty-one to get inside the clubs." That fact is I've never considered going. Checking out the strip joints has never seriously crossed my mind.

"Listen, you come and tell them you're my guest."

"Maybe I will," I muse.

"You go get my purse in the closet and take out thirty dollars."

I do as I am told and leave, locking Kitty's apartment door on the way out. Back in my room I plop down on my mattress and fantasize on Kitty dancing on stage, naked, for me alone.

I wake up happy. The commissioning of our elevator is planned for this afternoon; the little box will once again be ready to ride. I think it would be fun to have a ribbon cutting ceremony and ask Lykos to do the honors. The musicians in the building could provide the entertainment. We'll hand Kitty a bottle of champagne to crack against the steel doorjamb. I'll take special precautions to stand between her and Lykos, I wouldn't put it past Kitty to miss the elevator and swing the fucker down on my boss's head. Fun like this is what life is all about; however, it isn't meant to be. There doesn't seem to be much interest in a formal celebration. Have these people forgotten how good it feels to ride?

Inside the Student Union, I wash down a crummy muffin with a crummier cup of coffee and light a Marlboro to cap off my fine breakfast. Andreus slides into the chair beside me and drops his books on the table.

"Jonny, my fine friend! How is my building?"

"It's still standing. Nobody's tried to blow it up lately."

"What did you get on the physics test?"

"I scored a C," I answer unenthusiastically, flicking ashes into my coffee.

"C! That is good! Maybe we study together. I need help."

"A C blows, Andreus. I gotta do better."

"I asked Larry to study with me tonight. Maybe you come, too?"

"A study group? Sure… it can't hurt. Let me think about it." I reach into my ammo bag and pull out an envelope of cash; the weekly proceeds, and pass it over to Andreus who quickly opens it, flipping his thumb through the bills, silently moving his lips while counting.

"Did the police catch your thief?"

"Are you kiddin'? The only way that guy could ever get caught would be if he walked inside the station and turned himself in. I bought a new radio… I'm thinking of chaining it to the radiator."

"The elevator working?"

"It's happening today. Listen, man… Robert and I are planning to move across the hall into 6A. We want to change rooms. This okay with you?"

"Of course it is… I will ask my brother."

"Come on, let's hit it," I jerk my thump towards the exit. "I don't want to be late for Pederson's class." Professor Pederson, my engineering instructor, has been giving me a ton of shit for failing to complete assignments on time. I think he has it in for me.

Classes are through and I am anxious to get home and begin hauling our things over to the new apartment. Stepping off the trolley's underground dank and drippy Boylston Street Station, I ascend the rusty steel stairs to the street and pass through the door. Mesmerized, I stand frozen by the sights and sounds I'm witnessing down Tremont Street in the direction of my building. Dozens of red and blue lights are spinning and flashing from the tops of police cruisers and ambulances, dusk has dropped a veil over the scene making the lights flash that much brighter. Sirens scream through the air, shielding out all other sounds. Something terrible has happened. I begin running towards a gallery of onlookers lined up on their toes behind a human fence of police. My heart starts to race when I come within a few yards of this line and it becomes clear to me my building has been cordoned off. I force my way to the front of the crowd and wedge between several bystanders. An ambulance backed up near the entry has its rear bay door opened, ready to receive human cargo.

"What the hell's happening?" I ask the crowd.

"Not sure, exactly," says a black man standing beside me, looking on. "They say some people's been shot."

"Jesus, God," I whisper. Pushing my body forward, I approach the nearest cop. "I got to get in there!"

"Stop right there!" The officer shoves me back with both his hands.

"I live here," I say, speaking calmly and directly to his face, inches away from mine. "If somebody has been shot I probably know them. I'm the building superintendent."

The cop becomes courteous and speaks to me in a tone meant for my ears only.

"There are three people down, and one of them is a police officer. It didn't happen in your building… the shooting came from inside the bar next door."

I feel the warmth of relief.

The entrance to the Tam Café stands less than ten feet away from the door to my building, sounds of focused commotion pour out from inside, commanding voices of men directing the movements for other men to follow.

"Stand back! Go, go, go!"

A path is cleared in front of the door. Men pushing and pulling gurneys rush the wounded towards the nearest ambulance, rolling by in a blur. I recognize the first victim they whisk away, quick as a blink... Officer Johnson. His ambulance speeds off in the direction of Massachusetts General Hospital. I stand on the sidewalk stiff as stone, not believing what is happening.

This evening I sit by the radio with Van Helden and we listen to the news of the shootings:

"At about 5:15, Detective Philip Doherty and Patrolman Byron Geagan of the Boston Police Department responded to a report of shooting at the Tam Café, at 218 Tremont Street. John Sterling Stewart, a 46 years old drifter from Detroit, entered the Tam and displayed a revolver to the bartender, stating, 'This is a holdup. Put the money in the bag.' When the bartender indicated that he thought the man was joking, Stewart fired one round into the mirror behind the bar. The bartender then went outside and summoned Patrolman Francis "Bucky" Johnson, who was on traffic duty at the corner of Tremont and Stuart Streets. Patrolman Johnson was shot in the stomach when he entered the café and confronted Stewart. Two other bystanders were also shot; one had struck Stewart over the head with a beer bottle. Detective Doherty, Patrolman Geagan and Patrolman John Ryan of the Traffic Division arrested Stewart, and he was taken to the Mass General Hospital where he was treated for a laceration of the scalp, released and later booked into District One for attempted armed robbery and assault and battery by means of a deadly weapon."

And later, as the hours pass into the night…
"Patrolman Francis Johnson, admitted to Mass General Hospital early this evening, died of gunshot wounds to the abdomen. He was 49 years old, married and the father of six children."

PART TWO
LIGHTS ARE TURNING RED

16

Break On Through

The three of us sit cozy beside each other on Sam's bed with our backs to the wall like teenagers at a slumber party, the sole light in the room a candle poking out from the neck of an old wine bottle. Jasmine incense burns on the bedside table, masking the scent of cannabis sativa. The window facing the airshaft is thankfully sealed tight. Sam left the door to the hallway open a pinch, the room's only source of fresh air. Sandwiched between Charlie and me, she draws a hit from a joint and passes it along.

"Did you ever notice how quiet it is around here in the morning?" I ask.

"I wouldn't know," replies Sam. "I'm not a morning person."

"I was cutting through that alley between LaGrange to Boylston, I found this wino lying on the ground. He looked older than dirt. I thought he was dead.

"What'd you do?" asks Charlie.

"I checked him out, he sort of had an eye open, so I left him alone. This slick dude in a suit steps into the alley. The wino holds up a shaky hand like he's begging to be pulled from quicksand. Mr. Slick takes out a smoke, lights up, and passes it over to him. He dropped the whole pack down in the bum's lap, then just walks away, without saying a thing. That was pretty righteous. Pass me that jug, will ya?"

Sam hands me the bottle of Mateus she has propped between her legs. "So what of it?" she asks.

"It can get pretty ugly around here," I pause to take a swig, wiping my lips before continuing. "That dude put a little beauty back in the city. You gotta look up to people like that."

"Maybe the bum in the dirt helped Mr. Slick more than Mr. Slick helped the bum." Sam puts forward this hypothesis, but I have no idea what it means. I keep my ignorance to myself.

Charlie pulls a pack of Kools from his pocket.

"When did you start smoking those?" I ask.

"They're like breathing mountain air. You guys wanna try one?"

"No thanks," says Sam. "If I want menthol, I'll chew gum with my Camels."

Our elevator has been rejuvenated, but it's still an arthritic old box full of noise, groaning cranky aches and pains as it creaks its way up and down the shaft. The grunting machinery announces the approaching cab. Van Helden's laughing voice steps through the elevator door, joined by an unfamiliar baritone. Sam's door abruptly swings open. The fluorescence of the corridor's lights flood our darkened space as three figures emerge through the smoky fog.

"You're busted!" Robert points his gun-finger at us.

"Come on in, Robert. Put your gun away," says Sam, waving him inside.

Standing beside Van Helden is a handsome black man sporting a thick droopy mustache, dressed in dark bellbottoms; a pure white blouse opened at the chest, with sleeves billowed up above his wrists. He topped off his look with a black leather vest and a dashing cowboy hat. Hanging on his arm is a goddess; a remarkably beautiful young woman. Long, dark waves of silky hair enfold her shoulders, her elegant body wrapped tight within a violet satin dress. The lady's eyes dart beyond us into the corners of the room like a Siamese cat cautiously assessing the terrain before venturing ahead.

Van Helden introduces his new acquaintances. "This is Marvin…" an easy, affable smile emerges from beneath Marvin's bushy mustache; his eyes seem to twinkle… "and Winky." The tall beauty hugs up against her man, holding him tight by the arm. When she hears her name, the corners of her mouth turn up slightly as she softly says hello before looking away.

Van Helden spins to his side and gives Marvin a friendly slap on the back, happily declaring, "They're moving in." Marvin looks quite pleased by this announcement. "They're gonna be renting 5C. We're going around the building picking out a few things from the empty rooms."

I smile to my new neighbors, "Welcome home."

Van Helden waves goodbye and escorts the attractive couple on their quest for furnishings.

"Woofa! Did you check out Winky?" Charlie asks, his grinning face glowing in the candlelight like a silly jackolantern.

"I hate to pop your bubble, man, but I think she

has a boyfriend," says Sam, giving Charlie's knee a motherly pat.

"I felt a good vibe coming from Marvin. Did you pick up on that?" I ask.

"No, I missed it. I was too busy eyeballing Winky," chuckles Charlie.

"Why don't we take a walk? It's nice out tonight. I could use a little air, what do you think?" I ask, hoping for some company.

"Where?" asks Sam.

"No where, anywhere... I really don't care. Let's just go."

Charlie jumps up and rolls his fists in the air. "Let's do Washington Street! We don't have to go anywhere. It's a trip just walking in it. The circus is in town every night; it's a freak show."

Sam passes on the prospect of touring the neighborhood, calling the suggestion dull, "I'm out there every night... What's the big deal, Charlie?"

On the corner of Essex and Washington, Charlie grabs hold of my shirt and gives it a yank. "Check it out... exotic, man," he says under his breath as he points his chin across the street at two ladies, a flaming red-head and tinsel-blonde who look as if they stepped off the set of a Russ Meyer production. The pair cross Washington Street and are coming directly towards us. I suddenly recognize them: dancers I met inside Kitty's apartment.

"Hi, Jonny," says one, easily.

"Out having fun tonight, Jonny?" harmonizes the other.

I can't remember their names, and I am shocked they remember mine. Too stumble-minded to reply, I give a feeble wave as they continue floating on their way.

Charlie gives my shirt another yank, "You *know* them?"

"I've seen those two a couple of times in my building. I think the red head's name is Venus."

"Woofa!"

I flash a shrug and adjust my posture, standing several inches taller than I was a few seconds ago.

Sparkling lights of the marquees beckon the course of gentlemen drifting along Washington Street. I feel a charge of excitement as we blend into the flow. The sidewalks are brimming with men of all shapes and colors eager to tap into the sexual fantasia that pours from the strip clubs as easily as the liquor and the beer inside. Many travel in packs of threes and fours; a few are in uniform; the majority are your average, loud-mouth, boozing, adolescent rednecks, office creeps, and college boys. They all share one common fascination: female subjugation. Among the visitors, local scammers, pimps, and drug dealers troll the gutters, feeding on innocence, pleasure, and greed. Black musicians – romantics and entrepreneurs – walk the street with an air of confidence and superiority, affecting an attitude that is urbane, and debonair. Affecting no attitude at all, except maybe boredom, are the bartenders, bouncers, and capitalists living off the local entertainment.

And then there are the girls…

You can clearly discern the various patterns of female life in the Combat Zone. Three classes distinguish the ladies. The first group – the Entertainers – makes up the majority. They include strippers, dancers, and cocktail waitresses. The second is the Girlfriends. They consist of women who are along for the ride with the men in their life; the men are definitely behind the wheel. And finally there are the Hookers. They are further distinguished by two subclasses: the Winners and the Losers. The Winners are semi-successful, work out of their apartments, and service a steady customer base. At the bottom of this sexual swamp are the Losers, the ones that hang out in the street, often alone. But don't underestimate their power. They can be the most dangerous, mostly because they've got nothing left to lose. One in thirty people out tonight is a woman, and one-hundred percent of the women fall into one of these three categories.

"Those chicks we bumped into back there… they hookers?"

"No, they're friends of Kitty. They dance in the clubs."

"Strippers?"

"Yeah… maybe, I don't know. Most of her friends that come by call themselves dancers."

"Does Sam dance naked?"

Like me, Charlie's never seen the inside of a strip club. I've never actually caught Sam in action, but I've seen the outfits she wears when she heads out for work.

"Sam just gets up on the bar in her hot pants and a slinky top and slides around to the music. She's not into stripping," I comment, like I know what I'm talking about. "I met a friend of hers a little while ago, a pretty little blonde chick named Angel. I heard them both talking about the crummy bread they make dancing. They said the bucks would skyrocket if they took off their clothes. Sam won't do it, though. She says her tits are too small. But Angel's thinking about it. There's a huge difference between strippers and hookers, but it's not so much in the way they look. It's in the way they act; it's their attitude that sets them apart."

"Attitude?"

"Yeah… Hookers will come on to strangers, put their hands all over them, flirt like maniacs; strippers won't give a stranger the time of day. Fact is, they tell most guys who hit on them to fuck off."

"Strippers and hookers," Charlie says the words slowly while gazing across the Washington Street landscape. "The woods are full of them."

At the entrance to the Normandy Lounge, a middle-age man in a white shirt and tie and neatly combed hair is standing on the edge of the sidewalk reading from a Bible. The guy reminds me of my high-school vice-principal. He's preaching repentance and salvation to a world that has ignored his existence.

"*Jesus loves you!*" the vice-principal shouts into the face of a wino shuffling by clutching a paper bag. The top of a green bottle pops out from the bag like the head of a turtle.

"Whiskey loves you!" The wino shoots back, raising his turtle in the air.

The Normandy Lounge is familiar to me only because I know a few girls who dance here. We stand beneath its brightly lit marquee; bare incandescent bulbs trim the edges of the letter board. This is the first time I ever stopped and lingered by the entrance. Charlie and I begin checking out the glossy black and white photos of girls displayed on wall panels flanking the door. Kitty's picture is featured in a prominent spot. It's a full-body shot of her standing naked in high heels looking directly at you over her shoulder;

back to the camera with hands on hips. The only stitch of visible garment, a thin bit of white lace tied around her waist supporting a G-string. She looks positively breathtaking. There is also an action photo of Julie dancing nude on stage before a circle of men, tassels twirling from her glorious breasts, like little fans cooling the faces gazing up at her. Her breasts are out of focus. I imagine Julie moving them in dizzy-fast circles with the skill of a juggler. The name with the photograph identifies her as "Candy".

"Charlie, let's go in."

Two men in shabby dark suits materialize out of the woodwork as we cross through the darkened foyer. The smaller of the two, a stocky guy with no neck and a complexion like raw hamburger, informs us the club has a two-drink minimum policy. The taller dude, looking like a close relation to Herman Munster, blocks the double-door to the inner sanctum where muted rock music can be heard spilling through the cracks, "May I see some ID gentlemen?" he grunts politely.

"We're Kitty's guests," I say without hesitation. "She invited us to stop by and catch her act."

"May I see some identification?"

"I'm a friend of Kitty's," I repeat, earnestly.

"Gentlemen, if you turn around and leave now, we can avoid a situation. Do we understand each other?" says Herman Munster, without a trace of emotion.

"No… Yes!… I mean, listen, I really am a friend of hers. No bullshit. She'd be pissed off if she found out I came by and couldn't get in. Please, please… go tell Kitty her Super is standing out here waiting to see her."

Something I said must have clicked with the taller dude. He brings his hands together as if in prayer, raising them to his chin, all the while fixing me with a cold stare. He appears to be either considering my request or contemplating the optimum way to dispatch two teenage punks without messing up his suit. He leans over and whispers something to Meat Head, who turns quickly and darts through the doorway into the club. In the brief second the door pivots on its hinges, a quick blast of rock music escapes from inside the venue. Charlie and I step to the side, away from the incoming traffic lane and beyond the earshot of the tall goon still staring at us.

"What the hell's going on?" asks Charlie, sounding somewhat apprehensive about our chances. "Are we staying or leaving?"

"I think we're going in," I smile, feeling a little confident.

After a short wait, Meat Head returns and ushers Charlie and me from the foyer through the set of double doors and into a dark, cavernous room that has the atmosphere of a subterranean chamber. We pass scores of tables crowded with drinks surrounded by seated gentlemen forming a deep horseshoe pattern around a stage, which is actually nothing more than a raised platform. A young raven-haired lady with alabaster skin and a firm body moves in perfect syncopation to the throbbing, sensual beat of drums, base guitar and Jim Morrison's strong baritone voice persuasively singing to us, *Break On Through to the Other Side*. She is naked, except for emerald-green sequin pasties the size of healthy shamrocks covering her nipples and a matching G-string cupped between her legs.

The entrails of silver cigarette smoke waft through yellow beams of light encircling her performance. To my delight, we are given a table up front.

A cocktail waitress leans over our dartboard size table, displaying a warm smile and welcoming cleavage, "What can I get for you boys?"

"Oh, I don't know…" I pause, I could really go for a Coke, but instead think better of it. "How'bout a couple of beers. That okay with you, Charlie?" I look over at my buddy, grinning like a banshee, his eyes locked on the dancer.

"Yeah, that's cool with me," says Charlie, beaming from ear to ear.

Our waitress returns a few minutes later and drops four bottles of Budweiser on the table; two in front of both of us.

"Excuse me," I say. "We only ordered two beers."

"Two-drink minimum, honey," she says, adding with a friendly wink, "These are on the house, compliments of your girlfriend."

Half-standing, I crane my neck above a sea of male heads, hoping to catch sight of her, but the room is dark and smoky, making it difficult to see much of anything but the stage. I suddenly recognize Julie cutting through the fog, zigzagging in our direction. Several men are straining in their seats trying to grab her attention as she passes by. She twists and turns her hips to avoid tables, and the slip of a few hands. Highlights of her blonde hair are set off from the black satin jump suit that hangs loose over her frame, she crosses beneath the girl on stage, her curvaceous silhouette backlit by the performance lights. Julie approaches our table and smiles as we make eye contact.

"And who are these two good looking men we have here?" she says, sitting down between us.

"Charlie, I'd like you to meet my neighbor."

Charlie continues grinning, showing all thirty-two teeth.

"Julie, that picture of you out front..."

"Do you like it? I can get you a copy. I had a *ton* of publicity shots taken of me last month. I'll come by and show them to you, if you'd like."

"Yeah, sure… that would be cool. The name below the photo says, 'Candy'. What's up with that?"

"Candy's my stage name. My real name is Julia. You can either call me Candy or Julie. I don't much care which; just don't call me Julia. I always thought Julia sounded too snooty."

"Julie, where's Kitty hiding? I want to thank her for the beers."

"She's coming out next. But Kitty didn't buy them for you… that was me."

The lights on the stage suddenly dim. A spotlight falls on a forty-something white dude with a face like a rat, dressed in a crummy tweed sport jacket. He steps to the far corner of the stage and grabs hold of a microphone, clears his throat, "A couple goes into an art gallery," he says, talking at high-speed. "They find a picture of a naked lady with her privates covered with leaves. The wife doesn't like it and moves on but the husband keeps staring. The wife asks, 'What are you waiting for?' The husband says, 'Autumn.'"

After telling a couple more lame-ass jokes the rodent gets down to business and announces the next act. "Ladies and gentlemen, the Normandy Lounge is pleased to welcome back this evening's very special guest, the forever fabulous, eternally enchanting, cosmically captivating ... KITTY!"

In perfect syncopation with the opening chords from the Doors, *"Light My Fire"*, a blast of a white light sparks off a crimson-clad black woman at center stage, the light falls across her reclined body, barely seated on a cane-back chair. She's wearing a spangled-ruby skirt and vest over a white, silk blouse, opened wide from the neck down to her belly, revealing the hint of a beaded, scarlet bra. A choker of pearls grip tight around her throat, matching the pair of garters clutching her upper thighs, her head tilting back; a flowing, thick mane nearly brushes the stage. Kitty's posture becomes even more compromising as she begins to languidly lift her hips in rhythm to the music, bringing them down slowly, and gliding open her legs in a dreamy motion. She doesn't seem to acknowledge the adulation of the swarm of men surrounding her, howling through the darkness, their shouts, a jumble of vulgar taunts and wanton admiration. Kitty gyrates off the chair, losing her vest in the move. Standing tall, she plays with the crowd, feigning disapproval; shaking a long finger in their face, like a schoolteacher scolding her misbehaving students. The howling amplifies, practically drowning the music. Suddenly, as if to satisfy pent-up fantasies, Kitty rips her blouse from her body and throws it to the floor like it was on fire. As the music continues to flow, her skirt is shed from her hips, not in haste... but slowly, teasingly, leaving behind only a scarlet heart tied to a G-string. The bra slips to the floor, giving all eyes a look at Kitty's breasts, her nipples topped with pasties like red cherries. After there is nothing more to remove but her pearls, the climax complete, she continues to dance, spent, till the end of song. The light lifts from the stage and along with it Kitty and her garments.

"Whoa," I say, looking towards Julie. "Not bad, huh?"

"I can do better," she winks. "You ain't seen nothing yet."

I glance over at Charlie to see how he is doing. Still grinning like a banshee, he hasn't touched his beer.

17
Robin

We now have a window facing the street giving us the power to communicate with the outside world. Now and then, Robert and I stick our heads out and holler down at the people below our fire escape. We tell them to shut up if we're trying to get some sleep, or there may be a foxy chick crossing Tremont deserving of a compliment. Perhaps we recognize a passerby and we simply want to say hello.

"HEY, BARRY! BLOW ME!"

Watching the street gives me the advantage to screen our visitors. After they buzz us and retreat to the sidewalk, I furtively check out who's there before deciding to respond. My friends know enough to hit the buzzer, dart outside and wave up at me sneaking a peek.

The late afternoon sun is pouring through our window, bathing my bed in warm light as I lie here reading, relaxing comfortably until the electric bzzzzz slashes a hole in my peace. I scooch over the edge of the bed and lean my eyes down to the street, waiting for my intruder to appear. The figure of a girl emerges from our entrance and begins to walk away. I hastily crank open the casement window and call out to her.

"HEY!"

She spins on her heels, looking behind her back, completing the circle, searching the air around her.

"UP HERE!"

The girl raises her face towards the sound of my voice… I immediately recognize Robin, our old tenant from 3A. I give a little wave and tell her to wait, "I'm coming right down!" I can see her eyes go bright, even from six floors above.

The elevator door closes and I reach behind Robin to push the button for the sixth floor. She seems to enjoy me brushing up against her. She's acting ditzy; maybe she's loaded.

"What have you been up to, Robin? Are you stoned?"

She begins to giggle. "Nooo, why? Do I look high?" she says, touching my sleeve and batting comically coquettish eyes.

"Spaced out, I'd say."

"I just feel good. Can't a girl be happy without having to explain herself?" she says, adopting a Betty Boop quality to her voice, followed up with more giggles.

"Sure, you can be goofy if you want to… It doesn't bother me."

We walk together into my room. Robin is following me tight, like she is trying to glue herself to my back. I turn into the kitchenette to fetch my cigarettes; Robin right behind me, sticking to my pants like lint, her breath on my neck. Flashing on Donnie and the simplicity this girl flaunts when it comes to free-love, I figure this is my chance to finally get laid, and roll a tight one-eighty into her arms.

"Robin, let's go to bed."

"All right," she says, brightly.

Robin disrobes breezily, yanks open the covers, and plops her naked body under the top sheet, pulling it up to her waist. Leaning an elbow on my pillow, she pats the spot next to her where I belong. There is no chance in hell I am going to screw this up. I drop my clothes and eagerly jump in. Robin's robust frame straddles over me with cowgirl gusto.

"Whoa, slow down a second… don't go so fast," I appeal to her while gently pushing free from under her weight. I'm as flaccid as an empty balloon. I want a successful performance, and I desperately need to stiffen up my act. I prop up beside her on one elbow and focus my eyes on her large breasts, while slipping my other hand between her open legs. It feels surprisingly like steel wool. All of a sudden I'm not so sure of myself. This is not going to be as easy as I thought. Thankfully, Robin seems to know how to handle the situation and fondles me gently while sending kisses over my neck and down my chest. Soon, she is back in the saddle again… this time successfully drawing me in.

So, this is it… sinking into mud… up and down… like pulling footprints stuck in a silky bog. I look at her face while coming, expecting to see a little reaction, but she is lost in a world of her own. I keep myself inside her, feigning potency, but eventually fall free, sliding down a slippery precipice. This whole thing lasts maybe two minutes.

"That was nice," I say, thinking I'm quite the stud.

"Yeah. You got a cigarette?" Robin acts a bit more detached than she was five minutes ago. I jump up and grab her a smoke and slide back down under the covers. She lights up and concentrates on her Marlboro. Lying intimate inches away from her I feel remarkably distant and disassociated.

"So, what did you do today?" I ask, trying to sound interested.

"Well… before coming here I stopped to see a friend of mine. He lives in the North End."

"He? Who he?"

"His name's Michael. He's nice."

"So, what were you and nice ol' Michael doing all afternoon?"

"Balling."

"You guys had sex?" I feel squeamish.

"Yeah… it was fun. Of course, not as much fun as you and I just had."

My first real dip into sex and I'm gonna get the clap! I bolt into the bathroom, frantically searching the medicine cabinet for some kind of disinfectant to douse myself, grab the green plastic bottle of hospital antiseptic, jump into the shower and squeeze like a maniac gobs of white goo over my dick, scrubbing vigorously. I place my faith in Doctor PHisoHex, praying it will kill any spores before they begin to nest and multiply. I walk back into the room nonchalantly, drop the towel I have around my waist and pull on my pants.

"You took a shower?" Robin looks surprised.

"Yeah, it felt great. I like a good, hot shower at the end of the day. It's very relaxing. If you feel like taking one, knock yourself out."

"Maybe later," she quietly says, her head peeking out from beneath the sheets.

"Ah, Robin, where are you going… I mean later, after you leave?"

"Jonny ... can I stay with you tonight?"

"Here? Sure... why? Ugh, it's perfectly okay... don't you have your own place?"

"Of course I do, but it would be nice if I didn't have to leave right away, that's all."

After dwelling for a moment on the idea of Robin sleeping with me and figuring it can't hurt, I slap my hands together, "Get dressed! Let's go grab a bite."

"Okay!"

The diner downstairs is empty of customers, as usual. "How do these guys manage to make a buck," I wonder out loud as I poke some rubber meat around my plate.

"What?" Robin asks, sipping Coke from a paper straw.

"Nothin'... You know the last time I saw you, Robin, was the night you got it on with my friend, Donnie. Whatever happened between you and him?"

"Who?"

"Donnie Pyle, about a month or so ago... remember? My friend, the Marine... he was here visiting. You two had sex together."

"We did?" Robin's eyes look to be searching over the horizon as she chews on the end of her straw. "Oh, yeah! The Marine Man." She drops her straw and takes a gulp of soda, "He couldn't get it up."

"Whoa..."

"I thought Marines are supposed to be men?"

Balling, I guess, isn't as easy as everyone makes it out to be. I feel I should treat her for the meal, so I pay the check, besides... the dinner was cheap.

We step outside and stand in front of my building. The night air feels comfortably cool, much more inviting than my stuffy old room.

"You want to take a walk," I ask. Robin smiles and shakes her head okay. We take our time strolling down Boylston, pausing at storefronts to window shop. I probably should hold her hand, but I don't want her to get any wrong ideas, like I'm her boyfriend or something.

"Wait right here," Robin says, leaving me standing alone on the sidewalk as she ducks inside a tiny florist shop, emerging two minutes later clutching a bouquet of yellow roses. "These are for you," she smiles kindly, extending her gift to me.

"Thanks… ugh, why?" I stare at her with my hands stuck in my pants.

"That *blah* room of yours needs something pretty to cheer it up," Robin feigns a frown. "Take the flowers."

We cross the street side by side, the flowers tight in my hand, and step onto a path that leads to the center of the Public Garden. Coming to a stop on the bridge that spans the duck pond, I lean over the railing and peer into the water. Robin follows my queue and leans in beside me. After a quiet moment I turn towards her; the moon reflects a path of light off the pond straight into Robin's face, applying a soft glow to her features.

"This bridge is my favorite place to be in the whole city," I confess, adding, "day or night."

"It is pretty, isn't it?"

"Listen…"

"Listen to what? I don't hear nothin.'"

"My point exactly. It's so calm and peaceful here. Everyone takes their time passing through;

you can't help feeling reverence for this place. It's as if this garden is a church and the bridge its altar.

"Does anyone ever come here to get married?"

"I don't see why not. You know… that's not a bad idea," I say, truly believing it. I take Robin by the hand and walk home.

Stepping into my room, I flip on the light and search for a pitcher to hold the flowers. Robin goes directly to my bed and removes everything but her white cotton socks. I douse the lights and jump in naked. Once we get past the preliminary kissing and fondling, she mounts me and impales herself. This time, I stay with her for nearly fifteen minutes, a huge improvement over my first shot. We flip over flat on our backs, breathing heavily, like we just chased each other around the block.

"That was nice, Jonny," Robin pants.

After a subdued minute, I pull a cigarette from my pack and light up; the smoke never felt this refreshing.

The elevator comes alive; I feel its vibrations rumbling up the shaft. It grinds to a halt outside my door and the voices of Van Helden and Omar emerge in the hallway. I recall Robert saying something earlier about Omar coming to spend the night.

"You remember Omar?"

"Yeah, sure… why?"

"He might be crashing with us. It could get a little crowded in 6A tonight."

"I don't mind being stuck here with three pretty boys. It might be fun." Robin laughs like a little girl having her feet tickled.

Robert and Omar walk into our darkened

room and hit the light. I sit up straight with my back to the wall, Robin lies low holding the covers up to her chin, like she is peeking over the neighbor's fence trying to see into their backyard.

"Hi, guys! We have an old friend visiting… Say hello, Robin."

"Hello Robin," she smiles.

"Hey!" Robert, instantly drawn in her direction, steps over our clothes and sits on the corner of my bed, "Long time no see."

I squirm out from under the covers and scoop up my pants, slipping into them while these two catch up on old times.

"Omar, you remember Robin, don'tcha?"

"Of course… Good to see you again!" Omar beams a smile in her direction.

Robin raises her arm and wiggles four fingers in the air like she is trilling piano keys.

The four of us all get comfortable sitting together in a tight ring around my bed listening to music, joking with one another and telling stories. Robin hasn't bothered getting dressed; she simply drapes the bedspread around her shoulders like an Indian maiden.

As midnight approaches we break up our circle and my buddies begin preparations for sleep. Robin and I slip back under the covers. I feel her hand tickling between my legs, "Come here, big boy."

Romancing Robin is not something I care to be doing all night. In fact, now that I have done the deed, I'm sure I don't want to do it again with her. I whisper across my pillow, "I want to ask you something… don't take this the wrong way."

"What?"

"Would you like to sleep with all three of us?"

"When… now?"

"If Robert and Omar are cool with it, you can take turns going from bed to bed."

Robin's face, expressionless, slowly evolves to curious, finally breaking into an agreeable smile, "Okay."

I hop out of bed and huddle with my buddies.

"How's this supposed to work?" asks Omar.

"Robin will spend time in bed with one of us," I say. "When she feels like leaving, she hops in the sack with someone else." I walk over to my dresser, reach in the top drawer and pull out my box of Trojans, still sealed in its cellophane wrapper. "I'm gonna pass out protection." I open the box and tear off three condoms.

Robin gets up from my bed and steps beside us in the center of the room. She looks thoughtfully at each of us in turn, as if this is a ladies-choice dance and she's judging potential material, pulling her chin with her hand, "Who's going to be first?"

"I'll start the ball rolling," I volunteer.

Robin spins around like a ballerina, and retreats directly to my bed.

With the lights off and the music turned down low, Robin and I make love quietly, one last time. She lies on her back, not moving, waiting for me to finish, kisses me softly and leaves my bed. I look up, watching as she crosses the room and disappears into the darkness to slip beneath the covers with Van Helden. The melancholy ballads of Tom Rush, perfect for this early hour of the morning, play sweetly from the radio as I drift off to sleep.

My head lifts and turns to face the window, morning sunshine cascades bright light across the table where my yellow roses are wilting, having neglected to fill the jar with water. I drop back into my pillow and stare at the ceiling. I feel empty inside, like I'm made out of dust. I could be blown away by a baby's breath. The radio, left on all night, is playing faintly; the smack-head monotone of Leonard Cohen's *Suzanne* adds more shades of grey to my funk.

Robert and Omar are still in bed sleeping, I presume; Robert on his pullout couch, Omar on the thin cot with Robin precariously deposited beside him. How can they possibly be comfortable on that thing? It's like sticking a size 12 foot into a size 6 shoe. Robin and Omar have their arms wrapped around each other, like they're hanging together to keep from hitting the floor.

Van Helden rises from his bed. After stretching the sleep from his limbs, he walks a straight line over to Omar and Robin.

"Get up, you two! We got a nice day! Let's go do somethin'!" He yanks on their covers trying to get a reaction from a pile of inertia.

"Okay, okay," Omar grunts, batting his hand in the air towards Robert like he is swatting an annoying fly.

I shift myself out of bed and pass them on my way to the bathroom. "G'morning! How you guys doing?"

"Shut up," Robin mumbles as she slides off the cot and transfers her body to my bed, burrowing beneath the covers; apparently not ready to join the world.

The four of us leave the apartment, taking pleasure in a lovely Sunday morning stroll in the Common. A magnificent spring homecoming of fresh foliage surrounds us; the cold, barren products of winter now entirely gone. Robin links arms between Omar and Van Helden; I walk behind them. We cross Charles Street and pass through the Public Garden, marveling at the glorious collection of flowers framing our path in colorful flames. Crossing the bridge spanning the duck pond, we pause to capture the beauty of it all.

"This is where I plan to be married," Robin announces.

18

Snakes, Gypsies and the Secret Service

"I came by to pick up your rent."

"Wanna see my snake?" Barry asks.

I'm standing impatiently in the hallway outside his apartment. Barry, naked from the waist up, is clutching the end of a natty burlap bag the size of a large pillowcase. The bottom of the bag looks as if a bowling ball is dropped inside.

"Do I have a choice?"

He ignores my remark and proudly steps forward, opening the bag for my inspection.

"What the hell is *that?*" I recoil back a half step.

"It's my python," Barry says. He places the loaded bag on the linoleum floor, reaches in and extracts his trophy; a lethargic, three-foot long, multi-colored reptile, as thick around the middle as a child's arm. Barry holds it up by the neck, choking the creature. Together, they looked like something out of a Tarzan flick.

"Where did that come from?" I ask, withholding the more honest question; where did you steal it?

"The lab at Harvard let me take it home."

"Is it poisonous?"

"Of course not, it's as gentle as a lamb."

"That goddamn thing could eat a fuckin' lamb. Where the hell you gonna keep it? Not here, I hope."

"Of course here," says the big guy, challenging me with his eyes. "Fang's going in my room, man."

Fang?

"Barry! Come in here!" an unfamiliar female voice shouts a command from inside Barry's room.

"Colette wants me."

Colette?

"Barry, NOW!" An ugly white girl stomps out from his room and positions herself behind Barry, one hand on her hip, the other clenched like it's getting ready to throw a hand grenade. She's dressed like a lumberjack, or a bull rider, wearing a red flannel shirt and jeans.

Barry and Fang withdraw from the doorway and disappear with Colette. I continue on my rounds.

"Sam, it's time to pay The Man."

"Come in, come in," she says. "I'm getting ready for work."

For Sam, this means slipping into hot pants and a halter-top, putting on makeup and getting stoned. I join her with the 'getting stoned' part of the ritual. Final preparations complete, standing to leave she asks, "Can I pay after work?"

"Sure, no problem."

"Why don't you come with me," Sam suggests, as she locks the door on the way out of her apartment. A cigarette pokes out from between her red painted lips. She turns and looks at me, "You can have a beer and can keep me company."

"Sam… I don't have any bread," I pathetically

confess. I also worry about being denied entry to the club for being under age, plus I have homework that needs to be turned in tomorrow, but I keep these concerns to myself.

Sam laughs, "You don't need money; you're with me. The bartender, Bruce, he owes me. He'll spot you one."

I run into my room and change into something bar-worthy, reappearing wearing an elegant shirt acquired from our former tenant Jamie before he left the building. He was broke and owed us one-week's rent. I took his fancy shirt. He said it was too big for him, anyway. I think it belonged to one of his boyfriends. Van Helden procured Jamie's black leather stove-pipe pants. I love this shirt. It's a dress-blue, white pinstriped, buttoned down affair with French cuffs. He also gave me a cheap pair of imitation onyx and silver cuff links to trim it out.

Sam loops her arm through mine. We cross the street the short distance to the Four Corners Lounge. It is mid-afternoon and the entrance to the club, facing the corner of Stewart and Tremont, is covered in blazing sunlight, an extreme contrast to what greets me on the other side. Passing through the door, my eyes struggle to adjust to the black innards of the club, without a pinch of light, save for the spotlights above the bar. I can't see the corners of the room. Sam's girlfriend, Angel, is dancing on the bar to Stevie Wonder's *My Cheri Amour*. Angel is swaying to the music in a graceful, dreamy motion, drifting through the air, as if lifted by a gentle wind. She smiles and waves to us as we find our seats beneath her legs. Sam pulls a cigarette from her pouch. The bartender instantly materializes at Sam's side, holding a lighter to the end of her smoke.

"Thanks, Bruce."

The lighter snaps shut.

"I want you to meet a very good friend of mine. Bruce, say hello to Jonny."

"Pleased to meet you, Jonny. Sam speaks highly of you." Bruce is an affable looking character with pleasant eyes and a winning smile, features too soft for a bartender. I always imagined bartenders as tough guys. He places a cold bottle of beer in front of me at Sam's behest.

After a smoke and a gin and tonic, Sam follows Angel on top of the bar and begins to dance. Compared to Angel, Sam seems wooden, disinterested in her performance. I scan the twenty or so guys parked around the bar, acting as if they couldn't be bothered by her performance. Sam might as well be up there filing her nails, for all they care. The surprising thing to me is Sam looks good, even if her dancing is lame. She's still a foxy chick with great legs.

Sam's set ends and she steps down and joins me for a drink. I am on my fourth beer, having befriended Bruce, gratefully accepting the freebees he keeps plopping down in front of my face.

"Have you seen that girl Colette hanging out with Barry?" I ask.

"Maybe, what she look like?"

"I only caught a peek of her... white chick with thick, dark wooly hair; dresses like a dude, wears glasses. Kinda ugly."

"I haven't seen anyone like that inside the building. Why, is this important?" asks Sam.

"It's not. I'm just curious what they're up to. I

can't figure Barry living with a chick. A girl would have to be pretty low to hook up with him."

"Or pretty slow… maybe she's a retard."

"She might be mental, but she's not retarded. I heard her giving Barry some shit; she sounded pretty together."

Bruce leans in from behind the bar, "Sam, another gin and tonic?"

"Sure, hit me. Dresses like a dude? What's that mean?"

"You know, dungarees, Roy Rogers cowboy boots, flannel shirt."

"That's not a dude, my man, that's a dyke," Bruce says, tapping his finger down hard on the bar for emphasis.

I wasn't ready to commit to his assessment, the idea of Barry with a lesbian just doesn't equate.

Sam and Angel work all afternoon. I flip back and forth watching them dance and chatting with Bruce, while downing somewhere in the neighborhood of eight or ten beers. For some odd reason, I took to calling Bruce, Boober.

"BOOBER! You gotta come over to my building sometime…We'll have a party."

"BOOBER! Do ya wanna play some pinball? I'm great at pinball!"

"BOOBER! Where the hell's the toilet in this place?"

Sam and Angel finish their last dance and step over to me. "Let's go home, Jonny."

I lift myself off the stool and stand between two pretty bookends with hot pants, escorting me from the bar. Its late afternoon and a pale-blue twilight sky hangs above Tremont. We walk the short distance back to our building; they each have an arm looped through mine.

"Did ya know we got a snake in the building?" I ask the ladies.

"What did you say... a snake?" Angel laughs. "What the hell are you talking about?"

"Barry... A *snake!*"

"Yeah," says Sam. "We know. Barry's a snake."

"No no no," I say, fighting out words to get my point across. "Barry *has* a snake. A fuckin' python!" I pull away from the girls, standing in the middle of Tremont Street, stretching my arms out as wide as physically possible and shout, "THIS BIG!"

Back in my room I fall into bed. My clock shows 5:45 pm... could that be right? Man, I'm tired. I have sketches I'm supposed to complete for tomorrow's drafting class. I'll get to that later. I'll just lie down for a little while... close my eyes.

Our place is looking pretty slick. Whenever an apartment is vacated Robert and I drag the best furniture up to our room and replace the old crap we started with. The corridors have been jumping with the addition of new arrivals filling all our vacancies this past month. Marvin's younger brother, Benny, is now living in 4A, along with his sleazy girlfriend, Jackie. A family settled into Apartment 5A, a middle-age guy named Tomas brought along his young wife and infant son. Tomas looks well fed, but the girl and baby look like refugees from a concentration camp. Kitty switched rooms and moved up into our old place across the hall. In her wake, we rented to another musician. A guy named Michelangelo filed into 3B with his girlfriend, Maureen; we like to call them Mickey & Minnie. Including Barry and Colette, a quality common to these couples is their biracial ingredients, a black man with a white woman. It's funny, except for Marvin and Winky, all the couples in the building share this distinction.

A lot of strange agents are living among us, but in my opinion, only two tenants in the building should be regarded closely; Barry, of course, and a bizarre family of Gypsies living in 2B. I think I got a handle on Barry, but I'm not quite sure what to do about the Gypsies. A matriarch apparently runs the show. She looks like a Romanian bag lady; walks around with several layers of clothes, her soiled skirt falling just above ankle-high black socks, long dark hair rolled in a tight bun planted on top of her head. I've counted at least two kids, perhaps as many as four, orbiting around her. It's hard to tell… they never look quite the same. I think Mom shuffles the kids around with her in public, bringing them out in shifts of two at a time. It's possible she has a troop of them stashed inside that little room. Once in a while, a guy appears to join this assembly, a scrawny dude with a face like an olive topped with a shock of red hair that pops from the top of his head like a pimento.

We've had very few dealings with these people, and never go down to their room. A kid always shows up at our door to pay the rent. Lately, the family has been setting up shop in front of the building. Mom sits in a chair she hauls down from her room. A boy, about ten years old, places a shoeshine kit a few feet away, and a girl, about the same age, pushes single stem flowers to folks strolling past our front door. The flowers look remarkably similar to the tulips in the Public Garden. Our tenants say the true nature of their enterprise is pickpocketing. When some unsuspecting schmuck lifts his shoe up on the boy's box for a buffing, the little girl presses up against him to push her flowers and buffs his wallet from his pants. Mom keeps an eye on the business in case something should go wrong and things get ugly. I never witnessed any crimes, but I have a reliable source that can substantiate theses facts. Marvin says they're all a bunch of grubby thieves and warns everyone to keep their doors locked.

As a security feature, every door in the building has these little peepholes to discreetly view visitors. We call them fish eyes. I knock on the Gypsies' door and have the sneaking suspicion of being eyeballed through the fish eye. I hear faint mumbling coming from inside the room. The door opens just wide enough for Mom to pop her head out.

"Yes, what can we do for you?" she asks in clipped English.

This is the first time I've seen this chick up close… I have no clue how old she is. She could fall anywhere between thirty and seventy. Her hair, pulled back severely from her high forehead, is pitch-black, not a strand of gray in it, obviously dyed. The hair yanked so tight it stretched all the wrinkles from her forehead flat. Not part of the same solar system, the skin below her eyeballs is as crinkled as my Grandmother's.

"I'm one the building superintendents. I don't believe we've met."

"My toilet doesn't have a seat!" she squawks at me.

"That's fine. I'm here to ask you to quit hanging out by the front door. You're freaking out the people who live here."

"Freaking out? What is that?"

"I've been told you're bothering folks that come and go into the building."

"You have been told? Who told you this? I want to see their face!"

"Listen, I'm asking you nicely, move your operation up the street. I hear the Boston Common is lovely this time of year."

"Operation?"

I thank her and turn to leave.

"Get me my toilet seat!" she squeals into the hallway as the elevator door closes behind me.

I get off at the third floor to check up on Barry, Colette and Fang. Barry's door is opened. I tap my knuckles on the jamb and walk in. Barry is lying in bed on top of the covers with his head buried in a magazine.

"How you doing, my man?" I ask. He doesn't move an inch. "Do ya think it wise to keep your door wide open with a snake crawling around your room?"

"Snake's gone," mumbles the voice from behind the magazine.

"Good!" I say, relieved to hear this news. "Where'd you take it?"

"I didn't take it anywhere," he says, dropping the magazine flat to his chest. "I put him down on the floor last night to give him a little exercise; the sonofabitch squeezed down that tiny hole where the radiator pipe comes out. Can you believe it? The thing actually fit through that skinny fuckin' hole. I wouldn't bet on that happening in a million years. Ain't nature amazing?" Barry says, giving me goofy smile.

"Jesus! Do you have any idea how *not cool* this is? Fuck amazing nature! The only thing amazing around here is you," I say, throwing my hands in the air. "Stick your fingers down that hole and pull that goddamn snake out!"

"That ain't gonna happen, Chief, and you know it. That snake's a goner."

Looking around the room I see no evidence of Colette. "What happened to your girlfriend?"

"Colette's gone, too, and she ain't my girlfriend."

"Oh… I thought you two were kinda together."

Barry sits up fast and drops his big feet to the floor. "If I ever see that slut again, I'm going to smash her face. That bitch robbed me blind. She took my stereo, she took my speed, she took my pot, she took my wallet."

"Not your detective shield? She didn't take that, did she?" I ask, secretly amused by this news.

"She took my badge," says Barry, fuming anger from his eyes.

"Love is a fickle thing, my man." I say, on my way out the door.

I see the world made up of two distinct classes of citizens: Those that are straight, and those that get high. I was once a vocal advocate of the first class, extolling the virtues of abstinence and preaching condemnation of drug indulgence. The creed, marijuana leads to harder drugs, kept me scared straight. The line went something like this, "If you smoke dope, your choices in life are over; harder drugs sailed on thermal currents overhead like vultures killing sky time waiting for you to die." That's a lie. I'm always looking forward to turning on, hopefully within the next 24 hours, and I could care less about harder drugs.

I make it to class most of the time, but it's become increasingly difficult to keep focused. The energy it takes to remain seated is slipping away. Morning sessions are finished. I amble into the Student Union cafeteria and queue up with my tray, waiting in turn to be served. Looking around at these future technocrats, first class citizens all, I feel more out of place than ever. I take my meal and sit alone in silence.

"Hey, Jonny! We have lunch together?" Andreus asks, interrupting my peace, depositing his tray on the table next to mine, not waiting for an answer.

"Knock yourself out." I gesture with my hand towards an open seat.

Andreus begins shoveling down his food. "How's our building?" he asks, while wiping his mouth with the cuff of his shirt.

I report the news of the snake to Andreus. Neither Fang nor Colette have surfaced since their disappearance several days ago.

"Do you think the snake could be pregnant?" asks Andreus, visibly nervous.

"Jesus, how would I know that? I don't think it had a boyfriend."

"If it makes snake babies, we can have a big problem. I better tell my brother."

We finish our lunch in silence.

"Let's get outta here," I say. "I can't be late again for class."

We slide back our chairs, but before I take a step Andreus pulls me over by my shirt.

"Why did you stop coming to my study group?" he asks.

"I got too much to do running that place of yours." I wave him off. I don't need that scene.

Why should I spend my nights studying with a bunch of clowns?

At the end of my last class of the day I return home and find a business card wedged between my doorjamb. I pull it free and discover my name written on the back of the card with a note scrawled below it:

> Jonathan,
> I am looking for your assistance in an important criminal investigation.
> Please call me at your earliest convenience.
> Thank you,
>
> Tim Westinghouse

I turn the card over. It looks rather ordinary, except for the titles:

Timothy Westinghouse
United States Secret Service
United States Department of the Treasury

Hello?... this is interesting. I slip the card into my shirt pocket and open the door to my apartment. Dropping my books on the table, I pull a Coke from the fridge and plop down on the couch. Retrieving the card from my pocket, in between sips inspecting it, wondering about its message and its authenticity, I reach down, pick up the phone and dial. After a single ring, a woman's voice comes on the line, "Secret Service."

"No shit!"

"I beg your pardon?" says the woman.

"I'm sorry," I say, instantly regretting my utterance. "I'm just blown away by the way you answer the phone. You said, 'Secret Service'. It sounded funny hearing you say that."

"Yes, sir. Do you wish to speak with anyone?"

"One of your guys stuck his calling card in my door today; told me to give him a ring… so that's what I'm doing."

"What is your name, sir?"

"Me? My name is Jonathan Tudan. The name on the card is Tim Westinghouse."

"Hold please, while I connect you to Mr. Westinghouse."

After a short pause and a click, a man's pleasant voice comes on the line, "Hello Mr. Tudan, this is Tim Westinghouse. Thank you for getting in touch with me."

"No problem."

"We're looking for someone we think you might have been in contact with recently. Do you mind answering a few questions?"

"Naw. Go ahead, shoot."

"Do you know a Catherine O'Reily?" he asks, spelling her name for me.

"Never heard of her."

"She may be living under an assumed name. Have you met anyone recently named Colleen McGuinnis?"

"Nope."

"Colette O'Hare?……… Mr. Tudan, Colette O'Hare?"

"What does this girl look like?"

Westinghouse begins to describe Barry's girlfriend, right down to her Roy Rogers cowboy boots.

"I think she hung around here for maybe a week… hardly saw anything of her. She ran out several days ago. I don't think she'll be coming back."

"Why is that?"

"Ah, she took everything with her."

I gave the agent what little information I knew about Catherine Colleen Colette, without mentioning Barry. I imagine I sounded circumspect, maybe causing Westinghouse to be a bit suspicious of me. Even though I can't stand Barry, I didn't think it proper to be blabbing to the Feds about how he spends his time. When I asked Westinghouse why they were after this girl, he blew me off. "We want to question her," was all he would say. He chose not to be forthcoming with me, so why should I be Joe Citizen and give up Barry?

19

Julie

Julie's three-year old girl is crawling around on the floor beside the couch where John Taylor is resting his broken leg, propped up on the coffee table. A dozen or so empties are scattered about the table beside a clutter of spent Chinese take-out and overflowing ashtrays. The little girl wiggles and squirms, passing under John's leg like it's her fantasy bridge. John ignores the kid. He has a beer in his lap and a distasteful look on his face. Julie asks if he has a couple of tens to put towards the rent.

"You pay the man! You're the one with all the money!"

Julie opens her purse and fishes around, "Here you go," she says, smiling for me. Her fingertips gently stroke my palm sending a jolt of electricity down my pants. She proceeds to drop five-dollar bills, one at a time, floating them down into my open hand. Julie looks me in the eye and winks, sending me on my way.

Earlier this evening, I caught Julie in the lobby on her way out. She asked me if I would be staying home tonight. I told her of course, where else would I be? She asked me if it would be okay for her to come up and visit. I told her certainly, you can come up anytime you want. She asked me if I would like to see some new promo shots taken of her dancing on stage. I said absolutely, I bet you photograph very well.

I have been sitting around doing nothing except nervously waiting for Julie since I walked through my door two hours ago. I open my calculus book and force a little homework. I wonder how old she is.

"Jonny?" Her voice comes across my room in a loud whisper, intended to be heard by only me. Julie is standing by my opened door. She must have taken the stairs, because I didn't hear the elevator clanking up the shaft.

"Oh, hi… come on in," I say; icy smooth, like I entertain older women all the time. I casually put out my cigarette, raise myself from my chair and walk over to greet her, discreetly checking the hallway before shutting the door as she makes her way into my room. Julie sticks a large manila envelope in my hand.

"These are for you."

I thank her for the package and place it on the table. "Have a seat," I gesture towards the most comfortable spot in my room, a cushy armchair we moved into our room last week.

"No thanks. I feel like standing. I'm kinda wound up. My little sister's visiting and I don't want to leave her alone too long with my old man."

I flop into the chair Julie passed on. "So, how old's your sister?"

"I don't trust him with her. Melanie's fifteen. She's *really* a sweetheart."

"Maybe you shouldn't be up here. She might need you."

"I've been with John long enough to know when he's a threat, and when he just being an asshole. Right now he's an asshole, flirting like an old fool, telling my sister how pretty she is, building himself up, acting like he's some kind a big man."

"When does he become a threat?"

"Melanie's no fool. We had a talk when she got here. She sees right through his bullshit. I get worried when he's drunk, and he ain't drunk right now. But, just to be safe, I want to get back down there in a little while."

Julie walks over to the bed and sits down. I guess talking about being wound up helped her unwind, because suddenly she stretches out, looking comfortable, resting her head on my pillow. She turns to face me. I remain seated, but lean out towards her, elbows on my knees. We look at each other in silence for several long seconds.

"Why are you with John?" I quietly ask.

Julie has a far-away look in her eyes. She takes a deep breath and sighs, "My last old man ran out on me, leaving me alone with my baby. I needed someone to take care of me, and John was the best thing going at the time, so I grabbed on. He was kind to me, made me feel safe. Before we moved in together, he would tell me all the time how much he loved me. Now all I hear is how he would kill any man who tries to take me away from him… John thinks that's supposed to impress me."

Julie sits up and swings her legs to the floor. Her face takes on a distressed look. "I'm almost twenty-eight. You think I would know enough by now not to get myself mixed up with the wrong kind of man. Well, let me tell you, it ain't easy being me. Why didn't you look at my pictures?"

"Now? Do you want me to?" I say, quickly getting up from my chair.

"No. Sit down."

I drop back into my chair. The room becomes awkwardly quiet, so I fill the space with the first thing that pops into my head. "Why are you a stripper?"

"M-O-N-E-Y," Julie says.

"What are you gonna do when it's over?"

"What do you mean?"

"You can't be a stripper all your life. Someday, your body won't be so glamorous, then what?"

"I'm not stupid. I'm saving up to buy me a house. When all this is over, I'm going back to Canada. I don't know what I'll be doing five years from now... but I do know this, at least I'll have a place to call my own."

"That's cool, Julie." I'm surprised by her resourcefulness.

"Would you like to look at my bank book? I'll show it to ya." Julie's mood brightens. "I've shown you everything else," she laughs, pointing to the envelope on my table. "I might as well give you a peek at that, too."

"No, thanks. I don't need to see your personal stuff."

Julie jumps up and squeals, "I forgot to tell you! Kitty and me are gonna be in a movie!"

"A movie... no kidding?"

"Well, it's actually kind of a soft porno film. The producer approached us at work. He's super nice, his name's Lionel. His company is making a movie about the Mafia and they wanted a couple of professional dancers to play themselves. I signed a contract yesterday, after John took a look at the script, of course. Isn't this exciting!?"

"I'm happy for you," I fake a smile. It sounds a bit dubious to me.

"I have to get back downstairs, but I would love to come back tomorrow and read my part to you. You can help me rehearse my lines."

"That would be cool." I will happily submit to giving up a night of homework to assist Julie with her fledgling acting career.

"One thing, though, you gotta swear to me not to mention any of this to John."

"Mention any of what?" I smile.

Julie blows out of my room and flies back down the stairs. I watch her go and wonder about the mood inside her apartment. Turning back, my eyes fall on the envelope she left behind. I spread its contents out across the table; a half-dozen attractive publicity photos, 8 X 10 black and white glossies of Julie dancing across a stage in her G-string and tassels. I look on the back of the pictures; thinking maybe she signed them for me… she didn't.

A matinee is always a great way to fill a Saturday afternoon, and when Marvin asked me this morning if I would be interested in joining him and his buddies on a trip to the Paramount to see the western, *The Good, The Bad, and The Ugly*, I accepted his offer on the spot. We hook up inside Marvin's apartment. Marvin is sitting at the kitchen table with his younger brother, Benny, and another gentleman I haven't met before, introduced as an old friend, named Orlando, "Me and Orlando have been tight since 1956," Marvin declares. "I bet you can't guess his age. Go ahead; tell me how old you think he is."

I look at his old neighborhood pal, searching for some revealing trait to distinguish him. I haven't had very good luck lately playing this game. I take a stab at it, "Twenty-eight?"

Orlando grins back at me with perfect, white teeth. Marvin and Benny laugh... not even close. Marvin, feigning astonishment announces, "Would you believe thirty-five?" and adds, with an infectious smile, "Look at him! Don't he look great for an old dude?"

We all felt good about how young old Orlando looks, and smiles are shared all around the table. Orlando, beaming the widest among us, has yet to utter a word. I take his laconic nature as a sign of maturity.

"Where's Winky?" I ask.

"Working the liquor store next door to Jack's Joke Shop," says Marvin.

"I didn't think she was twenty-one," I say, completely mystified when it comes to guessing someone's age.

"She's not, Winky's nineteen. Age is not important for what she does." The three of them look at each other knowingly.

"So, how does a nineteen year old get to work in a liquor store?" I ask.

"When the owner is your Sugar Daddy," Marvin replies, his voice hardened. Benny and Orlando chuckle, but Marvin's serious expression doesn't budge a muscle.

"Why don't we get going? It's almost two; the thing starts at two-thirty," Marvin informs us. "I don't want to miss the cartoon." He grabs a black cowboy hat and steps in front of the mirror by the entry, placing the hat gently on his head with both hands, adjusting the slant in a perfect incline over his right eye.

"Nice hat, Marvin," I say. "Makes you look like a black Paladin."

"I loved that dude! He's one bad motherfucker! Nobody messed with that man. What's his name, Boone? Daniel Boone… Pat Boone?"

"Richard Boone," I answer.

"Yeah! Richard Boone." Marvin claps his hands together. "Let's go to the movies!"

The four of us file out of the room, squeeze into our skinny elevator, and hit the street with a flourish. The day could not be more spectacular. It feels great to be alive. Drenched by the warm afternoon sun, we walk along the sidewalk on Washington Street, four cool guys in a collective, blissful mood. There is no line at the Paramount, so we breeze through the ticket booth and make our way to the snack bar. After stocking up heavily on provisions, we find our seats, sit back and get ready to enjoy the show.

"Old Paladin was one bad-ass dude," Marvin shares his thoughts with us. "But Clint Eastwood, now he tops all them motherfuckers."

We all murmur concurrence.

I add to the discussion, "Watch out for the guy who plays 'The Bad'. His name's Lee Van Cleef. Talk about bad motherfuckers." I didn't tell the others I had seen this movie already. I wasn't going to spoil it for them.

Before the Coming Attractions and the ubiquitous Tom and Jerry cartoon, the theater plays something called a "Public Service Message". An animated television set with a drooling mouth and a voracious appetite is gobbling up dollar bills. Its human owner, a dim-witted white guy is feeding the TV, woefully pulling dollar bills from his wallet, dropping them into the set's open mouth. The owner tearfully watches as the TV insatiably devours bill after bill, licking its lips.

"What the fuck is this?" Benny asks.

A voice-over comes on and hits us with the "public service" part of the message,

"What you are seeing may appear amusing, but this is no laughing matter. In the very near future, you may be charged a fee to watch the programs you now enjoy free across America's airwaves. Cable television is coming, Ladies and Gentlemen, and unless you stand up to these forces of avarice, this silly cartoon will become a reality. Stand up for your rights! Stop cable television from entering your homes and keep our airwaves free. Contact your local Representatives in the State House and tell them to fight for you on this cause. Keep Cable Out! Paid for by the Committee for Free Broadcasting."

"I'll be damned if I'm gonna pay for my motherfucking TV shows," Benny whispers loudly for our benefit.

"Benny, do you know how stupid you sound? You don't even own a TV," Marvin cuts into his little brother.

On the way out of the theater I stop in the lobby and purchase a large poster of Lee Van Cleef; he's got to be the coolest bad dude on the planet. We return to the building, I say my goodbyes to my friends and walk up the stairs to my apartment. Opening my door, I look back in the direction of Sam's room. I feel like talking, so I turn and take the few steps over to her room and knock.

"Yeah?" Sam's muffled voice yells from within.
"It's me!"
"I'm busy… I'll be over in a minute!"

Back in my apartment, I step into the kitchen, fall to my knees and rummage through the fridge.

"Where you hiding?" Sam calls out as she enters the room.

"Can I make you a sandwich?" I ask, popping my head over the counter.

"I'm fine." Sam drops into my armchair and crosses her legs. She is working a ball of chewing gum into a little pink balloon.

I stand and rifle through the cabinet drawer for a knife. "I was talking to Marvin," I say, as I slap meat on my bread. "He said something about Winky having a Sugar Daddy."

"Really?" Sam says with a curious smile. "That's interesting."

"Yeah… What's a Sugar Daddy?"

"When a girl lets an older guy set her up financially, you know… pays for her apartment, clothes, TV, jewelry, shit like that. Well, they call that guy a Sugar Daddy."

"What's the girl gotta do," I ask, biting into my sandwich, "let the guy screw her?"

"Basically, yeah. It's a pretty simple case of being an exclusive whore."

I have the image in my mind of the toffee lollypops I used to love to suck as a kid. I think about the arrangement between Winky and the liquor store owner. "Maybe Winky's got somethin' else going. Maybe she doesn't screw the guy."

"Like what?" Sam asks, blowing a pink bubble and letting it snap in her face. "Blow jobs?"

"Maybe sex got nothin' to do with it." I shrug my shoulders. "Maybe he just likes her company."

"Jon... grow up."

"I'm having trouble figuring this out. Marvin is obviously nuts over Winky, right? Who wouldn't be? Hell, he might even love her for all we know. So, how can he allow her to do somethin' like that?"

"Jon, does Marvin have a job?"

"I don't think so."

"Where's his money coming from? Marvin may be behind this thing with Winky, but it doesn't mean he likes it. He just happens to like the money more. I see this kind of shit all the time. Pretty soon, he'll be beating her up for doing what she's doing. Winky's a loser, and so is Marvin. It's really pathetic when you think about it."

"I'm not going to write them off as losers, Sam. I think they're good people."

"I didn't say they weren't good people... I said they were losers. What else would you call someone who trades sex for goodies?"

John Taylor's left leg is wrapped up in a cast from the knee down. He hobbles around without the aid of crutches or a cane. On the bottom of the cast his doctor placed a hard rubber peg to protect the plaster from wearing off. When John walks through the building's hallways you can hear the dull sound of a rubber thump coming long before he gets to where he's going;

Step, thump, step, thump, step, thump...

We pass each other on my way into the building tonight. The friendly smile I give is not reciprocated. He answers with what I clearly detect as a mean glare.

"Bye, John! Have a nice evening."

Step, thump, step, thump, step, thump...

"Julie! What a cool surprise," I say, happy to see her standing in my doorway. Julie is dressed in one of her classic man-killer outfits. "You going out tonight?"

"No, I thought I might come by for a visit... Do you mind?"

Julie's voice is so sweet, only a fool could refuse her, I stick my head out into the hallway checking for spies or miscreants who might be tailing her. Coast is clear. I quietly shut the door and return my attention to my guest. "Can I get you a Coke or somethin'?"

"Something? What else do you have?"

"Cherry Kool Aid."

"Sure... that would be nice. I brought along the script to my movie like I promised. Sit down... I'll read to you."

I get comfortable in my armchair. Julie, standing at my feet, takes a sip from her glass and places it on the table.

"All right, promise me you won't laugh. I haven't done any acting since the third grade." Julie becomes animated, displaying the scene with hand motions; "We're inside this big, magnificent mansion of a millionaire tycoon. Kitty and I have been drugged and taken there by his business associates..." Julie reads from the script for the next few minutes, giving a childish inflection to all of her lines, "Where am I? Who are you boys? What am I doing here? Where are my clothes?"

The story seems more like corn-porn than soft-porn. I think she notices I am trying hard to remain interested.

"Well, enough of that... the whole thing sounds

kind of silly, don't it?" Julie tosses the script on the table and finishes her drink, walks over to me and sits down on my lap, throwing both legs over the side of the chair's overstuffed arm. She wiggles her hips and reaches inside the waistband of her skirt and removes a thin red booklet.

"I want you to see something." Julie opens what appears to be a ledger. "This is my bank book."

Scores of typed entries follow the course of her savings account over the past two years. She flips to the second page and points a painted nail to her current balance of $5,675.46. "See this?" Julie has a proud look on her pretty face, closes the bankbook and slips it back under its hiding place.

"You're gonna get that house."

Julie starts kissing me, slowly at first, then with rising intensity; she holds my face in her hands and covers my mouth in a kissing frenzy, surpassing the most red-hot high-school make-out sex I had ever experienced. She stands up, taking me with her. I hold her tight in my arms, binding her against me, but she wiggles to pry herself free. I yield and step back. Staring at me with vicious eyes, her arms free, she begins to pull off my clothes, ripping open my shirt, buttons flying through the air like wedding confetti. Julie strips off her blouse and bra and pulls me down to the bed on top of her. Our teeth crack when our heads hit the mattress. I am falling into a sexual abyss and nearly fail to hear the elevator as it begins to rattle and clang.

"Ssshhh," I whisper, pulling my lips away from Julie's face.

"What?" she asks, breathlessly.

"The elevator is coming up. I want to hear where it stops."

"Why?"

The cranking of the old gears tug the cab slowly up the shaft. I listen uneasily, praying for it to stop somewhere below us. It continues up, passing each floor, finally coming to a dead stop in the corridor outside my room. The elevator's cage door opens. We are breathing so heavy, I swear we can be heard from across the street.

"Ssshhh, don't say a word," I whisper in Julie's ear.

Step, thump, step, thump, step, thump...

"Jesus Christ, no," Julie shrieks under her breath, and begins to tremble.

I motion for her to be still, quietly lift myself off of her and begin gathering her things, sliding them all under my bed.

A fist is hitting my door like it's a punching bag. "JULIE! YOU IN THERE!?"

I lift Julie by the hand and gesture for her to follow my instructions. She silently lies down on the floor and slowly wiggles her frame beneath the box spring.

"Hey! I'll be right there! Quit banging!" I shout as I grab a clean shirt from my dresser before swinging open the door. "Shit, John! Just what the hell do you think you're doing?"

"Where's Julie!?" asks John, smelling boozy and swaying slightly from side to side.

"How the fuck would I know?" I answer in a properly stern voice.

"JULIE!" John pushes past me and enters my apartment; his eyes darting this way and that.

"John, I don't remember inviting you in," I say, stepping in front of him to block his path. "I told you I don't know where she is. I suggest you back your ass out of here."

"My black ass?! Whut did you say?" John angrily slurs his words. "I have a gun! I'll use it, goddamit... I'll kill you both!"

"John, there's no point in talking like that. I don't know what's going on with you and Julie... That's between you and her. I think you should go home, relax. Wherever Julie is, I'm sure she'll be coming home to you soon," I speak my words calmly, hoping to settle him down.

"I'm sorry... I'm sorry," he mutters quietly, more to himself than to me.

I lead him gently into the hallway and bid him good night. Closing my door, I fall back against it and blow out a lungful of air. The thumping sound of his steps recedes down the corridor.

Walking back to my bed, I drop to my knees and lift the blanket hanging over the edge; peeking beneath it feels odd, like looking up a woman's skirt. To my shock, I find nothing under there but dust and a ratty old sock. I spring to my feet and shout in a restrained whisper to my empty room, "Julie!?" She reappears from the bathroom, completely put back together, exactly the way she was when she first arrived.

"Did you hear what he said!?" I nervously pace a wide circle in the center of the room. "What the hell's going on? Why did he come up here? He thinks you and me are fooling around... where did *that* come from? Did you talk to him about me? By the way, we're *not* fooling around, are we? At least not anymore... and we haven't anyway, have we?"

"Calm down, Jonny." Julie postures a cool bow, resting one hand on the curve of her waist, "He's not going to hurt you."

"Oh no?! Which John was I just talking to a minute ago? Was that John the Threat, or John the Asshole? Cause if you ask me, I was being eyeballed by John the Threat…and it scared the hell out of me."

I decide it would be wise to lay off seeing Julie as long as John's still in the picture.

20
Kitty

"I have had *eenuff* of this shit!" Kitty stomps into our room and digs her feet in front of Van Helden, pointing a long finger at his nose, then jumps it over into my face, "You children better start doing somethin' about it!"

Robert and I are slumped down low beside each other on our couch.

"Do I gotta call *Lykos*...huh!?... Drag his white, candy-ass up here? Just what the fuck you boys doing, anyhow?"

Kitty bursting into our room this way knocks us stupid. Robert and I are sitting on the couch like a pair of marble statues. Whatever it was we did, I wish to hell we hadn't done it.

I fumble out a clumsy, "What's going on, Kitty?"

"What's going on? You fillin' this building with whores, that's what's going on! I want them out! I want them out NOW! You boys better take care of it, or I'm gonna get the police in here!"

"We got whores in the building?" I feign surprise. Robert and I know damn well what Karen does for a living, but we generally ignore this fact since no harm seems to come of it, besides... we like her.

"Don't play dumb-ass with me!" Kitty hisses, swishing a long finger in my face like a wiper cleaning my windshield. "You know what I'm talkin'bout. We got hookers down there doing it right now," she says, pointing to the floor. "That fool pimp below you leaves that girl alone all day long with that lil' child, turning tricks in front of that sweet thing. What's that fool pimp's name?" Kitty demands, as if we are hiding it from her.

"Tomas, that's all I know. I don't know the chick's name. Do you, Robert?"

Van Helden shrugs.

"You seem to know a whole lot of nothin'! Open your eyes! You got hookers downstairs on every floor!"

Kitty spins on her heels and marches from the room, Robert and I remain frozen to the couch, not saying a word; the silence broken by a gaggle of honking taxi cabs coming from our open window.

I straighten my back and turn towards Robert, clicking my lighter and holding it to the end of my cigarette. "How old do you think Kitty is? She told me once she was twenty-five. Does she look twenty-five to you? She's gotta be a lot older than that."

"Twenty-five... I don't think so, thirty-five... maybe. Jesus, are we supposed to be responsible for all the shit that goes on in here?" Robert asks, getting up from the couch and scratching his backside. "What are we supposed to do about it?"

I blow smoke from my lungs and tip my cigarette in the ashtray. "I don't believe this. Kitty's full of shit. We might have a couple a hookers, but not on every floor. That ain't happening. Who do you think she's talkin' about?"

"Karen," Robert answers, flatly.

"She's not bothering nobody." For some crazy reason, I feel like protecting Karen, besides, I think she likes me. I haven't given up on the possibility of taking her out sometime.

"Jackie!" Robert snaps his fingers. "What about her?"

"Who?"

"That skinny chick living with Benny, Marvin's always calling his brother's girlfriend a whore. He says she does some kind of a freaky sex show at stag parties, crawling around naked on top of a table. She could be doing that shit in her room."

"Maybe... they got a table in there."

"You know, Jonny, there are a few girls here we know nothin' about."

"Yeah," I nod, "and they all got boyfriends... some dude always comes by and pays the rent. Maybe these guys are pimps?"

"All right, so we got whores... now what?"

"I don't know," I answer, totally lost. I'm not about to go running around the building accusing a few seedy guys of pimping off their girlfriends.

Van Helden slumps back down on the couch, "Should we be calling Lykos; tell him what's happening? He might give us some advice."

"Or he might just throw our asses out the door. He'll blame *us* for bringing in the hookers."

Monday afternoon I report for work at the library. After saying hello to Wentworth's matronly librarian, Mrs. Butterfield, I walk into the supply room and rummage through the cabinets, snagging pieces of cardboard and Magic Markers. I do a quick layout for my signs making sure I get the point across without being too offensive, mark up five colorful posters and prepare to slip them into my ammo bag. Mrs. Butterfield steps inside the narrow room, startling me. "What are you making, Jonathan? Are you doing an art project?" She peeks over my shoulder to read.

> *Attention Hookers!*
> *Several girls are disturbing their neighbors*
> *(And you know who you are!)*
> *Stop turning tricks immediately or you will be deported from the building.*
> *Thank you,*
> *The Building Managers*

"Oh, my goodness." Mrs. Butterfield has her hand cupped over her mouth, the lines on her forehead rough as a washboard.

"I have a little problem I got to deal with." I quickly gather the signs and stuff them inside my bag.

On my way home from class, I confront the Gypsies working the sidewalk in front of the building. The matriarch and her two kids flank the entrance. I give Big Mama a hard look as I step between her and the two bambinos. "You gotta quit doing your business in front of the building," I say, wagging a finger in her face. Trying to keep my tone friendly, but firm, I add, "Have a nice night." She replies, saying something for my benefit as the door closes behind me. I don't recognize the language, but the expression of her voice leaves little doubt of her intentions; she is either placing a black curse upon my soul, or accusing me of a carnal association with my mother. This chick and her brood pose a real threat to my building, and I want them out of here. Living among thieves is not an option. The last thing I need is to come home again to a ransacked apartment.

Stepping off the elevator on the fifth floor, I walk to Marvin's door and knock. I can hear the tight soul sound of James Brown playing down low on the stereo. Winky greets me barefoot in a lacy lavender teddy, revealing a gossamer figure both men and women dream of possessing. Marvin stands a few feet behind her wearing only a long, black terry-cloth robe. "Enter, my man... cop a squat," he says, teeth smiling brightly beneath his droopy mustache.

"I thought I'd stop by and see how you guys are doing." I return his smile as I plunk down into one of a pair of soft easy-chairs I haven't seen before. They look expensive; nothing like the crummy pieces of crap Lykos hands out. My eyes scan their apartment; lots of new stuff: cushy furniture, colorful art on the walls, a luxurious white shag carpet nearly covers the entire floor, and a new portable black and white TV! "It looks like you guys are doing just fine."

"You like it?" Marvin asks, proudly waving an outstretched palm across his domain, "Me and Winky been out shopping."

I look into Winky's face, slightly bent towards the floor; her vacant eyes hold none of Marvin's enthusiasm. I know why Winky looks so sad. All this pretty stuff comes from licking on her Sugar Daddy.

"Yeah, cool pit ya got here. I dig your rug."

"I picked dat out," says Winky flatly, without a shed of emotion.

Marvin sits down in the chair beside me to relax, Winky continues standing. "You wanna beer?" he asks. "Winky, fetch Jonny a beer," he directs, not waiting for my answer.

"Sure, I'll get it."

"Sit! Baby, get this man a beer." Marvin snaps his fingers, and points at the refrigerator.

I sit back down and wait to be served. Winky pads over from the fridge in her bare feet and places an open can on the table in front of me, like a dutiful Geisha. Marvin reaches over his coffee table and lifts a small wooden box into his hands. It looks like the jewelry case my mother keeps on her bedroom dresser.

"Here," he places the box in my lap, "do the honors."

I flip open the lid and find it contains an ounce of sticky, leafy grass along with several packs of Zags. I dutifully roll a fair-sized joint, lick my lips, pull and twirl the number through my moistened mouth, and hold it up for inspection.

"Did you hear we're gonna land a guy on the moon in a couple of months?" I ask Marvin, handing him the joint.

"No shit? I don't suppose they plan to let a Brother be the man to do it."

"Not unless you know any Brothers named Buzz."

"Buzz? Shit! Is that the dude's name? Ain't no black man on the planet named, Buzz," says Marvin, blowing a little cloud of smoke in the air and passing the joint back to me.

"I read in the paper the guy's name, Buzz Aldrin… gonna be the first man to step foot on the moon. Check it out," I pause, trapping smoke inside my lungs before continuing, "The whole thing's gonna be on TV!"

"Ain't no black man named Buzz, and even if there was, they ain't gonna let his black ass on the moon. Never… no way," says Marvin.

"We can catch this whole thing on your TV." I point to his portable, adding permissibly, "If you're into it."

"Sure, why not… we'll cop a buzz watching Buzz buzz around on the moon." We both howl with laughter.

After a few sips of beer, I start wondering again about Winky and her Sugar Daddy. I would kill myself before I ever let any girlfriend of mine get naked in front of another guy, let alone screw him. I turn to Marvin, "What do you do with yourself all day, man?"

"Marvin don't do nothin,'" Winky answers for him, barely audible, from the confines of her bed, her head buried behind a movie star magazine.

"Hey, Baby, that ain't true and you know it." Marvin gently defends himself. He appears pleasantly stoned and a poor match for a confrontation. "I've been trying to start a painting business," he gives his attention back to me. "I went to the bank and asked The Man for a loan to start my business."

"You got a loan?"

"I got a whole lot of nothin'. But I don't need their help… I got a little money. I have a few guys lined up to work for me. If the assholes ever show up, I just might be able to get somethin' going."

"Don't hold your breath," Winky slips in another comment. "Baby, you can't count on nobody but you. You waiting for somethin' dat ain't gonna happen."

"I had this painting job lined up for an apartment on Columbus," Marvin says, with a plaintive look, "could a made two-hundred for two days work, and my boys never show up. My brother was one of 'em."

"Baby, don't count on nobody but you," says Winky.

I thank them both for their hospitality and stand to excuse myself. Marvin suggests we hit the street tonight for a little fun.

"Sorry, man, no can do… not tonight, I really need to study."

"How about we do somethin' Friday night?"

"You're on."

I make it back to my room and drop my ammo bag on the floor. *My signs!* I have forgotten all about them. They still lie tucked inside my bag. I pull them out, grab a handful of tacks from our junk drawer and head out the door. Starting from the bottom floor and working my way up to the top, I tack them on the walls facing the elevator door, impossible to miss by anyone stepping from the cab.

Sam has her door opened. Tapping my knuckles on the jamb, I walk in and see her standing in her kitchen facing the sink, fixing a cup of tea. She turns her head a fraction, catching me through the corner of her eye, and begins shaking her head from side to side in a gesture of disbelief. "Nice signs," she says, laughing.

"What?" You think they're funny?"

"They're a riot."

"I want to give the girls a chance to stop their shit before we gotta get heavy."

"Sit down, Jonny."

I drop myself unto the edge of her bed. Sam sits down close to me; our knees touching.

"Sweetheart, these girls aren't going listen to anything you have to say. Where do you think they get their marching orders? You don't have a hooker problem," she pauses to blow on her tea. "You have a pimp problem. You start shaking these girls around, you're asking for trouble."

"I need to think about this," I say quietly.

"Yes, you do."

"Did you know Kitty is screaming she'll go to the police if we don't do somethin'?"

"Good. It takes the heat off of you. Let her boyfriends in the Vice Squad deal with it. If Kitty puts it out there she's looking for help, the cops will fall over each other on the way to her dressing room. She gets the Law to throw a few girls into the street... so what, at least no one comes gunning for you," Sam smiles, sipping from her steamy cup.

A minute of silence passes as I reflect on Sam's advice. I light a cigarette and turn towards her. "I want to tell you something, but you gotta promise not to laugh."

"Tell me what?"

"Promise!"

"Sure, okay... what?"

"I've been asked to a Junior Prom next month... an old girlfriend called and invited me to be her date. I might do it. What do you think of that... pretty lame, huh?"

"I don't know. You could have some fun with it. You should go… it could be a goof. Is it one of those tight-ass, preppy schools?"

"Naw, nothin' like that."

"Well, what? Where's this happening?"

"It's at my old high school."

"*High school!* Jesus, Jonny, how old is this girl?"

"Sixteen… we met last summer. Her name is Lara. We saw each other for a little while. I used to like her a lot."

"What happened?"

"We broke up, but I think I want to see her again. She called me and told me how much she misses me… she sounded so fine, I started missing her a little, too."

"Sixteen… don't you think that's a wee bit young?"

"I don't know… I'm only two years older than she is. That's not too weird."

"So, why'd you dump her?"

"Why do you think *I* dumped *her?* Maybe *she* dumped *me.*"

"Why'd you dump her?" Sam asks again, narrowing her eyes.

"I told her I didn't want a rope tied around me when I moved up to Boston. But that was just bullshit. I found out she screwed around with other guys."

"Sixteen year old girl… really?"

"Yeah… This happened before we met."

"Do you mind if I ask how many guys we're talking about here… five, ten?"

"One," I answer, nearly under my breath.

"One guy! Jesus… you dumped her for screwing *one guy!* Shit, boy… you're a hard dude."

"It seemed like the right thing to do at the time."

"Jonny, take Lara to her prom. Give her a night to remember."

"Jonathan, when you're through stacking those books, would you mind running over to get the mail," Mrs. Butterfield asks, her voice as sweet as the Good Fairy.

I head off in the direction of the Administration Building to retrieve the library's mail like I do every day I come in to work. My first stop is always President Beatty's office suite where I sign in before making my way down to the mailroom. After sauntering up to the receptionist, smiling with my hand out (the girl knows the drill), I whistle a tune while waiting as she disappears into the back room to fetch the key.

Miss Ripjaw materializes two paces in front of the receptionist. Phyllis Ripjaw, President Beatty's craggy private secretary, has the personality of a Bolshevik camp counselor watching over the Romanov kids. She marches up to me in her stiff cardigan sweater, buttoned to the neck, carrying a disdainful expression on her face and the mail room key tight in her fist. She looks as if she wants to hit me with it.

"I need to pick up the mail for Mrs. Butterfield," I announce very business-like, holding out my hand.

"I understand... I'm here to escort you," Ripjaw's icy voice cracks, her face frozen in a distrustful scowl.

She accompanies me down the corridor, shoulder to shoulder, walking in a clip, her black square-toed shoes, Pilgrim footwear, hammering on the terrazzo floor. Halfway en route, I turn toward Ripjaw and ask in a silky, seductive voice, "Would you like to hold my hand?"

Ripjaw's face looks as if it is about to explode in a ball of flames. Jesus, what's the big deal? She's acting like I had just asked her to peek down my pants, or something.

Mrs. Butterfield has a sick look on her face when I return to her office, dropping the morning mail on her desk.

"Jonathan, I just got off the phone with President Beatty. Whatever happened over there between you and Miss Ripjaw, you made everyone terribly upset. The President directed me to terminate you from the Work-study program if you don't apologize at once."

"I won't do that. *She* should be the one who should apologize."

Mrs. Butterfield picks up the phone and politely asks me to leave her office while she dials-up the President.

A few minutes later, I learn I can keep my job, but for my transgression I'll never be allowed to pick up the mail… never again. Big deal.

Friday afternoon, I return home after classes are through, my mind fixed on going out tonight and having a few beers. The elevator door opens and I face a blank wall where I hung my sign yesterday. Some bastard must have torn it down. I do a quick inventory of the other floors. All the signs are gone. I take the stairs up to my room, thinking about my next move. Fumbling for my key, I hear music filtering through the door. I walk in and find a very attractive brunette sitting up in Robert's bed amidst a pile of crumpled bedding. She's naked, a single sheet barely concealing her from the shoulders down. Her legs extend beyond a patch of blanket that runs across her mid section, exposing most of one thigh and all of the other. She wiggles her feet when I approach the bed.

"Hi!" she greets me all bubbly. "I'm Jennifer. You must be Jonny."

"I must be," I give a cheery reply to match her effervescence. "Robert here?" I ask Miss Twinkletoes. The toilet flushes and Van Helden pops out of the bathroom in his underwear.

"Hey, Jonny! You're home. Did you meet Jennifer?"

"Yeah, we met. I don't want to spoil your party… I'm gonna clean up and get out of here. I'm hooking up with Marvin."

"You don't have to hurry. We're going out, too. Hey, your signs got trashed. I came in this afternoon and found them on the floor ripped to pieces. I cleaned them up."

"Pimps!" I snap. "Robert, I've been thinking. We shouldn't get in Kitty's way if she wants to call the cops."

"I wasn't planning on it. Last night I found a bunch of strange looking white dudes hanging out in front of 5A."

"Johns!" I snap again.

"You have prostitutes *here*, in *your building*?" Jennifer asks, a little too gleefully, like she is inquiring about some famous movie star living next door.

"Yeah, lucky us," I sigh.

Marvin and I drift north on Washington Street with Winky between us, my head floating nicely along in a marijuana miasma. We coast through the doors of the Normandy Lounge and happily find Julie on stage dancing to the beat of *Backdoor Man*, rotating her ass suggestively. She is nearly finished with her act, I assume, since there is nothing left to shed from her body. Watching her gyrate to the music under the smoky spotlights, and listening to the men in the crowd howl in the darkness over her every move, my mind wanders back to the night in my room when she tore off my clothes and pulled me on top of her. God, she looks great. The music ends and Julie is gone in a flash.

"What do you wanna drink, baby?" Marvin reaches out across the table to hold Winky's hand. He caresses her fingertips gently; the lady looks positively gorgeous, like Motown royalty. I can't fathom how any guy could share this girl.

"Ah don't know... somethin' cold."

"How about you, Jon... beer okay?" Marvin is being gracious. He gets this way when he's stoned.

"Yeah, a cold one would be nice, if you please."

The cocktail waitress takes Marvin's order for beers all around, coming back a few minutes later dropping six Buds on the table. We polish them off in short order and have another round sent to the table. Julie appears in front of us, stepping out of a shroud of fog.

"Hello, friends," she smiles pleasantly. "Can I join you?"

I quickly stand and pull open the chair beside me, smiling back into her eyes.

"Oh... what a gentleman," she gushes. "You

didn't see my old man in here earlier, did you?" Julie shifts a bit uneasily in her seat. "I had his black ass kicked out of the club… he is such a weasel. I wouldn't be surprised if he finds a way to sneak back in."

Our cocktail waitress returns and asks, "What can I get you, Julie?"

"Club soda, honey." Julie says brightly. She returns her attention to us; and with a grave expression leans into the conversation, "John is drinking all the time… it starts when he crawls out of bed in the morning and ends when he passes out at night. Everything in between is pure shit." She glances over each shoulder and leans in tighter, "I'm going to tell you something that could get me killed if my old man ever found out I said it."

"Maybe you should keep yo mouth shut," says Winky.

"No… John wouldn't *really* kill me. I meant that as a figure of speech. My old man is wanted in Baltimore. Today, he found out Kitty's speaking to the police about our building, and now he's scared shitless they'll find him and send him back to Baltimore. He came in here earlier all sloppy drunk, looking for her."

"What's Kitty doing talkin' to the police?" asks Marvin.

"She's fed up with them whores we got, and I don't blame her. It's disgusting having all these Johns inside the building. They're as dirty as rats! And the girls that attract them are garbage! We don't need their kind."

"Why are the cops lookin' for your old man?" I ask.

"He happens to be married with a couple of

kids. I found out this bullshit a little while ago. All I know is he messed up his wife somehow, and the police are looking to arrest him. Whatever it is, it's got him all freaked out."

Our cocktail waitress places the club soda on table, and hands Julie a note. "What's this?" Julie asks, staring at the folded piece of paper in her hand.

"See those three guys sitting at that table by the stage," the waitress nods with her chin in their general direction. Julie looks at the men seated about thirty feet away; they are all beaming as they raise their glasses in the air in a toast in her honor.

"They want to buy you a drink… and they handed me this note to give you."

Julie unfolds the paper, and closes it immediately, slapping it down hard on the table. I pick it up, open it and read.

> Leave the niggers.
> Come join our party.

The room feels ten degrees colder than it did a second ago. I close the note slowly and place it back down on the table.

"What's it say?" asks Marvin.

Julie slides the paper over to him, gilding it across the tabletop. He reads the note and starts to stand. I grab him by the arm and hold tight, but I can't keep him down.

"Don't do it, Marvin," I say, standing with him. "There's three of them and only two of us."

"You don't understand. I can't let this be. I'm going over there, and I don't want your help."

"Fuck it, Marvin! And fuck them! And you got

my help whether you want it or not! We've been smoking and drinking all night; we're not in any shape to be swinging fists. Look at those assholes," I point at their stupid faces, "They're just dying for an excuse to mess with us. If we fight them, we're gonna lose. And what would that prove... that we can take a beating? Fuck that shit!" I drop my voice, "They're assholes... We don't have to play their game."

Marvin stares at the three grinning animals who glare viciously back at him. "Let's get out of here," he says, spitting out the words.

"I'm coming with you," says Julie. As we walk by the three goons, one mouths a wet, kissy sound, and Julie lifts her middle finger, shoves it in his face. Behind our backs we hear them laughing like a pack of ugly hyenas.

Passing through the club's front door, the damp night air feels cool on my face; the welcoming mist a relief to breathe, compared to what we bathed in a second ago.

"What now, Boss?" I ask.

"Let's get something to drink," Marvin suggests, his voice blank. He links his arm through Winky's and heads south on Washington at a clip.

"Fine with me," says Julie. We follow Marvin's lead, weaving our arms together.

Turning west at the corner of Stuart Street, we pass several strip clubs as we walk down the block where we live. Our little parade stops in front of a club called the Gold Lounge. Marvin stares at the closed entrance door.

"Do you wanna go in?" I look at Marvin, unsure what to do.

"Has anyone been here before?" Marvin asks.

"No." "Not me." "Uh-ugh."

"Well," he says, with a touch of uncertainty, "Let's check it out."

The place doesn't have a stage, just a bar top wide enough for the girls to spin and dance without falling off. The music playing isn't the usual rhythm and blues or rock and roll numbers to accompany the strippers. A crummy organist with stiff fingers sits beside a lazy-looking dude with a two-piece drum set; together they bang out indistinguishable honky-tonk crap as backup numbers for the acts. The girls working as strippers are a collection of beasts and creatures that could barely be classified as feminine. The men surrounding the bar look as if they're all about to fall face first into their drinks.

A tall, masculine female with small, pointy breasts and dark, stringy hair takes to the stage and dances, if you can call it that, to the beat of a snare drum and two or three chords of organ sounds. Her movements are stiff and lack even a trace of imagination. As a finale to her clumsy performance, she gets down on all fours and bobs her body from her shoulders to her ass up and down in awkward syncopation with the drum beat, like a dog having sex ... boom boom boom boom boom. I glance over at Julie, who has her eyes locked on this appalling display; her face looks as if she's about to receive a spoonful of horrid medicine. Winky holds the same nasty expression. Marvin can't watch... he has his head in a beer, turned away from it all.

"Somebody ought to show this pitiful girl how to dance," says Julie.

"Yeah," Winky agrees. "This po thing lookin' like a fool."

"Come on!" Julie, grabs a hold of Winky's hand and steps up to the edge of the bar.

"What are they doing?" asks Marvin.

I shrug a response.

Julie asks a gentleman nursing a whisky to get off his seat, which he does without hesitation, and she and Winky use his stool as a stepping-stone to climb on top of the bar. My two lady friends flank the pathetic stripper, suddenly standing but otherwise appearing nonplused by this new addition to her act. Julie and Winky dance beautifully, swaying their lovely hips and rotating their shoulders. The provocative languid motions of these two fully clothed women magnify the sad, incongruent display made by the naked female they bracketed, like 24-caret bookends holding up a shabby comic book, and the men in the crowd come alive, loving every second of it.

The music ends; Julie and Winky thank the girl for her indulgence.

"That was fun!" Julie exclaims, hopping off the bar. Marvin and I reach the same conclusion, along with the unanimous vote of the two dozen clapping male customers. We drink our beers, drop a good size tip on the bar, and head out the door.

After walking around the corner to our building, the four of us squeeze delightfully into our narrow elevator. For the most part, it was a pretty good night on the town. I get out at the third floor and walk Julie to her door. She shouldn't be going back into that room. What the hell is she doing with that creep? I wonder if they have sex.

"You gonna be okay?" I whisper to her as she kisses me softly goodnight.

"I'll be fine… go," Julie's gentle voice sending me

off, her hand playfully patting my ass. As I turn to leave, I'm hit with the seriously disturbing sensation of being watched through the door's fish eye.

Morning rolls into afternoon and I haven't left my room. I need to gear up for final exams. They'll be starting in a few weeks and I require all the study time God will allow. Robert and Jennifer split over an hour ago on a lunch mission. I asked them to bring me back whatever it is they're eating. I'm not particular... just as long as it's not from Dirty John's or the diner downstairs. I've been eating too much of that shit lately; it feels like I got worms crawling around inside my gut.

Kitty walks into my room unannounced, cradling a tiny toy-poodle in her arms. Its color matches the dust I have built up under my bed. She sticks the little runt's face up against hers and begins kissing it on the lips, making silly, smoochy sounds.

"You got a dog?"

"Yes, Child, this is lil' Josephine." Kitty sounds like Minnie Mouse with a French accent. She places little Josephine loose on my floor where it immediately finds a convenient corner to take a crap.

"JOSEPHINE! How could you?" Kitty bends down with her ass up in the air and wags a finger in the clueless dog's face.

"Don't worry about it. I'll clean it up."

Kitty retrieves her mutt, cuddles it in her arms and locks eyes on me; her expression takes a right turn onto Gloomy Street, "You should know the police are coming. They know what's going on in here."

"When?" I ask. I have anxious visions of Elliot Ness and the Untouchables kicking down doors in the middle of the night, forcing people out of their rooms at gunpoint with their hands up.

"I don't know when. Today, tomorrow, whenever," she says, stroking pup fur from head to tail. "I didn't want to do this, but you not doing your job."

I look down at my feet. *Not doing my job?* I want to say we do a million things around here to keep things tight. We answer your calls at all hours of the night. We get your shit fixed when it's broken and clean up when you make a mess. We chase dead beats away from your door, along with the rats and the roaches. And you know what? Lykos couldn't care less about you. We play nice all the time with that dope, keeping him off your back. We carry a ton of shit on our shoulders for guys our age. How can you stand there and tell me we're not doing our job? But, I don't say anything, except, "Okay... police... fine." I look up and catch Kitty still staring at me. "Do you know me and Robert are just eighteen years old?"

"What's that got to do with anything?" she asks. She places her pooch on the floor, stiffening her stance.

"I think we do a pretty goddamn good job running this place for guys our age."

"Don't you tell me how old you are, you hear me! My little brother is fifteen, and he takes care of more business in a day than you got to deal with in a month! You're not helping nobody when you let pimps and hookers run this place!"

Kitty marches into the hall and back to her room; little Josephine's claws click across the tile floor, happily wagging her tail beneath Kitty's legs.

21
The Untouchables

"Pederson's class starts in two minutes!" Timmy Souza flings his lunch tray in the return-bin and darts from the room, his parting words echo in my head, "You're going to be late again!"

"Shit," I mumble into my plate. I've been late for class on several occasions, earning me more than a handful of reprimands. I wolf down most of my hamburger in two bites and jump up, throwing my head back to chug-a-lug a pint of chocolate milk while racing for the exit.

"Hey!" a voice yells from behind me, "Your tray!" A cafeteria attendant points to the spot where I was sitting, marked by the tray I left behind, which according to the school policy, requires that I stow it properly in the return bin.

I point to my watch and bolt from the cafeteria.

"Dickhead!" the attendant shouts at my back.

I run up three flights of stairs like a track star, taking the risers two at a time. Reaching my floor, banging through two pairs of double doors, I rip around the corner and sprint down the stretch to my classroom. *Yes!* The door to my class remains open. *I'm gonna make it!* As I get within three steps from turning into my room, I see a hand reach out and close the door. Class is seated. I'm late again. I stand still for a second to catch my breath, turn the doorknob and walk in.

"It's nice of Mr. Tudan to be joining us," says C.T. Pederson, glancing at his watch, "nearly on time this afternoon."

Fifty-six year-old Pederson is the head of Wentworth's structural engineering department, assigned to teach the science of how buildings are made so they won't fall down. I hate him.

"I'll make an exception for you this afternoon and won't mark you down late… seeing how yesterday was Daylight Savings Time, you probably haven't had a moment in your busy schedule to adjust your watch, heh, heh."

The mirthless old bastard made a joke. It is the first one he cracked all year. He pauses with a dumb smile on his face, expecting the class to yuck along with him. Nobody laughs. The room is filled with silent, gloomy faces all praying they were anywhere but here.

"Take your seat," he orders, quickly retreating to his more comfortable stance as an unpleasant prick.

C.T. Pederson is a tall, pasty-face bozo with thinning hair and a fleshy body shaped like an eggplant, cursed with chronically sour breath and a bitter disposition. Pederson begins his instruction scratching on the chalkboard calculations used to determine the breaking point of steel; excruciatingly dull stuff made all the worse by the expressionless, monotone delivery of his subject. The inflection of his voice sounds like he's speaking with his teeth glued together. I look around the room and witness a handful of students grappling to pay attention, taking notes and fiddling with their slide rules. Most of the others are trapped in Never Land, like me; lost in the wilderness, adrift in a somnolent daze.

C.T. plops his droopy frame behind his desk and dumps his face into a book. I feel the urge to pee. Only one student at a time is allowed to leave the room and Joey Whitney has his name up on the blackboard in the "permission to pee" spot. I wait anxiously for ten minutes, tapping my feet and drumming my fingers. Whitney finally walks back into the room and lazily erases his name from the board. I start to rise from my desk as Vinnie Petrozzi, sitting two rows in front of me, darts to the front and scrawls his name in the pee spot. I lower myself back onto my seat.

A few minutes have passed since Petrozzi left the room.

"I gotta go," I say to Jim Vanderhoffer seated beside me, as I walk to the front of the room. Stepping up to the blackboard, I etch my name in chalk below Petrozzi's and turn to face Pederson.

C.T. drops the book he held in his hands and glares at me for a long second, "Yes? Is there something you wish to say?" he drones.

"I'm next."

"I can see that. Now, take your seat."

"Mr. Pederson, this is stupid."

"I beg your pardon?"

"I gotta take a leak... I'm going to the restroom."

I was halfway to the door when Pederson says flatly, "If you leave without permission, I have no recourse other than to mark you down as absent. You know the rules."

I stop dead, turn and walk back to his desk. "These rules are for idiots. Would you like me to pee in the corner over there?" I point to the back of the class. "Or would you be happier if I just pissed in my pants?"

"*These rules are for idiots...* did I hear you correctly?" says C.T., glaring at me for my apostasy. This is the first time ever C.T. has put any muscle behind his voice. "You knew what was expected of you when you came here, and certainly nobody is forcing you to stay. *Rules* are structured to hold a society together. But the conformities that structure our society, they don't apply to you, do they? You want special treatment because you're an *individual*, isn't that right?"

"I didn't say that."

"That's exactly what you said, 'Rules are for idiots'. You, of course, are not an idiot, are you?" Not waiting for an answer, he continues, "You're special. You wish to be an *individual?*... Be prepared to face the consequences of your actions."

"You do what you gotta do," I reply. As I turn to leave, Vinnie Petrozzi ambles back into classroom and walks over to the chalkboard and erases his identity. I follow him, pick up a piece of chalk and draw a quick line below my name.

"Permission to leave the room, Sir," I say, giving C.T. a contemptuous smirk, heading for the door

The clock woefully reaches 4:45. I have muddled through another day of classes and pack my gear to leave. Slipping my bag over my shoulder, I walk down the row of desks towards the door.

"Mr. Tudan, may I have a word with you?" asks C.T.. He gets up from his chair and circles around his desk to address me. We stand face to face... sort of; Pederson has about six inches on me. He peers down through his bifocals, staring at me in an uncomfortable silence. I take a step back, trying not to get too close to this smelly man. C.T. heaves a deep breath and finally speaks, "You are failing my class. Are you aware of this fact?"

"I didn't know that."

"If you fail my class, you will be dropped from this program. That, of course, means you will never graduate. I could care less if that happens. Pass or fail, it doesn't matter to me one way or the other." C.T. narrows his eyes and brings his foul breath close to my face, "Any more misbehavior from you like we had in here today and I guarantee you will never leave Wentworth with your degree. Do we understand each other?"

"Mr. Pederson, I don't plan on flunking out."

"I take that as a 'yes,'" says C.T.. He returns to his desk and sits down, opening a drawer to retrieve a few folders. He ignores me as he goes through the motions of busying himself with paperwork. I get the message, the meeting is over.

I walk silently from the room, down the empty corridor. The stairwell is void of students; my feet echoing on the terrazzo treads as I make my way out of the building.

The trolley I board for the ride back to my apartment is packed with college students; all ready to call it quits for the day. I stand in the aisle facing the window, holding on to the metal railing for balance inside the rickety box. We enter a tunnel and I catch my reflection on the black glass staring back at me. "C.T. has it in for you," my face would say if it could talk. I think back to when classes began last fall with forty-two students. We've lost eight since then.

"You're next!" says my face. "Who the hell do you think you're fooling? You have no clue what it is you're doing, do ya? You want to be an architect? That's a joke!"

Last year, I confessed my ambitions to my high school guidance counselor. Mr. Savilli warned me not to shoot so high. His words were a slap across my ego, "I don't believe you're personally equipped to become an architect. If you like buildings, perhaps you should look into plumbing, or one of the other trades."

My reflection in the glass dissolves, only to be replaced by the face of Mr. Savilli, "You'll never be an architect."

"Fuck you!" I bark out.

The small crowd surrounding me edges back a couple of feet, as if I had just cut a fart.

I feel like talking to someone. I try Sam's door... nothing, walk down the hall to Kitty's room and knock; nothing here, either. Turning back to my room, I throw my bag on the floor and drop down on my bed. Swallowed up by exhaustion, I close my eyes and drift off to sleep.

Trapped deep in the woods... tied to a brawny pine tree tight as a mummy... my bare back pinched against the coarse bark. Pederson, laughing like a lunatic, orbits around me with a shotgun in his hands. He pauses... pokes the barrel hard into my gut... teasing me, mouthing blowy, guttural sounds of a shotgun blast. He circles again... stops and turns...

pumping the handle, aiming from the waist, pulls the trigger… blows a hole in me big enough to stick your head through. Can't move my hands to cover my ears… the shrieking is inhuman!

A siren howling past my window jerks me from my nightmare. The wailing fades, racing away into the night. I'm covered with sweat. I snap on the lamp beside my bed, walk into the bathroom and lean my clammy face into the sink, dousing it with cold water. Raising my head from the bowl, I lock on my look in the mirror, dark pot hole eyes stare back at me; water dripping from my nose, my hair a tangled muddy mop.

I wonder what happened to Van Helden… maybe he's spending the night with Jennifer. After fixing myself into a more presentable state, I leave the apartment to see if Sam is back. The elevator comes to life, clanking and rattling up the shaft in my direction. That's got to be Robert coming home, or maybe Sam. Either way, I am glad knowing company is only seconds away. I stand waiting by the elevator.

The box comes to a halt and the door slides open. Two straight-looking white dudes with oily combed back hair step out from the cab. Both guys look to be in their thirties, dressed casual with open-neck sport shirts, dark chinos and windbreakers, zippered down. The only difference between them, and it is striking, is their height; nearly a foot apart. I can smell Vitalis wafting off the smaller guy's head. He has an aggressive look plastered on his face.

"Who the hell are you?" he snaps.

"I'm the building super. Who the hell are you?" I don't particularly like his rude manner.

"I'm Detective Richard Boyko of the Boston Police Department. This is Sergeant Peter Dooley," says Boyko, pointing up to his tall pal. "We didn't get your name."

"You got any identification?" I ask Shorty. They each act put off by my question, as they flip open their wallets and shove badges in my face. "You got anything else?" I need to see something with a photograph to authenticate these goons.

"What?" The little cop looks mortified, like I have just asked him to drop trou.

"Anybody can have a badge… what else you got?"

He pushes his face up against mine, "What's your name, asshole?"

"Jonny… Jonathan."

"Where's your room, Jonny Jonathan?"

I point over my shoulder.

"Get in it!"

Mutt and Jeff follow on my heels. I have the feeling if I don't move fast enough they will pick me up by my belt and collar and toss me in headfirst. They ignore my offer to take a seat, electing to remain standing. I drop in a chair and light a cigarette.

"You're here to deal with the prostitutes?" I ask.

"Smart boy; we're going to take a little walk through your hallways and knock on a few doors," says Boyko. "Do you have keys to all the apartments?"

"Yes."

"We would like it if you came with us to make the intros." Boyko puts a slick smile on his face, greasing up his tone of voice, as oily as his hair, "You can do that for us, can't you, kid?"

"I suppose so… which rooms are we talking about?"

His partner slips out a small pad from the pocket of his windbreaker. "Apartments 2C, 3B, 4A and 5A," says Dooley, flipping the pad closed with a flick of the wrist.

"Enough chit chat… let's go." Boyko pokes his thumb towards the door. I stub out my smoke and the three of us file out of the room.

Boyko grabs my sleeve as I am making a beeline for the elevator.

"The stairs," he insists.

I do a U-turn and lead the way down to the fifth floor. We immediately hit pay dirt and find a John standing in front of the door to 5A, waiting his turn to get inside. He is about my age, dressed no different than the two cops. These three guys look like they would be comfortable sitting together at a Red Sox game.

"Does this man live in the building?" Dooley asks me, hard enough to put fear on the face of the John.

"Never seen him before."

Boyko nudges me out of the way and steps forward, flipping out his badge and establishing the agenda. "I would like to see some identification, please," he says, dryly. The kid fumbles in his pants and produces a driver's license. Boyko's eyes squint, looking it over. "Robert Drosdowski," says Boyko, reading the name off the license. "Mr. Drosdowski, do you understand it's a crime to solicit prostitution?"

"No, Sir," Drosdowski answers, barely audible.

Boyko hands the wallet over to his partner. I watch Dooley lift his pad from his pocket and pretend to scribble down information. It is all a sham. Poor Drosdowski looks like he is about to piss in his pants; he has no clue these clowns are putting him on. They return the kid's wallet. "Mr. Drosdowski, we want you to leave the building immediately and walk directly to the Police Station, number 7 Warren Street. Do you know where that is?"

"I think so… yes, Sir."

"Good… Go inside and report to the Desk Sergeant, tell him Officer Richard Boyko sent you, and you are being issued a citation for solicitation of prostitution. Do you understand me?"

"Yes, Sir."

"You can get in a whole lot of trouble being down here, Mr. Drosdowski. I don't ever want to see you in this neighborhood again. Now, get out of here."

"Yes, Sir." The kid turns and bounds down the stairs like his pants are on fire. Boyko and Dooley both laugh as they listen to the pounding of Drosdowski's feet retreating down the stairs several floors below.

"How these guys getting inside the building?" asks Dooley.

"They come in through the back sometimes… somebody props open the door," I say. "Sometimes, I think someone with a key lets them in the front."

Boyko turns his attention on the apartment Drosdowski had hoped to enter. "Let's see what's behind Door Number One," he chuckles, acting like he is starting to enjoy himself. He motions for me to step up and knock.

I tap and announce myself, "Building Super!"

"Wait a second!" a muted female voice comes

from behind the door. A minute later, the door hasn't budged.

Boyko pushes me aside and gives it a few good whacks, "Police! Open the door, NOW!"

The door swings into the room and we are met by Tomas' girlfriend standing barefoot in shorts, braless in a white T-shirt bearing a big number 69 stenciled in faded blue. She's holding a baby in her arms with nothing on but a diaper; and by the smell of it, in serious need of a change.

"Where's your John, lady?" asks Boyko, swinging his head back and forth inside the room.

"There is no one here but me and my baby."

Dooley walks over to the window facing the street. "Hey Rick, check this out."

Boyko and Dooley both have their heads stuck out the window, laughing. The John squeezed his body tight against the brick wall in the far corner of the fire escape balcony.

"Hey, Romeo! You're under arrest!" says Boyko to the trapped man who looks over the rusty railing to the street five floors below, presumably weighing his options. "Why don't you come back in and join the party?"

The John stretches his legs back through the window and drops to the floor. Boyko and Dooley repeat the drill they used on the last guy, and watch with quiet amusement as the John races down the stairs.

The smile vanishes from Dooley's face as he heaves a heavy sigh and turns his interest on the woman holding the baby. "What's your name, honey?" asks Dooley.

"Rosa Delasandro."

"Rosa, we can arrest you for prostitution and have you locked up. We can have that baby of yours taken away from you, as well."

Rosa doesn't flinch hearing these threats. She doesn't act scared, and she doesn't seem worried. She only looks tired.

"But we're not here to ruin your life any more than it already is. Consider yourself lucky tonight… you're only being evicted. The building manager here," Dooley slaps me on the shoulder like we're best buddies, "he's going to let us know if you aren't gone in twenty-four hours. If you're still here after tomorrow night, we will come back and place you under arrest. You got that?" he points a finger in her nonchalant face.

We say goodbye to Rosa, getting out of her way so she can get busy packing, and visit the other floors, stopping first at Benny and Jackie's on the fourth. No one comes to the door when I knock, so I use my passkey to get inside. Both cops start sniffing around like a pair of bloodhounds, picking stuff up off the shelves, opening and closing drawers. They ask me a string of questions, names of the occupants, ages, occupations.

"I don't know their names, I mean, I know their first names, anyway, not their last. Don't ask me about their birthdays, I'm awful at guessing that shit. I have no idea how they make their bread."

"You're a real disappointment, you know that?" says Boyko, shaking his head as he noses through Jackie's things hanging in the closet. "Nothing unusual in here," he says to his partner.

"The table," I say, trying to be helpful, pointing to the kitchenette.

"The what?"

"Nothing, never mind… I was just thinking out loud."

Down on the third floor, we find no one home inside Michelangelo and Maureen's place, either.

We enter the apartment and Boyko immediately begins poking his nose in and out of drawers and fingering things in the closet.

"You guys actually think this chick Maureen is a prostitute? That really floors me. I wouldn't have guessed that in a million years. We call these two Mickey and Minnie... did you know that? Did you know Mickey's a musician? He plays piano. I have no idea what Minnie does. I can't believe she's turning tricks," I say, trying to be helpful and conversational with my new pals. "Maybe you got the wrong room."

"Shut up," says Dooley.

"Let's move on," says Boyko. "What's the next place?"

Dooley glances at his pad, "2C." He turns to me and sarcastically asks, "Don't tell me, the girl living in 2C's a nun, right?"

"Her name's Karen MacArthur. She's a real nice tenant. Never ever gives us any trouble; always pays the rent. She's pretty quiet. When I first met her, I thought she might be a school teacher."

"She's a whore," says Boyko.

I lead the way to the second floor, stopping in front of Karen's door. "Would you mind if I do the talking," I ask.

"Sure, what do we care... just as long as you kick her ass out," says Boyko.

Karen opens the door on the first knock, just wide enough to speak with us. She is deliciously decked out, looking very classy in a black sequined dress held up by spaghetti thin straps over her bare shoulders. A string of pearls adorns her neck.

"Yes, what can I do for you?" she asks, puckering her brow.

"Can we talk? These two guys are police officers."

"I have a guest. We are about to go out for the evening."

"This won't take long, Lady," Dooley pipes in. "We'll have you outta here in a minute."

A handsome older man with a Florida tan and stainless steel hair is standing in the center of the room. His elegant grooming, dark suit and bow tie compliment Karen's evening dress. I introduce Boyko and Dooley. Karen says hello and introduces her fancy friend, Mr. Lee, as her date.

"We are on our way out to the theater and dinner. Is there something wrong?"

"Mr. Lee, do you understand it's a crime to solicit prostitution?" asks Dooley, getting face to face with Karen's date. Mr. Lee says nothing in return; he looks as if he is trying hard to become invisible. Perhaps it is working because Dooley suddenly ignores the man, spinning over to Karen, he continues, "You go out and have fun tonight… have a great meal, enjoy the show. But we want you out of this neighborhood in twenty-four hours."

"I'm being evicted?"

"Yes," I reply, "I'm sorry." I hope I get the chance to see her before she leaves; maybe find out where she's going next.

"Consider this your lucky night." The magnanimous Officer Dooley smiles, "You could be spending it in jail."

Boyko jumps in, "We're letting you off easy, but this won't happen a second time. If we catch either one of your pretty faces down here again, we'll rain shit all over your parade, Capiche?"

"Yes. Thank you, Officer," says Karen, softly.

"I'll be gone in the morning." Karen closes her door behind us.

Boyko steps in front of the elevator and presses the button, "Come on, Super. Let's go back to your room. We want to talk."

"About what?"

"We're going to leave you with a few simple instructions."

The elevator door opens and the two cops step inside the cab.

"Wait a second!" I say, holding back the door, "There's one more piece of business I think you ought to deal with."

"What are you talking about?"

"Gypsies."

"Gypsies? We don't ordinarily deal with gypsies," says Dooley. "They're not on our radar screen."

I want to boot Madam Zanzibar and her flying circus out of the building, and these two clowns can help me do it. "We get complaints all the time about the scams they got going out on the sidewalk; pick pocketing, selling stolen shit, begging, hustling... you name it."

Boyko shakes and scratches his head, "I don't think we want to get involved in this."

"Why not? They're thieves... you're the police. You guys are supposed to care about shit like that."

Boyko lets out a huge sigh and looks over at his pal, who in turn shrugs his shoulders. I take their indifference as a positive sign and bang on the door to Apartment 2B.

"Yes? What do you want?" says Mama, blocking the doorway, apparently not happy to see me.

"You're being evicted from the building. These men behind me are with the Boston Police Department, Officer Boyko and Sergeant Dooley." I point toward the pair, a little pissed off they didn't flash their badges. They simply stand still with stupid smiles on their faces.

"You cannot do this thing!" She appeals to the cops, "Can he do this thing?"

"You bet I can. You've been warned several times about peddling your shit around here. We've had enough of you not listening… now it's time to go. You got twenty-four hours to clean out. Thank you," I add, not wanting to be too discourteous. The door slams behind us as we turn for the elevator.

Boyko stares at me hard on the ride up to the sixth floor, making me feel a bit uncomfortable.

"What?" I ask, fidgeting under his glare.

"I don't like what you just did," he says. "You're on your own with this one, kid. We aren't going to back you up."

The elevator clangs to a stop. We squeeze out the door and walk over to my apartment.

"Why not?" I ask. We enter my room and shut the door behind us.

"I can give you three reasons." Boyko holds up an index finger, "We didn't see any laws being broken." He pops up a second digit, "Begging and hustling, as you put it, aren't reasons for evicting someone from their home. And I saw little kids standing inside that room," says Boyko, holding three stiff fingers in the air. "Leave the Gypsies alone."

I decide to change the subject. "You said something downstairs about leaving me instructions, instructions for what?"

Dooley pulls out a pen and his little pad. "We're going to call you in a couple of days to see how you're doing and to make sure things are going well. What's your phone number?"

I rattle it off for him.

"Who owns this building?"

"Lykos Theodokis. He lives out of town. You want his number?" I volunteer information while Dooley jots it down.

"I'm going to call this guy Theodokis and make it clear he has three days to clean up his building."

Dooley and Boyko make their way into the corridor. I follow them out.

"The two girls who weren't in their rooms tonight, we want them evicted," says Dooley.

"You want *me* to kick them out?" Don't I need you guys to be part of this?"

"I don't think so. You seem to pretty good at throwing people into the street."

"What if they don't show up in the next few days?" I ask.

"I suggest you remove their belongings and change the lock on the doors. If these girls cause any trouble for you, call us."

"It's not the girls I'm worried about."

"Call us," Dooley repeats, mimicking a phone with his thumb and pinky finger as he and his partner step into the elevator. I remain standing in the hallway after the door closes, listening to their faint laughter follow them down to the street. They didn't even leave their number.

22

Hit the Road Jack

The cops have Lykos thoroughly freaked. Our phone has been ringing off the hook since they called him two days ago. Thanks to us, he's having a nervous breakdown; screaming that his building's going down in flames. Two idiot teenagers are ruining his skyrocketing business career, destroying one of his precious real estate ventures. He's expecting Van Helden and me to make good. "Get them out of there!" he yelled the first time he called. "Don't let them play games with you," he warned the second time. "They don't deserve a refund; they're using my building to break the law. I will hold you responsible if you return their money," he pressured the third time. "Don't let them intimidate you; use psychology. You're smart boys," he coached the fourth time.

Robert and I sit on a bench inside the Charles Street Laundromat waiting for our clothes to spin dry. We come here a couple times a month. In the past, we dropped dimes in the machines and booked it down the street for coffee rather than hang out, but ever since some loser lifted all of Robert's duds from the dryer, we stay close by and eagle-eye our stuff. Our bench buddies include a bony-face speed-freak with sunken eyes and stringy yellow hair that sticks out from under his floppy hat like a scarecrow, and a slumbering wino smelling like pee.

"What did these dudes look like?" asks Van Helden.

"They looked like cops. You should have been there," I say. "I got to watch real crime fighters in action." We get up and begin folding our clothes, stuffing everything into fresh pillowcases. "How are you and Jennifer making out?"

"I quit seeing her. She tried to trap me into spending all my time with her."

"That blows."

"Yeah, right… and she's a ball sucker, too," says Van Helden, sounding annoyed. The scarecrow leans into our conversation.

"All she ever wants to do is suck my balls."

The scarecrow's eyes open as round as apples.

"You got a problem with that?" I ask.

"What about you, Jonny? You still going to the prom with your old girlfriend?"

"Yeah, what the hell. I gotta rent a tux. I'm thinking Edwardian, double-breasted, midnight blue."

"Cool."

"Peach dress shirt… ruffles down the front."

"Sounds nice."

"I don't have the right kinda shoes for this thing. Can ya rent shoes?"

"Bowling shoes… maybe you can get a pair in black," says Robert, laughing.

"Do ya want to take care of Benny and Mickey?" asks Robert on our way into the building.

"You know, man, I'm not cool with this. We

shouldn't be the ones to boot them. This is Lykos' building. He should be the one doing it. Why should we be sticking our necks out?"

"I'm hip. Let's call him and say we're getting a lot of static, nobody is leaving unless the landlord personally tells them to go. He'll run over here, drag them out with his bare hands. That gets us off the hook," Robert smiles.

"He ain't gonna buy that," I sigh. "He'll just tell us to change the locks when they leave their apartment."

"Screw him!" says Robert. "We don't have to do this."

The gypsies are not about to go voluntarily, so while they are out scamming, I personally round up their effects; which amounts to stuffing a couple of grocery bags worth of rags and junk and setting them out in the hallway. I'm standing guard as the locksmith I called replaces the cylinder on the apartment door. In the corner of my eye, Mama suddenly emerges from the shadow of the stairwell and rushes towards the locksmith, shrieking in broken English and swinging a handbag over her head. Down on both knees in the praying position, the poor bastard doesn't have a chance to duck. The bag comes down hard across his back.

"You crackers, Lady? What the hell you doin'?" the locksmith yells, falling to his ass.

She bludgeons him a second time before I am able to pull her off. The woman curses as she fights to wind back and toss another blow.

"Hold it!" I grab her by the shoulders and glare into her face, "Your room has been rented to someone else!" I lie. "What do you wanna live here for, anyway? Take your kids and go someplace nice."

Mama drops her weapon. My words flattened her spirit; she has a defeated look on her face.

"Your things are all here." I point to the two bags with her belongings and offer to help carry them to the street.

"I don't need your help," she says, lifting the bags. "I will be back!"

Van Helden and I have been out drinking with Benny and Mickey on a few occasions and can't quite come to terms with locking them out. Their girlfriends may both be involved in shady deals to make a buck, but I still don't believe they're full blooded whores, at least not in the classic sense. Robert and I decide to leave them alone. We don't bother to call Lykos, either. It's been four days since Officers Mutt and Jeff paid their little visit, and we now have three vacancies to fill; Karen, Rosa and Tomas, and the Gypsy Queen are all gone.

"Hello," I answer the phone reluctantly on the fifth ring. I'm sure it's Lykos calling again to pile on more grief.

"This is Boyko. What's going on over there?"

"Nothin.'"

"I know that! That's why I'm calling! You've had plenty of time to evict those two. What the hell are you waiting for?"

"We keep missing 'em. They're not home most of the time, or when they're in, Robert and I are out." I wonder if Kitty and Julie are feeding him information.

"You know what you're supposed to do; empty the rooms and change the locks. You got a problem with that?"

"Listen, I don't think this is necessary. We haven't seen one John in the building since you guys left."

"So what?"

"The word in the street is all the hookers are gone." I am hoping Boyko might swallow this line and cut us some slack.

"Do you think I'm an idiot? Take care of it or else we'll shut you down. You got it?"

"Got it," I dutifully answer.

"Oh, and one more thing; let the Gypsy Lady back in the building."

"What…why?"

"Never mind why. Just do it," he says, hanging up on me.

A few minutes later, the phone rings again. Lykos immediately begins snarling, "You two boys are useless! Why do I bother with you? I just spoke with the police. If you can't follow their simple instructions, you should leave; go live somewhere else!"

I decide to dust off Robert's plan; "Benny and Mickey want to talk to you."

"Who? I don't know any Benny and Mickey."

"They live with the girls you want us to evict. You can't evict the girls without booting their boyfriends, too; it's a package deal."

"Why should I talk with them?"

"They called the accusations a crock of shit, and you have no right to evict them. They said they have a lawyer who will back them up." I pile on the bullshit, particularly proud of my line about the lawyer. "What do you want us to do?"

"I'm coming right over. You make sure they're in when I get there," says Lykos, slamming down the phone.

I picture Lykos running to his garage, firing up the Lincoln and burning a line of rubber down Route 9.

Forty-five minutes after hanging up the phone, Lykos marches into our room impeccably dressed; like a diplomat calling on a camp of savages. Lykos paces back and forth with his hands clasped behind his back. "Where are these people who want to see me?"

Robert and I have no idea if they are home. Nothing has been prearranged. "They're in their rooms… waiting for you; at least that's where they were a little while ago."

"Maybe they got tired of hanging and split," says Van Helden.

"Tired of hanging!? What kind of crap are you feeding me?" Lykos stops in his tracks and scowls in Robert's face. "Who are these people? Which rooms are they in?"

Van Helden and I lead Lykos to Apartment 4C where Benny and Jackie keep house. Robert steps up and knocks.

"Yes?" says Jackie, looking skanky with bloodshot eyes and natty orange hair underlined by an inch of black roots. In one hand, she holds a caramel colored drink, and in the other, a cigarette. Ice cubes clink inside the glass.

"May we come in?" asks Robert.

Benny is sitting at the table behind a bowl of soup. He drops his spoon on the floor when he gets a look at Lykos in his Brooks Brothers suit and shiny wingtips.

"These boys tell me you refuse to leave," Lykos addresses Benny straight away, who stares up at him from his chair.

"Whut?" Benny asks, dumbfounded by this statement.

"I don't want to hear what you have to say. I want you to pack up your things today and leave my building."

"*What for?* We're ain't done *nothin!*" says Jackie, stepping up, facing Lykos in a defensive posture, poking the air in front of his face with her lit cigarette.

"What do you do for a living?" Lykos asks Benny.

"I'm a house painter."

"Where are you working?"

"I'm in between jobs at the moment," says Benny, sheepishly.

"And what is your livelihood?" he asks Jackie.

"I'm an entertainer."

"An entertainer… oh, really?"

"Yeah, you got a problem with that?"

"Where do you work?"

Jackie takes a drag off her cigarette, "That's none of your business," she answers. I smile, picturing Jackie naked on her table top, blowing smoke into Lykos's face.

"I will have the both of you arrested if you're not gone from my building by tomorrow morning!"

With The Boss leading the way, we take the stairs down to grill Michelangelo and Maureen. On the third floor, Lykos slows his pace by the open door to Julie's apartment. He sticks his head inside after tapping his diamond pinkie ring on the jamb. Robert and I follow him into the room. The whole scene is a model of domestic bliss: John, still hobbled by his cast, is camped on the sofa drinking a beer, ignoring us with his head buried in last month's *Playboy*. The toddler is crawling around on the floor wearing her mother's sequined G-string on her head like a tiara for a little princess. Julie, preparing a TV dinner in the kitchen, is dressed for work in a sultry scarlet pantsuit; her look topped off with an enormous blonde wig. Her kid sister, Melanie, sits nearby at the kitchen table polishing her toenails, her face draped in a cloud of smoke from the cigarette dangling between her lips.

"Hello there," says Lykos. He has an unctuous cadence dripping from his voice, "I just want you to know we are taking care of business around here." Lykos must have heard from the police that Julie and Kitty are spotlighting the hookers in the building. He wants to make sure she knows he is on top of things; maybe put in a good word to her cop buddies. "I hope everything is going well for all of you."

"Please, come in," says Julie. "Would you like a beer?"

John grunts something inaudible from behind his magazine.

"No, no thank you ... we must be running. We have more of this business to attend to."

On the approach to Michelangelo's room, Lykos asks, "What's the story on these two?" as he steps up and knocks.

"Nothin' special," I shrug.

When no one answers on the second knock, we open the door and walk cautiously inside. To my complete surprise, the cupboards, closets and drawers are bare. There is no sign of M&M; they must have checked out when we weren't looking.

"Where the hell are they? I thought you said they were waiting to see me."

"Shit, I don't know... maybe we scared em off," I say, not believing it.

"Good job," says Lykos. "Looks like they got the message."

"Yeah... I guess so." I highly doubt we had anything to do with their departure.

"Change the lock on the door."

In order not to repeat the disastrous collection of miscreants we allowed in the building over the past few months, Lykos passes along valuable reflections on tenanthood to help us weed out the lowlife. "A number of people in this part of town are dirty. Don't rent to anyone that looks like filth. You don't want to let that kind of thing in the building."

"You mean if they look like bums, we shouldn't rent to them?" I ask.

"Of course you don't want to rent to bums... that's not what I'm saying. I'm talking about smut... people with no morals, the kind of scum you find in dirty movies and peep shows; pornographers." Lykos continues, "Be careful... and don't rent to single women... they are nothing but trouble. And don't bother renting to any man who can't prove he has a job."

"Are we supposed to ask people where they work?" asks Van Helden.

"Of course. That's not privileged information. Ask them for the phone number where they work. Tell them you will call their employer for a reference. Ask them where they lived before coming here, and why they left. They should answer all your questions. Use psychology. People who act like they have something to hide usually do. Don't let them play tricks with you. You boys are smarter than they are. Also, and this is *very* important, don't rent to drug addicts; they're scum!"

"How are we supposed to tell if someone's doing dope?" I ask.

"We could ask them if they got any drugs," says Robert, smiling.

"You can't *ask* them that! They'll lie to you every time. You can tell if someone is hooked on marijuana by looking in their eyes. They're bloodshot... crazy dark holes surrounded by red splotches. These people are criminals... they're shifty and dangerous... they're worse than pornographers."

Lykos sums it up for us. "These types are dirt... troublemakers. They won't be allowed in here any more. I want to turn this place around. This building will be known as a good, clean, safe place to live. There's no reason why we can't attract nice families, like that pleasant man with the broken leg and his beautiful wife and children. That's the kind of people we want in here. Do we understand each other?"

"Yes sir."

Lykos leaves in better spirits than when he arrived; his confidence in our managerial abilities restored.

23
Twist n' Shout

A hand gently nudges my shoulder. "Jonathan... Jonathan," whispers Mrs. Butterfield. She catches me sleeping in a seated position on the floor in the library's reference section. I sat down to relax and accidentally dozed off. I was out late last night barhopping with Van Helden and Marvin. We closed the Downtown Lounge together and didn't make it home until after two.

"Jonathan, do you want to rest in my office?"

"Ah... I'm sorry, I went to bed late; didn't get much sleep." I say, rubbing my eyes.

"You needn't apologize. I remember what it was like when I was young, studying for my finals. There's never enough time at night to absorb it all."

"You got that right." Standing up and tucking the corner of my shirt back in my pants, I place my hands on the cart I'm supposed to be pushing around, shelving returned books into the stacks.

"Why don't you leave that for later," says Mrs. Butterfield. "Go sit at the checkout counter; we aren't too busy this afternoon ... you can rest up a little."

"Thanks, that sounds nice, but I'm okay, really." I wheel myself away and get busy.

"Dear boy," I hear her quiet voice say as I turn the corner in the direction of nonfiction.

Final exams are hanging over my head like a rusty guillotine. I woke up early this morning with intentions of performing some heavy cramming. Textbooks lay stacked on my kitchen table beside a pack of smokes, slide rule, and sheets of notepaper. I plan on sticking with this all day today and tomorrow; hopefully undisturbed.

"I'm going out to get the paper," says Robert. "Do you want anything?"

"Yeah, bring me back a brain. Mine's dead… I need to trade it in for one that works."

"Wouldn't that be cool if we could do that? What if you could go out and buy new brain cells, drop them in like replacement batteries for a flashlight."

Ragged screams send a shockwave through my body, a woman pleading to be saved from horror several floors below. Van Helden and I race down stairs toward the wrenching cries. At the dead-end of the corridor on the third floor I spot John Taylor, his back to me, a long kitchen knife gripped in his hand, the blade raised high, ready to stab into the body squirming at his feet. Julie lies curled up on the floor, screaming, flailing arms covering her head. I don't stop to think. Lunging forward, my right hand grabs the wrist that holds the knife. I lock my left forearm around John's neck and flip him back in the air, landing him solid to the floor. Pinning him down with my knees and straddling his chest, I bang John's wrist hard against the floor, forcing him to release the knife. Van Helden quickly pulls it free, away from the trouble twisting between my legs.

Our neighbors begin to fill in beside us within the narrow hallway. Over my shoulder, Ed Taylor stands beside Jasper, imploring his older brother to cool off. Marvin, standing shirtless with dabs of shaving cream on his face, makes the same appeal. John, bucking like a wild bronco, finally settles down, drained from his ordeal, until he recognizes who it is kneeling on his chest.

"YOU!" John hisses at the sight of my face, gritting his teeth, snarling; lifting his head to bite me. His rage is beaten back by several pairs of hands pushing his face, shoulders and legs flat to the floor. I ride on top of the man, shouting, commanding him to quit, my pleading lost among the screams coming from the others.

"You don't wanna hurt her, Brother!" Ed Taylor's booming voice rises above the din, "You don't wanna hurt nobody! Nobody wanna hurt you!" Ed's words seem to break through to the man, who goes limp between my legs. "John, you a good man! You a good man, Brother. Be cool.... be cool." Ed puts his hand on my shoulder, "I got him now, thank you," and he turns to face everyone in the hallway, "Thank you... thank you."

I lift myself off the beaten man. John stands, his body trembling, trying hard to regain some dignity by acting composed. "I love her... I wasn't gonna hurt her," he says, his eyes looking at no one. With Ed Taylor and Jasper guiding his way, John retreats up the stairs to his brother's apartment.

My eyes search for Julie. She has vanished in the chaos. Is she hurt? Did he cut her? "Where's Julie?" I ask Jasper's old lady, Dianne.

"She's all right. She's with her girlfriends. It's better if you let us take care of this."

Van Helden and I take the stairs back to our room.

"That was pretty freaky, man," says Robert.

"That guy scares me," I say, breathing heavily.

"He acted like he wanted to kill me… what the fuck's going on here?"

Sitting back down at the kitchen table, my trembling hands reach for my textbook and open to the chapter I was studying earlier. Staring at the content, the printed words and diagrams a blur, as if I'm peering into a well of water trying to read a page suspended beneath the surface. I can't do this.

I grab my pack of smokes and head for the door. "I need some air," I say, turning to Robert on my way out. I'm not sure where I'm going; I only know I got to get away.

The shady path leading through the Common has a calming effect. I follow it west, cross Charles Street and approach the Duck Pond in the Public Garden. Looking down at the little dock, several swan boat pilots are preparing their crafts for the lazy journey around the pond. I come to the center of the suspension bridge and lean over the rail. The sun feels comforting on my face, and for a second, my mind drifts along with the mallards in the water, forgetting how bizarre this morning began. John has fairy-tales in his head. I need to talk with him; tell him there's nothing going on between Julie and me. Sure, that's a great idea… he'll thank me for my sincerity just before he shoots me in the head. Sitting down with my back against the rail, I pull my legs up to my chest and light a cigarette. A current of tourists flows leisurely by my feet, some stopping to snap pictures of their mates enjoying the beautiful spring morning. I can't hide from this; I got to talk to the man. I get off my ass and head home to confront John Taylor.

Two police cruisers are lined up at the curb beside the entrance to my building; a third is double-parked in the street beside them; all lights are flashing. I don't see any ambulances, which is a good sign; at least no one's been shot. I pick up my pace, making a straight line down to the action. Several officers, looking disinterested, are milling around on the sidewalk. One holds open the door to the foyer as three men emerge from the entrance; two bulky white dudes in blue uniforms flank a wiry black man in handcuffs with his head bent low, his right leg hobbled in a plaster cast. A burly cop with a face like an Irish potato pushes John's head down as they tuck him into the back seat of the cruiser. Everyone jumps into their vehicles and within seconds, whisk off in the direction of the Warren Street jail. I stop a few feet from the parade and wave goodbye to John.

To fill in the blanks, I count on Raymond's penchant for gossip. He can be tighter than a clam's ass when it comes to opening up to expose criminal behavior, but he'll blab his face off if he's sure there no one's coming around the corner to whack him for his big mouth. Raymond sits on a folding chair near his doorway. He stands to greet me as I step from the elevator.

"Jon! Isn't it a beautiful day! Would you care to join me for a cup of coffee?

"Ray... do you know what went down here this morning?" I'm not feeling very sociable.

"Yes, indeed I do. Come in, come in." Ray is waving me into his room. "Care for some Entenmann's crumb cake? It's delicious."

"No thanks. What happened here, Ray?"

"Isn't Julie a beautiful girl?" asks Ray. "Have you

ever seen her dance? I intend to someday. That would be sublime. I would think she looks divine dancing naked on stage."

"Yeah… she's a knock out. *Ray, what the fuck happened in here!*"

"You don't have to raise your voice… I was getting to it. Well, you knew John attacked Julie with a knife. You probably heard all the commotion."

"Yeah, I had a front row seat. Where did Julie run off to?"

"The poor girl came here to my room to use my telephone. She called a friend. He's a cop. I believe his name is Rick."

"Rick Boyko?"

"Yes… I believe it was. Do you know him?"

"Yeah, we're real pals. Did she tell Boyko her old man tried to kill her?"

"You know, it's funny, but she didn't mention the altercation. She talked to him about something John did in Baltimore last year. She said the authorities down there want him. A few minutes later, the police burst in upstairs and arrested John. It's been quite an exciting morning, hasn't it?" Raymond beams a self-important smile of a privileged informant.

24
Prom Night

"Lara?" I ask the voice on the other end of the line.

"Hi," she replies, softly. "When am I going to see you?"

"I'm leaving here Friday afternoon after my last exam. I'll be thumbin'… I don't know when I'll get there."

"I got my mother's car for Saturday night."

"What she got?"

"What do you mean?"

"What does she drive… a Chevy, a Ford?"

"Oh, it's a '64' Dodge Dart."

Damn, a Dart… that kind of blows. "Why don't you plan on swinging by my house to pick me up around eight," I say. "How late can you stay out?"

Lara and I hatch a plan. She will ask permission to stay out extra late, telling her Mom we'll be going to one of the local after-hours prom parties. These affairs typically run till two or three in the morning. The Junior Prom is being held in my old high school cafeteria. We intend to make the scene there, stay for a few dances, duck out, fire up the Dart and sneak up to Boston. Marvin and Winky are throwing a party in their apartment that night. I thought it would be really cool to show up for it wearing my tuxedo.

Three vacant apartments were filled this week, one taken by Sam's girlfriend, Angel, and her boyfriend, Hector. Angel told me some college creep had knocked her up when she was in junior high. She has a five-year-old boy living in a Catholic orphanage run by The Sisters of Mercy, a troop of nuns in Quincy. The nuns plan on stopping by the building on special occasions to drop off her kid. Hector, an affable mulatto with a thick brown Afro, plays in a band. I think Hector, Angel and her kid qualify as the new breed of family Lykos is hoping to attract. Another tenant joining us is also a musician; a short, moon faced dude who kinda looks like Jack Benny's sidekick, Rochester. The guy's name is Joe Cook, but he prefers to be called Little Joe. He made a big deal of the fact he had a hit record about a century ago... a thing called, *Peanuts*. He asked permission for his band to jam in his apartment some afternoons. We gave him our blessing. Little Joe is staying in the room directly below us. The last apartment rented, 3B, went to a chubby black guy and his wife. "I'm a traveling salesman," he told me. "You won't see me around much." He flashed me his business card, *Lamar Bashear, Learning Incorporated*. All our new people seem to fit the mold Lykos is looking for, hardworking solid citizens.

    Little Joe Cook's band is set to jam. His group includes three guitars; lead, rhythm and bass; a full set of drums with a conga on the side, just for spice, and a small horn section. Speakers are arranged strategically around the apartment. A mike is set up in front of Little Joe, and two more are standing among the musicians in the field. Little Joe moves to the center of the group like a pitcher stepping up to the mound. He looks to his left, then over to his right... checking out first and third... nods to the drummer behind home plate; Diddle diddle diddle ... ba ba ba ba ba ba ba, BAAAOWW! Little Joe starts twisting and jumping like he has ants in his pants. "Ooooo, baaabby, baby, baby!!"

I retreat upstairs to my room, grab a Coke from the fridge and join Van Helden outside on the fire escape. Robert and I sit at opposite ends with our legs stretched out, facing each other, thoroughly enjoying the sweet, tight rhythm and blues below our feet. The music is outstanding! Little Joe has his apartment's casement windows cranked wide open, allowing the band's silky sound to escape below to Tremont Street. Van Helden waves to the crowd on the sidewalk passing by, stopping dead in their tracks, craning their necks up the wall towards the music. We sit outside till the sun hides behind the buildings across the street. The music plays on for a little while longer before the band calls it quits.

Van Helden dropped twenty bucks on a cheap stereo. The speakers are made from industrial grade cardboard stamped with a photographic image of polished walnut. When cranked up to full volume, John Bonham's drums take on a metal quality, like banging forks on pots and pans. We have three albums; each played a minimum of twice a day. Little Joe Cook stopped by our room this afternoon and added one of his own recordings to our collection, *Peanuts*, a 45 personally autographed by Little Joe himself. I suppose if played on a good system, his song could be bearable, maybe even enjoyable; but spinning on Robert's crappy stereo, Little Joe's high falsetto voice sounds like someone trying to stuff a cat's head into a soup can.

The air in my room is stale and muggy. I walk over to the window and crank open the sash. The down side of snatching a window breeze at night is the racket you let in. Organ music pipes out from the bar below, blending with the raucous action in the street, the blare of honking cars and the holler of men having fun. I walk back to the table to study, placing my head in my hands to cover my ears. Concentration is a losing battle.

Van Helden is standing in his underwear in front of the closet holding a pair of shirts by the hangers, judging their fashion potential. "Sam has some friends over. I'm going next door to say hello. You wanna come?" asks Robert.

"I can't, man. I gotta study." I look up and see Robert duck into the bathroom. "Maybe later. Who's over there?" I ask, dropping my face back into my book.

"A chick I met this afternoon." Van Helden is preening in front of the mirror. "She's hot!" he adds, sticking his head out the bathroom for emphasis.

"Anyone else?"

"Some dude... Sam's old boyfriend. I think he might be shacking up over there."

"No shit?" Sam never mentioned anything about this to me.

I close my books at 10:00 and walk next door. Van Helden is sitting at the kitchen table sharing a bottle of wine with the chick he mentioned. Sam lies on her bed nestled affectionately beside a diminutive, boyish looking guy with a dirty-blonde mop top; their legs entwined like vines.

"Hi," I enter the room a little tentative; feeling I might be imposing.

"Hey, Jonny! Sit down. Jonny's the other super I was telling you about." Robert introduces the new girl, Barbara. She is indeed stunning; colossal eyes, cocoa butter skin and silky Tahitian-maiden hair. I immediately have a crush on her.

Sam, kissing her guy hard on the lips announces, "And this is Joey!"

"Pleased to meet you," says Joey. "You got a nice building here."

Sam howls with laughter, as if Joey has said the funniest thing imaginable. She kisses him again, harder this time around.

I pick up on the conversation at the table, centered on Barbara's motivation to become a model.

"It's a lot of hard work… the competition is murder." Barbara's manner seems confident, like she's got the goods to make it happen. On the table, a glossy portfolio is opened to a chic layout displaying her in a variety of moods, head shots and full-body poses.

"You look great!"

"Thanks, my brother-in-law, Frosty, is the photographer."

Over on the bed, Joey focuses on petting Sam's bare legs. Sam is making little purring sounds. I turn to the two lovers. "What brings you to town, Joey, besides Sam?"

Sam makes a giddy cackle, hugging her little man.

"I play the drums," Joey answers, without taking his eyes off Sam's legs. "My band is touring the east coast. We're playing at Lucifer's. Why don't you come by and see us?"

"Where's that?"

"You've never been to Lucifer's?" he asks. "It's the hottest club in Boston."

"Never heard of it."

"Well… we gotta fix that. Let me know the night you wanna come. I'll get ya through the door."

"I rented Apartment 2C to Barbara. She's moving in a couple of days," Robert announces.

Barbara turns her mouth up in a pleasing smile. I flash on Lykos' list of forbidden fruit. He gave us a pretty clear warning about renting to single women.

"Are you moving in alone?" I ask, doing my due diligence.

"Her younger sister is coming, too." Robert answers for her, like he was her agent, or something. Lykos said nothing about single sisters living together.

"That's cool," I smile. "Where you working, I mean, until your modeling thing takes off?"

"Barbara works in the neighborhood, the Intermission Lounge," Robert fills in the last detail on Lykos's questionnaire.

"I'm a cocktail waitress… I don't dance on the tables, I wait on'em," says Barbara.

I finished my last final this afternoon, Professor Prick's. C.T. Pederson has a real hard-on for me. He would absolutely love it if I crashed and burned. If I don't get a decent grade, the next test I'll be taking is how to break down an M-16 in under ten seconds. Hell with it… no sense worrying about it. Sticking out my thumb in the direction of home, my real home, I ignore the "No Hitch Hiking" sign posted behind my back. I'm carrying my tuxedo and all the fixings in a bag they gave me at the rental shop on Winter Street. I found a royal-blue Edwardian, double-breasted with black satin piping. They didn't have the peach dress shirt I wanted, but I scored something almost as cool; a powder blue jobbie with tasty ruffles. I splurged on a shiny new pair of ten-dollar English Dappers from Tom McCann's.

Standing at the entrance to the Pike is strategically the best place to thumb if you're heading out of Boston. The road's wide enough for a car to pull over without causing a honking fit from the assholes behind it, people are moving slow enough to stop without slamming on their brakes, and I can make eye contact with the drivers behind the wheel, maybe get them to feel a little sorry for me standing out here.

So, why isn't anybody stopping? Maybe it's the eye contact thing. I should go a easy on staring through their windshields.

A candy-apple red Ford Mustang pulls over to the side, its engine purring. I open the door and flip the front seat forward, reaching into the back to lay my things down before jumping in beside the driver and nestling down on clean pearl-white vinyl.

"How far you going?" asks the attractive woman behind the wheel.

"Um, down to Hartford." I'm pleasantly shocked that a good-looking lady stopped to give me a ride.

"Let me guess," she says, catching me off guard staring at her shapely legs, "You're a college boy going home for the weekend to see his girlfriend. Am I right?"

"Bingo." Jesus, she's a pretty lady; her long red hair ignited by the contrast of a lovely white silk blouse. "I can't hardly remember the last time I saw her."

"Well, it's about time you paid her a visit," she says, jokingly evoking a stern manner in her voice.

"I'm taking her to her Junior Prom," I confess, feeling a little embarrassed by this.

We talk for nearly two hours. I tell her about my relationship with Lara and why I stopped seeing her. I fill her in on my life in the Combat Zone, detailing some of the things that have happened over the past several months. My car lady seems fascinated by what I have to say, following each one of my tales with a, "Oh, my… Really?… That's remarkable!" She's a very good listener.

The time driving to Hartford goes by so fast, before I know it the sun has set and we are coasting up to the curb at Constitution Plaza. I am sorry the ride is over. I want to stay in the car and go wherever it is she's going. The door opens and I step out, flipping the front seat forward to retrieve my things.

"Can I give you some advice for tomorrow night?" asks my car lady.

"Of course." My body leans back into the car.

"You're a nice boy; pick your girlfriend up at her door, bring her a corsage. Don't let her come to you… you go to her."

"But I don't have a car."

"I'm sure you can figure something out."

"Yeah, sure… thanks for the ride. You're nice, too." I close the door and watch her slowly pull away.

From downtown Hartford I board a local bus that drops me off a mile from my home. I hike the rest of the way. Turning down my street, I'm amazed by how peaceful and quiet it is. This serenity never caught my attention before, the stillness broken only by the sound of my feet crunching along the gravel, and a symphony of crickets and bullfrogs performing in the front yards I pass. Sporadic sparkles of fireflies guide my path from the driveway to my front door.

I enter my house and find my four little sisters in the living room parked in front of the television, exactly where I had last seen them six months ago. My parents are sitting beside my older brother, Jerry, in the kitchen, consuming beers, cigarettes and table talk. Everyone gushes over me, taking turns hugging me hard. I love it.

After dropping my bag in the old bedroom I share with my brother, I return to the kitchen table to join my family. My mother scrambles to make me a sandwich.

"And what would you like to drink?' asks Mom.

I'm tempted to say 'I'll take a beer', but think better of it, knowing my parents wouldn't approve. I pour ginger ale into a glass with ice and pull up a chair next to my father.

Last year, my brother joined the National Guard and has the haircut to prove it. Ever since he finished Basic Training my parents have treated him like a full-blown adult. That seems only natural; Jerry's acted like he was forty since the day he turned twelve. Early on in high school, he began addressing our parents by their first names, Lil and Vic. They reproached these references at first, but eventually came around to accept it. I do it, too, but switch back and forth. Once in a while it still feels good to call them Mom and Dad.

"I told Vic you're living with strippers and hookers," Jerry testifies. My father's eyes widen, his face suggesting interest.

"We don't have hookers anymore; they've been evicted." Reaching over the table, I pull a smoke from my brother's pack, light up and smile.

"When did you start using cigarettes?" my father asks, his bright disposition instantly vanishes, disappointment written all over his glum face.

"I like them now."

Vic shakes his head in harsh admonishment, pulls a sip from his beer and crushes his Pall Mall into the ashtray. The signal I'm getting; I have his blessing to cavort with exotic ladies just as long as I don't smoke with them.

My brother volunteers to drive me to Lara's house tomorrow night. This frees me from the indignity of having her pick me up. The downside is I might have to deal with her people. Lara's family is a solid ensemble of blue-collar Italian Americans; a hard working mother and three fiercely protective older brothers. Her father died when she was five; further intensifying the patriarchal claim the trio of boys yield over her life. I am anxious to call Lara and tell her the change in plans. I pick up the phone in my parents' bedroom and dial.

"YEAH!?" A guy gargling gravel snaps a greeting in my ear.

"Ah… is Lara in?"

"Who's this?" the voice on the other end of the line sounds as welcoming as a punch in the face.

"I'm her friend, Jonny."

"Jonny? I don't know any Jonny."

"Can I speak to Lara, please?"

Lara is screaming in the background, "Rocco, give me the damn phone!"

Rocco, Vinnie and Dominick sit at the kitchen table, regarding each other like strangers while feeding on plates of spaghetti and a bowl of meatballs and sausage. I stand against the wall like a mute, fidgeting with the box containing Lara's corsage. The brothers ignore me, all through their noisy chomping and gulping.

"So, up there in Boston, ya ever get to see the Bruins play?" Dominick, his mouth full of meatballs, surprises me with his question. The brothers all look up, staring at me while chewing. Their eyes, like spotlights, make me feel uncomfortable. I'm aware the Bruins are a hockey team, but I know next to nothing about the sport, having never been to a game.

"Oh yeah, all the time," I lie, sucking up to Lara's clan. "Those Bruins are killers! I love those guys." I embellish my deceit, hoping to score a few points, "I was watching a game at the Garden one night. They had this guy from the other team in the penalty box…"

"What team?" asks Vinnie, sounding vaguely interested.

"Ah… New York," I guess. "Anyway, the fans in the Garden are maniacs!" I overheard this statistic, I don't remember where. "These guys in the stands lean into the box and start wailing on the New York player; punching him out, whacking him on the head, dumping beer on him, a real freak show."

"How the hell did they get over the glass?" snarls Rocco.

"The what?"

"The GLASS. The penalty box is separated from the stands by a wall of glass. How the hell did they get over it?"

I turn to face Lara's mother entering the kitchen. With a smile as proud as a marching band, she announces the arrival of her adorable daughter, "Here she is everybody! Dominick, get the camera from the dining room hutch."

Dominick dutifully races from the room. Lara walks into the kitchen dressed in a strapless pale yellow satin gown. Golden waves of titian hair fall down her back and across her tanned shoulders. I am stunned by how lovely she is. I honestly can't remember a moment in my life when I dated anyone possessing more beauty than the girl standing before me now.

"Hello… I, ah, have flowers, ah, a corsage," I stammer, extending the small box I hold in my hand.

"Thank you, they're lovely," she smiles.

On the way out the door, I turn to Rocco. "They jumped over the glass," I say. I distinctly hear his comment as the door closes behind us.

"What a jaboni."

The Dart pulls into the high school parking lot and I kill the engine. Lara sits tight beside me; her baby finger touching my thigh. I turn towards her, gently hold her face in my hands and kiss her tenderly on the mouth.

"Ohhh, I've been waiting a long time for you to do that," she whispers.

Following another kiss, I confess to Lara it was all I could think about the second I saw her walk into the kitchen. "You're so beautiful," I softly say her name, "Lara," and kiss her again.

The two of us leave the car, walking into the building with our arms looped affectionately around each other. In the hallway outside the entrance to the cafeteria, a photographer is snapping pictures of couples queued up for their chance to pose between a pair of phony cardboard columns with a backdrop of a cheesy poster of the Parthenon in a fairy-tale landscape; five bucks a pop. I fork up the dough and lead Lara to the back of the line. In case you missed the point, a sign on the wall announces the theme for tonight's affair, Olympian Enchantment. A musical accompaniment to all this enchantment is coming through the doors behind us; a local band belting out a fair rendition of *Hang on Sloopy*.

The décor inside the cafeteria expounds on the excitement introduced in the hallway; a tacky arrangement of crepe paper and papier-mâché fashioned to evoke an ethereal landscape drenched in mythological magic; I think the footbridge cut from plywood and 2 x 4's laid over a stream of inky-blue construction paper is a nice touch. Regrettably, no amount of conjuring can hide the fact that I'm back inside my high school cafeteria. I look around for my guidance counselor, Mr. Savilli, but fail to find him among the adult chaperones strolling through the crowd with their hands behind their backs and smiles plastered on their dumb faces, struggling to act like they belong. I flash on the portent of Savilli's advice to me about becoming a plumber and my struggle through Professor Prick's final exam. Maybe old Savilli wasn't so wrong after all.

"Where are you right now?" asks Lara, pulling me close to her by the sleeve of my tux.

"Huh?"

"You look as if your mind is a million miles away. Are you sure you wanted to come to this?"

"Me?" I point to myself. "Of course I want to be here. I mean, this is a goof... you gotta admit it. But I wanna be with you. I wouldn't have missed this for the world."

"Then why aren't you smiling? Everybody in here looks like they're having a good time... but you. What's going on?"

"I'm sorry. I'm just a little freaked about my finals... that's all," I confess. "I promise not to leave you mentally, or physically, for the rest of the night."

Lara and I find a table in the corner of the cafeteria away from the action. The band breaks into a slow number, *Cherish*, and the floor begins to fill with couples hugging to the music.

"May I have this dance?" I ask, smiling graciously; hoping to make up for any misgivings I may have revealed.

"Sure," Lara returns my smile with a half-hearted one of her own. We dance our way through the crowd of her classmates; Lara occasionally acknowledging a friend, smiling hello with her eyes. I hug her hard against me as we dance through another ballad.

We've been drifting through the Land of Olympian Enhancement for nearly an hour, with me fawning over Lara every chance I get. "You wanna split?" I ask, as soon as she finished her glass of punch.

"What time is it?"

"It's almost nine. If we hurry, we can make it to Boston by eleven."

"Okay... just let me say goodbye to my girlfriends."

True to my word, at ten fifty-five we pass through the tunnel beneath the Pru and exit onto Copley Square. I look over at Lara; a streetlight beaming through the windshield shines across her face betraying her apprehension. She looks back at me, "Are we being bad?"

"Yep." I shoot the Dart up Boylston Street. Zigzagging over to La Grange, I find a parking spot in an alley a block away from my front door. "Let's go meet my friends," I say, turning to Lara, whose apprehension has evaporated; her beautiful face now takes on the look of an excited conspirator.

"Is the car safe here?" she asks.

"Nobody on the planet would bother to steal a Dodge Dart," I answer. "I'm more worried about someone lighting it on fire."

"*On Fire*! Why would anyone do that?"

"For fun." I reassure Lara that her mother's car is as safe here as anyplace else in Boston. No sense worrying about it.

Hand in hand, we turn the corner onto Tremont. The sidewalks on both sides of the street are crawling with people; mostly guys out looking for a good time. Passing by the open door of the Tam Café, we are hit with a discordant dose of organ music backed up by the crackling rattle of a snare drum. A rowdy cluster of men not much older than me spill out of the bar next to my front door and convivially ramble across the street in the direction of the Four Corners Lounge.

"It's noisy here," says Lara.

Upon entering my building, Jasper greets us in the lobby as he steps from the elevator. My dapper friend is sporting a canary yellow hat, with shiny pants, shirt and vest to match. In his right hand he holds an ebony cane topped off with a large crystal that resembles a glass doorknob.

"Hey, Jasper… nice walkin' stick."

"Wooo, man, you look slick," says Jasper, putting his fingers on the piping of my blue tuxedo's lapel. I gesture introductions with an open palm.

"Very pleased to meet you," Jasper bows his head slightly and taps the cane to the brim of his hat.

"Me, too," says Lara, giving Jasper a killer smile.

Lara and I begin making out the moment the elevator door closes behind us. When the cab comes to a stop at the sixth floor, we keep on going, kissing and exploring each other's bodies with our hands and fingertips.

"Would you like to see my room?"

"Yes."

We start kissing again, neither one of us making a move from the elevator. Lara's fingers begin struggling with the ruffles of my shirt, searching for the buttons.

"Maybe we should go inside my room."

"Yes," she kisses me hard on the mouth.

I place Lara's hand in mine and lead her from the elevator.

"Wow, nice place."

"It's a dump, but we like it."

"Who's that?" Lara points to a life-size poster of Lee Van Cleef I have hanging on the wall beside my bed. Mr. Van Cleef is dressed as Angel Eyes, the 'Bad' character from *The Good, The Bad and The Ugly*.

"I love that guy," I explain to Lara a little bit of his part in the movie.

"No… Who's that sticking out of his holster?"

asks Lara, pointing to the spot where the six-gun should be.

"Oh… that's Julie, she lives here." I got creative with one of the pictures Julie had given me of her stripping on stage, taking a pair of scissors to it and cutting out around her body like a paper doll. I snipped off her legs and placed the cutout of her naked torso inside Angel Eyes' holster. Julie's mouth has a sexy pout, and her hair and breasts are in motion. I think the composition of her and Angel Eyes together looks pretty cool.

"She lives *here*… in your building?"

"Yeah, we're friends. Maybe you'll get to meet her tonight after she gets home from work."

Lara parks herself at the kitchen table. "Do you have a cigarette?" she asks, propping both feet up on the chair beside her.

I oblige her and strike my Zippo in her face. Lara looks a bit indelicate in her classy gown at my kitchen table, puffing away in an aggravated manner.

"You want to smoke a joint?" I suggest,

"No thank you. You go ahead; don't let me stop you."

I decide to pass on the pot. Smoking is a communal thing, you know. There's no fun doing it alone.

"Would you like to go downstairs and check out Marvin's party?" I ask, believing a change of scene will do us good; I also want to make a big splash strutting into Marvin's pit in my blue tuxedo with a beautiful date on my arm.

Lara drops her feet to the floor and gives me an unenthused look, "Sure."

A confluence of laughter, loud voices and soul music greets us as we turn the corner on the fifth floor; the action erupting from the open door of Marvin's apartment. Twenty or more people have jammed inside the small room, passing around jugs of wine, bottles of beer, philosophy and dope. I hold on tight to Lara's hand and thread our way through the crowd. I recognize most everyone here, if not by name than at least by face. Van Helden is sitting on a couch in the center of the room framed by two gorgeous raven-haired ladies; one is Barbara, the girl that moved into 2C this week. The other girl looks like she could be her sister. Winky sits snugly on Marvin's lap in a big comfy chair beside the trio. Robert springs to his feet when we approach the group.

"Jonny, look at you!" says Robert, shaking his head in approval.

"Lara, this is Robert Van Helden." I present my friends to Lara. She sparkles at the sight of Van Helden. "Marvin and Winky," I continue the intros, pointing to the attractive couple, "Barbara... and... ah, this must be your sister."

"Yeah," Robert jumps in, "This is Joanne."

"Hi, nice to meet you," says Joanne, pleasantly, standing to shake our hands. "Robert said you were at a prom tonight. You both look like terrific! Lara, your gown is beautiful."

"Thank you."

"What can I get you guys?" Marvin asks. "Beer, soda?"

"I'm okay," I answer.

"Do you have any Coke?" asks Lara.

"Baby," Marvin faces Winky, "Go get Lara a Coke."

I pull up a couple of chairs for Lara and me and join a discussion Marvin is leading about his perception of why hippies and blacks are tight. "We got somethin' in common, don't we? We're all treated like outcasts."

"Hippies aren't outcasts; they're dropouts," says Joanne.

"Maybe," counters Marvin, "but they're still not accepted. They don't call themselves freaks for nothin; ain't that right? Most white folks look at them strange and move to the other side of the room when they come in the door. Hippies step on a bus and that nice little old white lady sitting all alone is praying they don't sit next to her. That happens to black folks all the time."

"Hippies love everybody," says Winky, handing Lara her Coke. "You don't do dat," she says, looking sideways at her boyfriend.

"Landlords don't want to rent to hippies," Marvin continues, ignoring Winky's comment. "You think Lykos wants them in this building? I don't think so. And hippies are always looking out for The Man, cause he's always out to bust them. The black man knows what that feels like, too."

"Whut you sayin', Marvin?" asks Winky. "Hippies know whut it feels like to be black?"

"No, no… I ain't sayin' that. All I'm sayin', there's some kind of bond happenin', and I'm just tryin' to figure out where it's coming from. Blacks are blacks and hippies are hippies, I know the lines don't cross."

"You got black hippies," offers Joanne. "What do you call them?"

"Black freaks," I suggest.

"Bleaks," says Van Helden.

"Blippies," says Lara, laughing.

Sam is standing by the window looking out at the dark night with her back to the party. At her side, Angel and her boyfriend Hector are engaged in animated conversation. I stand up and grab Lara by the hand, "I want you to meet someone." I introduce Angel and Hector to Lara on my way towards Sam, who continues to face the window. Reaching over to Sam, I tap her shoulder to get her attention; she slowly turns to face me and forces a smile.

"Hi, handsome," says Sam, taking a drag from her cigarette.

"Lara, this is my good friend Sam."

"Pretty gown… Did you have a nice time at the prom?" asks Sam.

"We didn't stay too long, it wasn't too spectacular," says Lara.

"Oh well, there's always senior year." Sam blows smoke and stubs out her cigarette in the ashtray parked on the windowsill. "Are you spending the night here?" She asks Lara.

"*Me?*" Lara points to herself. "No… we have to get back to Connecticut tonight. In fact, Jonny… what time is it getting to be?"

"Ahh… it's almost twelve," I say, scanning my watch. "You're right. We gotta be heading out." I look at Sam again, and turn back to Lara. "I need to speak with Sam for a second," I whisper in Lara's ear.

I pull Sam into the corner of the room, about as private a spot I could hope to find inside this packed apartment. "Are you doing okay, Sam?" I ask. "Is Joey coming tonight?"

"We aren't exactly hitting it off right now. I'm not sure we're going to see each other again. Why do you ask?"

"I was just wondering how you're doing, that's all."

"Jonny, go to your girlfriend. She needs you more than I do. By the way, I can see why you want to be with her... she's very pretty."

I return to Lara and hold her hand as we make the rounds through Marvin's room, saying goodbye to everyone. We take the stairs up one flight and walk into my darkened apartment. I shut the door tight behind us. Lara stops in the center of the room. I don't bother to turn on the light; the city night gleaming through my picture window is casting a luminous halo around her figure. Lara looks like an angel.

"You said you weren't going to leave me physically or mentally for the rest of the night. What was that, just words?" asks Lara.

"What?"

"I didn't like the way that girl, Sam, acted towards me. She was bitchy. Then you left me standing there alone to go off and be with her."

"Oh, that... Sam's boyfriend dumped her. She's feeling shitty about it. I guess she loves the guy; I'm not sure why. I didn't think she looked so good, I was asking if she's okay. But, I'm sorry... You're right to get mad. I said I wouldn't leave you and I did."

"Why did you bring me here?"

"I want to be with you, that's all. I'm up here studying hard, and I made a few friends taking care of this building, but that's it. I'm not seeing any of these girls. I've been thinking about nothing but you for I don't know how long. It feels so good being with you again. I never wanted to hurt you. I just..."

"Shut up," she speaks softly, cutting me off, "I'm not hurt. Come here."

I walk into her arms and kiss her tenderly, tracing my fingers slowly from her bare shoulders down to her hips. With my hand cupped around Lara's waist, I lead her to my bed. Turning to face each other, we kiss again; I gently coax Lara to sit down on the edge. I stand looking at her, slip off my bow tie, unbuttoning my shirt. Nothing in this world is more important than this moment.

"What are you doing?" Lara quietly asks.

"I'm going to make love to you." I whisper.

A few minutes after three, Lara and I step back inside her mother's car and head off for Connecticut. Lara sleeps the entire way with her head in my lap. I nudge her awake after pulling into my driveway at 4:55. We kiss goodbye. Standing beside the path leading to my front door, I wave to her as she drives away. The sun will be rising soon; already the robins are singing, announcing a new day is on the way.

25

Rags to Riches

Returning to Boston after a Saturday night romance, capped off by an exceptional Sunday dinner at home with my family, I should be quite satisfied with myself, but instead feel a little drained. Lara picked me up in the Dart and drove me to the Trailways Bus Station. Pulling away from her was a monumental effort. I promised ten times I would call, vowed twenty times I would think of her every minute we're apart, pledged thirty times I would miss her beyond belief, and wondered only once if I really meant it. But, that one doubt struck hard. Sitting in my seat as the bus pulls into Park Square, I ask myself, do I really want a girlfriend back in Connecticut?

The spring semester at Wentworth has grinded to an ignominious halt. Our grades will be posted by mid-week. I don't know if this is the end of my beginning or the beginning of my end. Everything I do from here on out is predicated on me passing. If I flunk out, I'll be drafted into the army quicker than you can say Ho Chi Minh.

After dumping my stuff inside my apartment, I decide to pay Sam a visit. Van Helden is nowhere to be found and I feel like talking to someone. "You wanna go out?" I ask, standing in her doorway.

"Sure... why not. Come in. Let me change into something." Sam walks over to her dresser, wiggles out of her shorts and slips into another pair, in denim, visibly shorter than the pair she kicked off her ankle.

"How did things work out with Joey?" I park my ass on her bed.

Sam pulls her T-shirt over her head and tosses it to the floor. Turning away from me, she begins hunting inside her closet, finally emerging with a white, cotton sleeveless blouse. Sam slips it on; fastening a couple of buttons on top and fashioning the front tails into a knot that blossoms directly above her belly button.

"Do you want to know if I'm available?" she asks. "Listen, I'm not hooked on the guy, if that means anything." She bends down and sticks her head back inside the closet, her ass poking out. Sam shovels out ten pairs of shoes before choosing open-toed red platforms she slips over her bare feet.

"Maybe I should mind my own business," I say. "I didn't mean to get personal. I was just wondering how you've been doing, that's all."

Sam completes her outfit threading a wide black, glossy plastic belt though the loops of her hot pants then tops off her look with a pucker of ruby-red lipstick. For the final touch, she waves a can of aerosol over her head, spraying a mist of sweet sticky-shit into her hair to fluff it up.

"How do I look?"

"Killer."

"Yeah, I'm doing okay," she smiles.

"Well, that's good to know." I slap my hands on my knees and stand.

"Wait… let's get right first," says Sam, pulling out a number from inside her pouch.

With our arms linked together, Sam and I amble across the street in the direction of the Four Corners Lounge. Inside, a dancer with her back to us is up on the bar looking sassy and sexually charged dancing to the Supremes, *Love is Like an Itching in My Heart*.
"She's good," I say to Sam.
Bruce, the bartender, drops a drink in front of Sam and a beer for me.
"You know who that is, don't you?" Sam takes a sip from her gin and tonic, lifting it in the direction of the dancer.
"No."
"Well, you should; you were talking to her Saturday night at Marvin's party. Remember your new tenant?"
"That's Barbara?"
"Uh ugh… her sister, Joanne."
"No kidding?" I'm genuinely surprised.
"Yeah… She moved in with Barbara this afternoon. Hey, check out Loverboy," Sam lifts a finger from her drink and points discreetly across the bar at Van Helden. He is seated behind a bottle of beer, oblivious to us, his eyes walking all over Joanne.
So that's where Robert is, I smile. "I'm going over there and snap my fingers in his face… see if he blinks."
The music fades and Joanne kills time by swaying easily in the interval between numbers; she busts out in a flash of hips, legs and arms with the powerful blast of the saxophone. Junior Walker and his All-stars cry out, "*Shotgun!*"

I stand, take another pull from my beer and push away from the bar rail. Van Helden notices me, grabs hold of his beer and races around to our side.

"When you get here?"

"We've been here all afternoon, hotrod," says Sam. "You looked like you were having so much fun, we didn't feel like coming over and spoiling your party."

"You bullshitting me?"

"Yeah… we got here a few minutes ago," I say, pushing Sam playfully on her arm.

Van Helden returns his gaze to the dancing Mediterranean beauty on the bar top. Tugging Robert by his sleeve to regain his attention, I gesture with my beer towards Joanne, "She looks good, no?"

"Yeah," says Robert. "We're going out as soon as she gets off."

Joanne completes her set and steps down from the bar to join our little group, sliding on the stool next to Robert; sweat runs across her forehead like tiny pearls. Bruce zips over and drops a Coke in front of her, which Joanne heartily knocks back. She rolls a couple of ice cubes into her mouth, crunching to dissolve them into edible contours.

"I hear you've moved in," I say to Joanne, adding sociably, "Welcome to the neighborhood. Hey, you're a fantastic dancer."

"Thank you," says Joanne with a shy smile, dabbing a cocktail napkin to her forehead.

"How's Lara?" she asks.

"Lara? She's great. I don't know when I'm gonna see her again… we, uh, she's uh, there's not exactly a commitment going on between us. But, I like her, you know… a lot."

"Yeah, you sound real tight," says Sam. "Kind of like me and Joey."

"I got classes tomorrow," I announce. "I'm heading back to the building."

Sam and I finish our drinks and say adios to Robert and Joanne. I suppose Sam could have stayed behind, but she decides to leave, too; probably feeling a little strange hanging around Robert and Joanne.

Inside the lobby waiting for the elevator, I remember needing to hit the drugstore.

"Sam, I'll catch you later. I gotta do Rexall. I need smokes and toothpaste."

"Oh, do me a favor?" she asks.

"Sure, what do you need?"

"Buy me a box of tampons… super-size."

"Whoa… those things you use when get your period?" I nearly choke out the question.

"You're not embarrassed to buy tampons, are you?"

"Of course not, super-size… uh, what's that, a big box?"

"No, sweetheart; that has to do with the kind of absorption I need. Are you sure you're okay with this… you're not uncomfortable, are you?"

"Me? Hell no… I'm cool."

"Let me give you some money."

"Forget it… my treat. Uh, how much do they cost?"

Sam peels off two dollars from a roll of bills in her pouch. "Here, you shouldn't have to pay for it."

Rags… I don't think chicks like that term. That's what us guys called those things in high school. Any girl in class took the brunt of ugly jokes if she was ever unfortunate enough to have a rag exposed in the contents of her purse, or worse yet, if somehow we found out she had one strapped on. I've never seen one outside the box. What kind did Sam say she used?

Inside Rexall, I pace up and down the aisles for several minutes, searching the shelves for supersize rags; where're they hiding those things? I stop by the counter where the pharmacist appears busy whipping up a drug potion for some grandma parked on a bench beneath him.

"Excuse me, Sir. Could you point out your Kotex section?" I ask in a loud whisper.

He looks down at me from his platform, "I beg your pardon?"

Shit, maybe I'm asking the wrong question. "Do you carry menstruation protection… you know, Kotex?"

"Kotex? Oh, yes, of course," he says openly, pointing to my right. "It's with the feminine hygiene products… second aisle over from the wall."

Christ, do ya have to blurt it out to everyone in the goddamn store!? Grandma on the bench looks up at me like she is smelling fish.

"Thank you."

I walk away quickly with my head down until I come face to face with feminine hygiene. My eyes dart back and forth across the shelves from one product to the next like a confused ferret. There are over a half-dozen brands, each with several selections of sizes and quantities. I spot the name 'Kotex' and lift the box from the shelf for closer scrutiny: 'FEMININE NAPKINS' is printed beneath the brand name. Jesus, I'm pretty sure Sam didn't say nothing about napkins. I scan the inventory on the next shelf up, 'Tampax – With Disposable Tampon Applicator'... *That's it!* I recall Sam saying the word, 'tampon'. I find a small box with the word 'Super Absorbent' printed on the front, grab it and head toward the check out counter.

Now I have to embarrass myself and show the box to the lady at the register. I pause, pretending to consider the design features of a certain toenail clipper. Maybe I should steal the box; slip it under my shirt. Okay... just hurry up and get this over with; pay the lady, have her drop it in a paper bag and run for home.

Back inside the building, I go directly to Sam's room, find her door open and pop my head inside. "Here ya go!" I say, proudly placing the bag squarely on top of her kitchen table.

"Thanks, Jonny. You weren't embarrassed doing this for me, were you?"

"Me? Naw, piece of cake; let me know if ya ever need any nail polish or a new bra and panties. I'd be happy to oblige."

The phone begins ringing the second I walk inside my apartment. I run to answer it and bang my leg hard on the coffee table. "HELLO! Oww... hello."

"Well, you sound like you could use a little help," says the female voice on the other end of the line.

"Lara?"

"No, Julie... who's Lara?"

"Julie! Hi, I whacked my leg on the coffee table answering the phone."

"Are you okay? I can come up there and kiss it for you."

"Where you callin' from?"

"I got a phone in my room now. John never wanted me to have one. After they took him away, I had the phone man come by and put one in," Julie's voice glitters.

"Where's John?"

"He's back in Baltimore, locked up in jail. The Prosecutor down there told me John won't be let out for at least three years; ain't that wonderful!"

"Yeah, break out the hats and horns. Do you wanna come up and visit?"

Her sweat gives an oily shine to her rolling breasts. I lie naked on top of my sheets, Julie sits over my lap rocking her hips back and forth in a flowing motion, like she is rowing up river and I am her dream boat. She must have reached her destination, after several languid groans she drops forward and rests her body over my chest. She tastes salty… like she just stepped from the ocean.

I learned that women have orgasms… they actually come! Not like a guy, nothing like that. The way Julie explains it, it really sounds better. Julie said she gets fantastic little blips that run through her in tickling waves. She gave me an anatomy lesson, describing the feeling while motioning with her hands to parts of her body, saying it's like pleasure jolts, "boop boop boop boop boop", starting between her legs, traveling up her tummy, through her chest across her shoulders and down her arms, and finally comes wiggling out through her fingertips. That sure beats what a guy gets by a mile.

"God, it's hot…"

"Why don't you buy a fan?" asks Julie.

"I'll see if Lykos will kick in for one."

I suggest turning out the lights. Maybe a dark room can be more comforting than one burning with light.

"I like'm on," says Julie.

After we made love a second time, Julie drops her naked frame over the side of the bed and reaches to the floor for her purse, bringing it up to the mattress. She lifts out a flat, pink and white plastic wheel with little pills arranged in a circle, breaks one free and pops it in her mouth and swallows.

"What's that?"

"My birth control."

"Isn't that stuff illegal?"

"Yeah… I get them from my doctor in Canada." She explains to me how they work. Fascinated, I finger the arrangement of tiny pills, set in a calendar sequence behind a thin veil of foil. It looks complicated.

Julie finishes buttoning her blouse and runs a brush through her natty bleached hair. She takes the end of the brush and taps her picture poking out of Lee Van Cleef's holster.

"Who said, 'Happiness is a warm gun'? Wasn't that the Beatles?"

"John Lennon."

"Well, I'll be your warm gun, baby. You can squeeze your finger on my trigger anytime you want."

I quietly laugh. "I've never shot a gun."

"You shoot just fine, Baby."

Julie finishes tidying up. Her mascara smells oily, like paint from a can. She applies a thick coat of red lipstick to her puckered mouth and a dab of blush to her cheeks.

"Who's Lara?" she asks, snapping shut her compact.

Wednesday afternoon, the last day of spring semester, my professors at Wentworth posted final grades outside their office door. I follow the crowd towards my destiny with hesitant steps. My classmates hover around the tally sheets like bees swarming the nest. Most seem pleased by the results. Some were virtually skipping out of the building on their way towards summer. I soon discover that I, too, will be returning next year, but my emotions hold more ambivalence than relief. I must have aced Pederson's final, otherwise that oaf would have failed me just as sure as the sun sets. Instead, he bestowed upon my record a charitable D. I fared slightly better in my other subjects.

At the end of the day, I meet Van Helden back at the apartment and give him my news.

"Congratulations, Bro!" says Robert, shaking my hand.

"I guess I should celebrate," I say, with half a smile.

"What would you like to do?"

"I don't know... how about we go out and score a six-pack, kick-back in the Common. It's a lot nicer outside than it is in this crummy room."

"Where can we go where they won't ID us?"

"Winky!" I snap my fingers. "The liquor store next door to Jack's Joke Shop, that's the place her Sugar Daddy owns. She might be working."

We bee-line around the corner to Boston Common Liquors and stare through the storefront window finding Winky slumped behind the cash register. She's propped up by her elbows looking like she is about to die from boredom. Ten feet over to her left seated in the corner behind the counter is her lumpy Sugar Daddy, an old thin-on-top flabby-in-the-middle ugly white dude with a stupid mustache like a tiny bristle-brush. He looks like Mr. Wilson from Dennis the Menace.

"Winky! How ya doing? Good to see ya!" Robert and I blurt out in unison.

Winky straightens up brightly when we approach the counter. "Hi, you guys!"

"We just came in to pick up some beer. What's Marvin doing?" I ask.

"Marvin busy being Marvin," says Winky, her voice droll.

Robert opens up one of the cooler doors, pulls out a six-pack and dumps it in front of the cash register. I wave to Winky's slime-ball caretaker, spying on her like a farmer watching over his daughter. "Nice place you got here; great location!"

"Why don't we all get together later?" says Robert, as we depart the store.

"Bye bye," says Winky, giving us a little wave.

It's the perfect time of day at the best time of the year; early evening at the start of summer. The heat of the day is gone, but not the glow. We walk up Tremont along the edge of the Boston Common. A few errant streetlights are starting to flicker on in advance of necessity. A practical joker deposited a box of laundry detergent inside the churning waters of Brewer Fountain and a thick layer of soapsuds is flowing over the monumental granite bowl into the surrounding plaza like white lava spilling from an amusement park volcano. A party of hippies is celebrating the event by dancing barefoot among the suds. Robert and I turn into the Common and cross over the grass, stopping beneath a giant hemlock, we sit beside it, leaning our backs against its beefy trunk. Robert reaches into the paper bag and pulls out a couple of cold ones.

"How's it feel to be through with school?"

"It's a rush, man. I never thought I'd make it. You know, we haven't talked much these past few weeks. What's going on with you, Robert?"

"I think something's happening with me and Joanne. I first thought about going after her sister, Barbara, but after meeting Joanne I changed my mind. We got somthing nice going."

I raise my can in the air, "Well... here's to that!"

"Yeah... and here's to a great summer," Robert smiles, meeting my beer in midair with a satisfied clunk.

26

Hot Town, Summer in the City

Someone is knocking, not one of those casual, social calls advertised by polite taps you don't mind answering, but the uptight, anxious sort you wish you could crawl away from. I pull a T-shirt over my head on my way to the door.

"Good morning," says Ed Taylor, standing shirtless and barefoot in a pair of red bell-bottoms. "Sorry to bother you, but you should know what's going on. Marvin sounds like he going crazy. I hear him throwing things, banging hard on the walls, Winky shouting for him to stop. He might be beating her up."

"I'll go down and take a look," I say. "Would you mind coming along?"

Approaching Marvin's door, I can hear loud thuds pounding against the walls from inside his apartment, like bodies being thrown, his deep voice booming angry protestations, I assume directed at Winky. I pause by the door apprehensively and look over at Ed for support, who nods back an implicit 'go on'. Stepping up, I bang a closed fist on the door panel; the commotion from within abruptly halts.

"WHAT!" a dark voice shouts from behind the door.

"Marvin, it's me."

"GO AWAY!"

I knock again. "Marvin, open the door. I wanna talk."

"Mind your own fuckin' business. This got nothin' to do with you!" his sharp words cutting through the wood between us.

"This *is* my business… It sounds like you're doing a number on your apartment. If you're tearing up the place, banging holes in the walls, smashing furniture and shit; I have to check it out." This talk is a ruse. I couldn't care less about Marvin trashing the building. It's Winky I'm worried about. "Open the door. I want to inspect the place."

"I haven't done none of those things… Leave us alone!"

"I'm sure that's true, but I gotta come inside and make an official inspection. That's my job."

The door swings open in a grand gesture. "Come in and see for yourself," says Marvin, stepping aside, his voice clear and cool.

I march to the center of the room; my eyes circumnavigating the environment: Walls - no holes; furniture - intact; Winky - trembling, but otherwise not bruised or bleeding. She is standing, wedged in the corner of the room, wearing that lavender teddy of hers.

"Hi, Winky, how's it going?" I ask, as if we were just passing the time of day.

"I'm fine, how're you?" Winky's voice is tiny, like a three-year-old.

"Not too bad. All right, everything looks cool in here," I say, clear-cut and business like. "Sorry to bother you."

Outside the room, Ed Taylor waits in the corridor, leaning against the railing smoking a cigarette.

I believe whatever it was that set Marvin off no longer poses a problem… at least for the rest of the morning. The situation in there is now being reconciled quietly.

"He's cool," I nod to Ed, who turns and goes downstairs.

On the way back up to my room I find Barry standing in front of Sam's room, jiggling the door knob. "What are you doing?" I ask.

"Sam asked me to stop by, but I think she's sleeping."

"No shit… Sam doesn't get up until noon." Barry turns fast, leaving without comment. My eyes follow him as he retreats down the stairs.

Julie's little sister, Melanie, is physically far-distant from her older sibling, like Pluto is to Venus, skinny as a pole, freckle-faced with a head of dark, straight hair. She stops by this evening and hands me a carton of cigarettes.

"What's this?" I ask, shaking the box in the air.

"They're cigarettes," she acts puzzled by my question.

"I *know* they're cigarettes. Why you giving them to me?"

"Because Julie told me to. I'm supposed to ask you about supper tonight. Julie wants to know if you're still coming."

"Tell her I'll be down later."

I've eaten at Julie's a few times. Its kinda weird… hanging out in her apartment with her three-year old kid and little sister, Julie fussing in the kitchen whipping up meatloaf and mashed potatoes, like we're some kind of family. Some nights Julie takes me out to dinner. Nothing fancy. I can use the free meals. I mentioned to Julie this morning if I don't find a job soon I'll have to leave Boston. "Lover, you don't have to work," she said, combing her fingers through my hair. "You're not going anywhere. I'm going to take care of you."

Charlie is on his way up to see me. He's always pumped up whenever he visits; especially at night. He gets off soaking up the atmosphere, thinks my lifestyle is exotic. It's not really, but I do nothing to dismiss that notion.

My friend makes himself comfortable on the couch.

"I'm dating a stripper. You've met her, Charlie. Remember Julie?"

"Woofa!"

"I don't have to work this summer. Julie wants to take care of me."

Charlie drops his jaw open. "What are you saying? Are you taking money from her?"

"Not really… it's more like… she pays for things."

"Be careful, Jonnyboy."

"What do you mean?"

"Did you ever hear that song Mose Allison sings about living in the city? Mose is a very wise man. 'If you stay up to the city, they're just two things I hope. Don't take money from a woman, and don't start messin' round with dope.'"

I brush off Charlie's warnings, although I don't feel quite as big as I did a minute ago.

"I can handle it."

The little electric fan Julie bought is humming beside me, blowing cool air in my face. I lie on the floor poised with pencil in hand searching the help wanted ads in tonight's paper, running my finger up and down columns of gigs I'm unqualified to apply for. I circle a couple of feeble prospects I may pursue further.

My door buzzer begins sounding off; in fact, all the door buzzers throughout the building kick in, making a long, annoying stereophonic drone. Johns in the street are still convinced we have hookers filling our rooms. The past couple of nights, a couple of drunken bozos camped out in the foyer pushing all the door bells, positive we got whores inside eager to drag them up to their beds and wrap their loving legs around them. Last night my bell must have buzzed fifty times.

Marvin explodes into my room in a rage, "If them assholes don't quit ringing my bell I'm gonna cut off their balls and stuff 'em down their throat!"

"Shine it on, man. It only lasts a few minutes before they give up and go away."

"I ain't shining nothin'! I'm gonna kill the motherfuckers!" He drops his frame down hard on the couch. "I don't need this shit right now."

"I can see that." I flash on Winky, wondering how she puts up with all his shit.

"No... You don't see nothin'!"

"So, what's happening?"

"I went back to the bank this morning and asked for a loan. They turned me down again. I'm sick and tired of their bullshit! I feel like going out and smashing my fist in The Man's face."

"What man?"

"You don't know what the fuck I'm talkin' about, do you?"

"Help me here, man, I'm trying."

Marvin lowers his voice and begins speaking deliberate and serious, "Sometimes... I feel like walkin' down the street and beating the first white dude I see. And I'll get away with it, too. You know they'll never be able to pick me out in a line up. You know what they say, 'They all look the same to me,'" Marvin's eyes roll and his speech takes on a 'holy cow' expression of some simpleton.

"You wouldn't do that." Elongated buzzing continues to resonant though our conversation.

"Don't tell me what I wouldn't do! Let me tell you what I did today." Marvin sits back and crosses his legs. "I was hanging out in front of the building, eating a bag of plums. Each time I finished a plum, I threw the pit at some white boy's face. I did this shit about five times. Nobody done nothing but run." Marvin has on a satisfied smile, like a gambler pulling in chips from a winning hand.

"You really did that?" I ask, shaking my head. "You're lucky somebody didn't drag a cop over here and bust your ass." The buzzing mercifully stops and the tension inside Marvin begins to subside.

"I was just burning off a little steam." Marvin slaps my leg and rises from the couch. "I'm not gonna hurt nobody."

I wish I could believe that.

My skin is sticking to the sheets like a wet shower curtain. A crushing heat wave hit Boston this week with brutal intensity, yesterday topping off at 102 degrees; the paper says that set a city record, today is supposed to be no different. Old folks are dropping dead in their apartments from heat stroke. By midday, everyone outside will be moving around in slow motion. It will take extreme effort just to lift your feet; like you have road tar stuck to your soles. I elect to pass on searching for work. It's way too hot to be dragging my butt up and down sidewalks, in and out of clammy buildings. Besides, Julie and Kitty organized a pool party.

A dozen of us gather in the front of the building at noon. We plan to walk over to the Lee Municipal Pool alongside the Charles River. Besides Julie and Kitty, our caravan includes Sam and most of the couples from the building. Angel's old man, Hector, has the presence of mind to show up with a box of fudgsicles. He begins passing one out to each of us in line, "Gotta eat a lot of ice cream today. Gotta stay cool. Gonna be a hot mothafucker.'"

A multihued parade of strippers, go-go girls, musicians, bar tenders, and one college boy lines up for a march to the river in a gala display of flesh and flash. Kitty, exposing most of her God-given gifts, is wearing a white lacy top over a slim pink bikini. Her top looks like a fabrication of several doilies stitched together. She holds a pink parasol above her head for both a sunscreen and a fashion statement. Julie, not to be outdone by anyone, is wearing an enormous broad-brim white straw hat that provides enough shade for the State of Rhode Island. Her prominent cleavage barely contained within a white bikini with blood-red tiger stripes, perfectly matching the color of her nails and lipstick. Julie has slipped on a sheer, diaphanous red blouse, opened in front and tied in a knot above her belly button. I wonder if Kitty and Julie are gonna swim with their wigs on?

The other girls are wearing an assortment of hot pants and bikini-tops, all sporting big sunglasses and each holding a beach bag full of lotions, toys, drinks, snacks, towels, transistor radios and extra clothing. The boys have on colorful flowered shirts, hanging open over swimsuits in various styles and colors. I don't own a bathing suit, so I pulled on a pair of old cut-up Levis. My Red Sox hat is keeping the sun out of my eyes.

 Kitty leads the way with a happy send-off twirl of her parasol. Our route takes us through the Common. We cut a wake in the center of Frog Pond, kicking our way through the six-inch deep tepid water like little kids playing in their backyard pool. The girls make a delightful scene strolling down the middle of the pond, giggling like children and waving to the crowd sprinkled along the banks. The boys follow the girls, sharing the irony of trying to look tough and aloof while at the same time secretly, utterly enjoying themselves. We cross Beacon Street and step onto the brick sidewalk path along Charles Street, stopping here and there to buy more refreshments and to peer inside storefront windows. I catch Hector nudge Jasper with an elbow, registering shocked regard over the comic book appearance of a trio of stoned hippies. The hippies are falling over each other crossing the street; I think they're laughing at us.

 "You want me to rub sun tan oil on you, honey?" Julie asks. I lie my towel down on the flat cement landscape bordering the pool's rectangular edge. Most of our group is already in the pool splashing around. I look over her way, squint my eyes from the glaring sun hitting me square in the face.

 "Naw, I'm okay. I'll rub some on you, if you want."

Julie spreads her towel down next to mine and slips off her hat, blouse and platform sandals. "All right," she chimes, as she scavenges inside her bag to retrieve a few beach accouterments and turns on her transistor radio.

"Here, honey." Julie holds out a tube of suntan lotion and flips over on her tummy. I squirt a glob into my palm and dutifully lather her white skin from the nape of her neck down to the back of her toes; she hums as I slide the cream up between her thighs.

"I found the most beautiful suit for you yesterday," Julie dreamily speaks into her towel. "It's deep red, double-breasted, *very* slick, *very* sexy. You would look *so* handsome in it. I want you to come with me later and try it on."

While rubbing my hands over Julie's body, I get this uneasy feeling of being watched. I look up and down the pool scanning the general public, finding everyone engrossed in his or her own existence. On my second pass over the crowd, I catch a glimpse of her on the opposite side of the pool, staring at me. The look on Sam's face stops me cold. I wipe the leftover lotion onto my shorts and roll my shirt into a makeshift pillow, lie down on my towel and turn on an elbow in Julie's direction.

"You have to stop giving me things," I say in a whisper.

"Sweetheart," Julie's eyes twinkle, "I don't mind treating you right. You can't fault me for that."

"I'm thankful, don't get me wrong, but… I just don't feel good about it."

"Oh, you're being silly. I want you to come over tonight. I'll cook you a nice sit-down dinner."

Sam is sitting alone on the opposite side of the pool. What's going on with her? She looks like she's been dragged around the block by her hair.

"Well?" Julie asks, raising her head to face me. "You coming over?"

"Okay, sure…"

Hector, Jasper, and Ed Taylor run up to Kitty and ask to borrow her diamond ring for a game they wish to play. Kitty slips her ring off her finger and holds it straight out in front of their faces, pinched between her fingertips.

"What you want with this little piece of my goodness? This ring is no play thing, children."

"No harm will come to it," Hector promises. "We need somethin' to throw into the deep end of the pool that sparkles."

"How about throwing me in?" Angel laughs.

"Come on… how'bout it? The first one to find it wins!"

"Wins what!?" Kitty snaps.

"We haven't decided yet," says Hector. "Hey, Jonny! How'bout putting up a prize for the winner, free rent for next week!"

"All right you guys," I say. "But I get to play, too. What happens if I win?"

My friends stare at each other trying to find an answer, but after a long minute come up dry.

"Sorry, man," I say. "I can't risk losing somethin' with nothin' to gain."

"Here!" Kitty throws her ring at me… I catch it with one hand.

"Do it for fun," she laughs.

For the next hour, we all take turns throwing Kitty's diamond ring into the deep end, as a pile of bodies dive in after it. Each time, the diamond is recovered from the deep yielding a champion with the honorary prize of most skillful swimmer in the pool. We do this until each of us holds that honor at least once.

At the end of the afternoon, we retrace our steps back to our building. Halfway up Charles Street I notice Sam at the back of the line, lagging behind everyone. I stop and wait for her to catch up, leaning against a gas-lantern streetlight.

"Hi, Sailor," says Sam as she approaches me, "Want to buy me a drink?"

"You look like you could use one, Sam. How you doing?"

"I'm pregnant. Other than that, I'm great."

27

Getting Buzzed

"Hi, Lara."
"Why are you calling me?"
"I miss you."
"No you don't. If you missed me you'd be here. You said you were coming back to see me."
"Now's not a good time. I have new people moving in, apartments to clean, locks to change, the building's a mess. I have a lot to do around here."
"You promised me."
"I know… I am… just as soon as I can get free.
"Jonny… do I mean anything to you?"
"Of course… you know that."
"You have a funny why of showing it. What's going on? Are we going anywhere together?"
"Yes… we are. Believe me. I miss you, Lara."
"Come home, Jonny, I love you."
I don't know what to say…
"Jonny… did you hear me?"
"Yeah… me, too. I'm comin'. I promise."

"Robert, you know about our friend getting knocked up?"
"Yeah… How'd you find out? I thought Barbara wanted to keep this quiet."
"Barbara? What she got to do with it?"

"Isn't that who we're talking about?"

"No, I'm talking about Sam."

"Sam's knocked up!?"

"Barbara's pregnant?" I shake my head.

"Shit!" Van Helden gives his face a slap, "I think I just fucked up. Joanne told me not to say anything about her sister."

Van Helden and I reflect on the consequences that lie ahead of both girls. The two dudes who caused their predicament ran out of the picture like they were being chased by a pack of crocodiles. Perhaps that's a blessing in disguise.

"What would you do if you knocked up a chick?" I ask.

"I wouldn't run away like those assholes."

"How they gonna manage this shit? What are they gonna do for bread?"

"They can have my job. I'm thinking about quitting."

"You're leaving Filenes?"

"Charlie was right about fags in department store windows, the business is crawling with them. I'm the only guy doing this shit who's not a homo. My boss, Albert, has a crush on me." Van Helden sighs, "It's getting pretty fuckin' weird just showin' up for work."

"You wanna know what's weird?" I take a deep drag from my cigarette, "Julie wants to buy me a three-piece suit. It's red."

"Like, how red?"

"Neon red. Can you see me in a getup like that? Maybe I can be her pimp." I crush out my smoke. There's a bad taste in my mouth.

Pimp is actually the wrong end of the stick. I'm beginning to feel like Julie's my Sugar Daddy, if such a thing like that is possible. We had gone by the store on Avery Street where they had my fancy new threads waiting. I looked through the storefront window at the cheap trash they peddle as fashionable menswear. The inventory reminded me of the crap I used to see in Hartford's North End; pointy shoes with Cuban heels and tight shiny pants displayed alongside a collection of weapons. She tried to pull me inside, but I fought back like a pit bull, tugging in the opposite direction. I told her that shit is not my style, so we settled on a pair of Levis to replace the ones I had cut up for swimming. They fit okay.

I shouldn't bitch. I'm getting laid every day now. Julie likes screwing before going off to work. She says stripping in front of a hundred guys right after balling turns her on. It's great for getting tips, she says, because it makes every guy in the room want to hump her. This should probably bother me, but it doesn't. I'm not a kid anymore, so I'm not going to act like one and get all freaked out over little things like sex.

He walks into the middle of my room and freezes, flat-footed, staring at me as if expecting an explanation. "Jesus, Jonny... I thought you said you lived in Apartment 6C."

"Jerry! What are you doing here?!" My brother is holding a small suitcase in his hand, looking like a councilor at a church picnic in his short-sleeved Madras plaid shirt and his G.I. Joe hairdo. "We moved... why didn't you tell me you were coming?"

"I wanted to surprise you. I went to the wrong apartment. What kind of friends do you have living here, anyway?"

"I don't know... just friends, why?"

"I knocked on that door down the hall," he points over his shoulder to Kitty's place. "Two black guys were sitting at the kitchen table. One guy was eating a sandwich; he acted like I just pissed in his food. The other guy was cleaning a gun; he had bullets lined up on the table. I thought he was gonna drop one in my head. I told them I was looking for my brother, Jonny… the Super. They started laughing, invited me in and told me to pull up a chair. I said, 'Thank you very much, maybe later. Where I can find my brother?' They pointed me over here." Jerry grins, holding it a little too long. "So, how you doing, little brother?"

"Everything's great."

Charlie and Van Helden walk in, returning from lunch at the diner downstairs.

"Jerry! Look at you!" Charlie gives my brother a slap on the back. The two old friends greet each other with beaming eyes.

"What's going on, Charlie?"

"They're dropping Agent-Orange in my pit today," says Charlie. "The cockroaches are on the march. My Super called in an air-strike. The shit they spray would defoliate a jungle. I don't want to breathe in that crap so I'm crashing here tonight."

"Hi… I'm Robert." Van Helden shakes my brother's hand.

"I should have let you guys know I was coming," Jerry surveys our digs. "This is bad timing. You don't have any room for me."

"It's cool, Bro. You can have the mattress from my bed; we'll put it on the floor. I can sleep on the box-spring."

"Sounds cozy," says Jerry.

It was the fart that woke me; a long, metallic sound, like someone zipping up their sleeping bag. I lift my head from my pillow into an atmosphere like a varsity football team's locker room. The dank morning air inside our apartment is thicker than steam. My puny electric fan provides relief only if you have your face stuck in it. It's whirring away on the kitchen table surrounded by a collection of empty beer cans. Everyone's clothes lie in clumps on the floor, including some of my own. After Van Helden opened his bed, Charlie spread out on the cot, and I split my bed in two, there is hardly a free spot on the floor left to step, given all the clothes and trash we have scattered here and there. The counters are spilling over with last night's garbage; dirty plates and bowls hardened with the entrails of cooked spaghetti. My three roommates are out cold, dead to the world. It's only 8:00, too early on a Saturday morning to be showing signs of life.

The knocking on our door hits harder than what we normally expect at this time of the day. I slowly lift myself from the box-spring. The knocking comes again, now more intense… urgent.

"COOL IT! I'm coming!" I don't bother to put on my pants… underwear is appropriate attire to greet whoever this rude asshole is that's banging and making me drag my ass out of bed.

"Lykos… what are you doing here?"

He pushes past me in heavy silence, entering the room like he owns the place. Andreus, following tight on his heels, looks about as pleasant as sour milk. The other guys are all sitting up now in their beds, topping off the sheets in their underwear.

"You ask *me* what I'm doing here. Are you kidding me? That's the question I should be asking *you!*" Lykos points his finger in my face, showing obvious disgust. Turning, he waves his arm in a sweeping arc, "WHAT THE HELL IS GOING ON HERE!?"

"Uh… we have some guests," I say.

"These 'guests,'" sniffs Lykos, "they living here with you?"

"They're just visiting," I answer, watching Lykos' face turn red.

Our Boss angrily rails on for several minutes, first bitching about how skuzzy the room looks, then expanding his critique to the whole goddamn building, saying what a pile of shit the place has become.

"We are waiting for the weekend to start cleaning." My excuse sounds lame, even to me.

Andreus leans down and whispers in his brother's ear; Lykos shakes his head in affirmation and begins to slam us for renting an apartment to Barbara and Joanne. "You ignored my orders! No single females! How do you know these two aren't whores?"

Robert quickly rides up to their defense, "They're decent girls, Lykos… They have regular jobs."

"Where do they work?" Lykos barks his question in Van Helden's face.

"They work around here."

Lykos wrinkles his nose in response to Robert's endorsement. "Give me their rent money," he extends his open hand.

"We haven't got it yet," says Robert, adding, "They get paid this weekend."

"Give me the money for the other rooms," Lykos is gritting his teeth, his hand now balled into a fist.

He explodes like the Hindenburg when we report no rent money has been collected over the past week.

"We promise to bring some in this afternoon after everybody wakes up."

"You two guys are nothing but promises. Either you're both stupid, or you're a couple of smart-asses. Which is it?"

Robert and I don't respond to his bullshit remark. We just stare at him in steamy silence.

"You boys are spending my money; that right? You collect it and spend it; that right?"

"That's crap!" I fire back, narrowing my eyes into his.

"If you play tricks with me, funnyboy, I'll have you arrested." He points his finger between my eyes. "Don't you make the mistake and think you can fool me. I want my money!! I want this mess cleaned up! Get your..." he pauses, regarding Charlie and Jerry like they just murdered his mother, "*guests*, out of here! I want the hookers downstairs thrown out!" Lykos slows down his rant for a second and rearranges the knot in his tie. All this screaming must have tightened the blood vessels in his neck. "Andreus will be back here tomorrow; don't disappoint him."

The Theodokis brothers march from the room like a pair of Storm Troopers. Andreus, that chickenshit, said nothing the whole time he was here, not even hello. "Nice fellow," says my brother.

"Yeah... he's a real peach."

I take Jerry on a spin through our building, introducing him to my friends, occasionally picking up rent along the way. Barbara invites us to join her tonight at the Intermission Lounge after she gets off work; she plans to meet Joanne and Robert there and suggests, "Maybe we can all do something." Sam asks us to stop by and see her in the Four Corners Lounge, "If you're not doing anything later, come across the street. I'll be working there all afternoon." Julie tells us to come to the Normandy around midnight, "You can watch me dance," she says to my brother with wicked eyes, turns to me and flicks a button on my shirt, "and *you* can walk me home."

We pass by Barry in silence coming down the stairway, ignoring one another as we brush shoulders. He stopped talking to me since I found him messing around Sam's door. He knows I caught him in a lie; Sam said he had no business being there.

"Who's that guy?" asks Jerry.

"That's our resident thief."

Continuing the tour, I knock on Marvin's door. Winky opens up, greeting us with an affectionate hello. Marvin steps out from the bathroom shirtless, his fingers in his hair massaging his scalp; a towel draped around his neck. He's working on his Afro and the creamy shit he's rubbing into his hair stinks worse than a bull fart.

"Hey! Those dudes are going to the moon next week. We're gonna throw a party and watch it on TV," says Marvin.

"Peee yooo! Whut's dat smell?" asks Winky, pinching her fingers to her nose.

"It stinks... don't it? I have to leave this chicken poop in my hair for fifteen minutes; it takes that long to work."

I introduce Marvin and Winky to my brother. Marvin asks if we would like to join them for their moon party.

"You bet," I say. "You think we should score some good champagne; pop it open when they land?"

"Sure… but I can't tell Chateau Brianne from Ripple. You go over to Winky's store and pick out somethin' expensive," says Marvin.

As I turn to leave, I remember they haven't paid their rent for the past week, and I ask them for their thirty-five bucks.

"We paid, man. I gave it to Robert about five days ago. Ain't that right, Baby?" Marvin turns to Winky for confirmation.

"Yup, we paid up."

"Nice group of folks you got living here," my brother hooks his hands behind his head as he stretches out on our couch, plopping his feet up on the coffee table. Van Helden walks in from the kitchen with a glass of ice tea in his hand and parks down beside him. I pull up a chair.

"The girls here are all dancers?" asks Jerry.

"Some are…" I answer, slightly inattentive to my brother's question, my mind drifting in another direction. "Robert… what happened to the rent money Marvin gave you?"

"I borrowed a few bucks," he says, without a trace of guile. "Why?"

"Why? Shit, Robert! Lykos thinks we're pocketing his cash, and you're taking out loans!"

"Hey, it's no big deal. I pay it back every time."

"What do you mean, 'every time'? You've done this before!?"

"Come on, Jonny… you never borrow any money?"

"Not from Lykos, I don't!"

"Jonny, you're getting all freaked-out over nothing. We're clean. I always put the money back. Lykos is just being an asshole."

I pause for a second to reassess... I trust Robert as much as I trust my mother. I believe him. My real problem is I got Lykos-on-the-brain, screwing up my fundamental principles of friendship. I'm getting all weirded-out over nothing.

"You guys all done talking about business?" asks Jerry. "A creepy thing happened to me inside Trailways yesterday. I walked in the john to take a leak and this guy comes up beside me, grinning at me while I'm standing there holding my dick. He freaked the hell out of me. I went outside... looking around to get my bearings; another fucker comes up and propositions me. Your bus station is a goddamn meat market. I couldn't beat it out of there fast enough."

"Ah, you're just playing hard to get."

Buttoning up my favorite shirt, the blue and white pinstripe jobbie with the French cuffs, I leave the bathroom to join my brother and Charlie. We're getting ready to go out and hit a few clubs. Charlie takes his hand from his pocket and places three little white aspirin-size tablets in a line on the kitchen table.

"What's this?" I lift one up for closer inspection.

"Crossroads."

"Cross what?"

"Crossroads... speed... Dexedrine; they give you a nice little boost, just the right amount of fizz, nothing serious. Jerry, you want a hit?" asks Charlie.

"Me? No thanks... Things are fizzy enough for me around here."

Charlie passes an opened bottle of Coke to wash down the pill, which I do without hesitation.

My door bell begins to buzz. In fact, all the door bells in the building are buzzing; an annoying electric cacophony echoes through the hallways, bouncing from room to room.

"Shit… they're back."

"Who's back?"

"The Johns," I sigh. "They're looking for hookers."

The noise is unbearable; I'm tempted to go downstairs and chase the fuckers into the street.

"Aren't you going to do something?" asks my brother.

Marvin bursts into my room like an escaped mental patient; his face twisted in anger, his right hand has a fierce grip on a knife with a five-inch blade. "I'm gonna kill em! I'll cut their fuckin" hearts out!" he snarls through his teeth.

"Marvin, drop the knife, man… come on, give it to me," I step in front of him, reaching for the weapon. Marvin pushes me out of his way and charges towards the elevator. Charlie, Jerry and I stick tight to his heels. The infernal buzzing seems to be sending Marvin electric shocks, giving his face a jolt with each sustained blast. Three of us barrel into the box beside him, pleading against his deadly threats.

"Don't do it, man!"

"Give it to me!"

We make our descent to the street; the disturbing racket receding above us. The tension in Marvin's face loosens as he appears to consider his next move. He looks down at his weapon, relaxes his fingers, offering the blade in his open hand for the taking. Jerry quickly snatches it.

The elevator cab knocks to a stop at the lobby floor. Two white dudes, drinking buddies, no more than thirty, dressed like Dads' at a Little League game, stand beside each other in the foyer riotously laughing, pushing their fingers to the panel of call buttons. Marvin slides back the elevator's folding gate and charges, like a wild animal springing from a cage. One John's playful expression instantly transforms into wide-eyed panic; he breaks free and runs, but his partner appears confused, facing us with puzzled ambivalence.

Marvin rams into the man, the force of the broad span of his shoulder lifts John Number Two off his feet, spinning him onto the sidewalk. The two men spill into a frenzied clump of swinging fists. The John deflects a dozen blows raining down on him, feebly attempting a few of his own. Marvin grunts with each powerful punch he delivers. The John, covering his face with his arms, cowers in a pitiful crouch. Marvin beats him, over and over again, bashing his fists down like a pair of hammers clubbing an anvil. I can't bear to watch. I push myself between the two men, "That's enough, Marvin! Fight's over!" Lifting the loser up straight from his bent position, I lead him out of harm's way. The John surprises me, snapping up straight, coming alive in a flash of anger, lashing his left hand around the collar of my fancy shirt, pulling me towards him by my throat, he spits into my face, "FUCK YOU!" as he clenches his right fist, raising it to deliver a punch between my astonished eyes. I spin to my right and slam my left arm down across his grip, breaking free. My right hand jabs straight into his face with a violent thrust, hitting him hard across the nose and mouth. He reels back on wobbly legs, a long step away. My right leg kicks high into the air, catching him square in the face. The John's feet leave the ground, his body airborne, flying up and back, landing ten feet from where I stand, his head cracking down with a lethal thud on the concrete curb, coming to rest beside the gutter, his body stiff, lifeless.

Inside my mind, I go deaf to the noise from the city surrounding me.

"Jesus, Jonny… you killed him," Jerry bends over and looks into the man's unconscious face.

I had hit him on instinct. I don't know where that came from. I lean down and point a finger at the comatose lump, my body quivering, "WHY DID YOU DO THAT? I WAS TRYING TO HELP YOU! WHY DID YOU GRAB ME?" I suddenly notice other people in the street, strangers, joining my brother's concern for the man.

An unfamiliar voice asks, "Should somebody call an ambulance?"

Jerry repeats gravely, "Jonny, I think you killed him."

I nudge the man's face with the toe of my shoe, lifting it gently to the side.

"Ughhh," the John groans, his eyelids begin to flicker like the wings of a spastic moth trapped behind a pane of glass.

"He's okay, let's get out of here," I say. Without a fraction of remorse, I address the face awakening below me, "You shouldn't have grabbed my shirt, man." I look up the front wall of my building; rows of staring faces are pressed up against the window glass, fixing their eyes on me. I stand still for a second and stare back at them, put my head down and walk inside.

It's almost 3 a.m. and I can't get to sleep. A high octane fizz is flowing through my veins. Jerry went on a little too much tonight about how I creamed that guy, happy to repeat the story to anyone who missed it. Marvin seemed even more juiced about it than my brother, "I must a hit that guy fifty times," he exaggerated, "and I couldn't put that fucker down. And you come along… BAM!… knock him out with one punch." Julie rubbed her hand up and down my arm cooing something about loving men who know how to take care of themselves. I feel a million miles away from home right now, and I don't like talking about what had happened. Something about it bothers me, and I'm not sure how to deal with it. What I can't admit to anyone, the truth is even hard for me to admit to myself, because it scares the shit out of me… I nearly killed a guy… and it felt great!

28

Pornographic Priestess

Sam and I sit beside each other in the steamy hot trolley, clunking down the tracks to Copley Square; her pretty face is shiny with sweat. She hasn't looked too happy lately. Sam doesn't speak at all about her condition; I think she's hoping it might somehow go away. I'm afraid she might do something stupid, like search the streets of Chinatown for an abortion witch doctor. How the hell is she ever going to raise a kid? She's freaked out, no doubt. Maybe it will make her feel better to talk about it.

"Is Joey coming back?" I ask.

"Fat chance... why do think he left town so fast?" Sam gives a caustic chuckle.

"Nice guy. What's next, Sam? What are you gonna do? You can't stay here, can you?"

"I certainly won't be dancing on top of any bars."

"Where you gonna go?"

"Oh, I don't know... maybe I'll move to a big house in the suburbs, get a nice raised ranch with a white picket fence and two-car garage. In a few years I'll join the PTA, put my kid in the Brownies or Cub Scouts, go to church on Sunday, sing in the choir... FUCK! I don't know what I'm gonna do! Stop asking me questions, okay."

"Sure... I was just trying to help."

"No, you're not!" Sam spins her body a full turn in my direction. The lights inside the moving trolley flicker off and we sit in dark silence. Sam comes back to life when the lights return. "Well, enough about me, what's going on with you? Do you talk to your girlfriend anymore?"

"Who, Lara?"

"Yeah, Lara. You got more than one?"

"Well... there's Julie."

Sam sniffs, "Julie's your girlfriend?"

"No... we just... you know?" I'm not sure what you call it. "Lara and I talk a lot on the phone. She wants me to leave here. Julie wants me to stay."

"What do you want to do?" Sam locks her eyes on mine.

"Me? I don't know what I want."

"Think about what you're doing with these girlfriends, Jonny, and do the right thing."

The right thing to do is put a little space between Julie and me, spell out my intentions and make it clear she will have no part in my future. We can still see each other, of course, but I can't promise her anything. I steer her inside the Intermission Lounge for a heart to heart talk. She is puckering in the seat beside me, applying lipstick, her mouth overwhelming the mirror in her compact. I knock back a bottle of beer and drop it down hard on the bar to get her attention.

"Maybe I'll go out west someday." My eyes search the ceiling. I take a drag from my cigarette and blow a line of smoke high in the air. "You know... Arizona or Colorado... live on a ranch, or on some mountaintop, maybe get a horse."

"A horse? What are you talking about?"

"I don't know... I'm just thinkin'. You know... someday I'm going places. You don't think I wanna hang around here for the rest of my life, do you?"

"Crystal is coming to Boston!" Julie's friend Venus slides into our conversation with breaking news, her eyes flashing.

Julie jumps high in her seat and waves her hands out, like a Jack-in-the-Box popping open. "Does Kitty know!? We *have* to tell her!"

"No... You tell her! She'll be tickled pink!"

"Who's Crystal?" I ask.

"She's the hottest thing stripping in New York City, that's who," Venus raves. "Crystal is famous!"

"We're old friends," adds Julie. "We go back to Montreal together. What club will she be dancing in?"

"The Four Corners," says Venus. "We *must* have a party for her after work. This is going to be fun!"

The two of them squeal, clapping hands like giddy teenagers; you would think some megastar celebrity is coming to town.

I had been inches from making a clean break from Julie, neatly laying the groundwork for a smooth get-away, and Venus has to come along and break my rhythm. I don't feel like listening to them reminisce about the good ol' days, so I excuse myself, push away from the bar and head for home.

A police cruiser is parked beside the entrance to our building, its business lights flashing. The car pulls away from the curb before I reach my front door. Inside the lobby Van Helden is waiting by the elevator and spots me when I come in.

"Jonny! We had a little trouble. Somebody attacked Dianne. She's all fucked up. The cops just brought her back from the hospital."

Robert and I hurry into the elevator, taking it up to Jasper and Dianne's room. The fifth floor corridor in front their apartment is jammed tight with the couple's friends. We weave our way into their room and find Dianne propped up in bed with her back against a pair of pillows, drinking cold apple juice through a straw. She looks up at us with raccoon eyes, her jaw is wired shut, and a bandage covers the bridge of her nose.

"What the heck happened" I ask.

"Airry," she says through gritted teeth… Barry.

Dianne says she didn't get a clean look at him, at least not while he was assaulting her, but she is almost certain she recognized Barry on the fire escape before he entered through the window. Dianne can't speak normally, but she is capable of communicating well enough to be understood, grunting out her story through clenched teeth. She had been asleep, lying naked in bed with her head on a pillow inches away from the window that looks into the building's airshaft. At first, she imagined the hulk of a man on her fire escape peering inside her open window as some foggy element of a bad dream. The giant squeezed through the narrow opening, breaking through that cloudy moment between sleep and wakefulness and entered the room, crossing over her body. Dianne's head snapped up from her pillow, only to be met by his large hand, silencing her scream. He grabbed her by the chin and twisted her face away with a vicious jerk, breaking her jaw as effortlessly as cracking an egg.

"He said, 'Don't look at me. If you move I'll kill you.'" Dianne, sobbing and taking heavy breaths, continues to recount the attack, telling us her face had been crushed hard into the bed. The man ran from the room, leaving through the door and out the corridor. She lay motionless for several minutes, crying into her pillow, afraid to get up.

Dianne's girlfriends stay to comfort her as us boys leave her side to discuss retribution. The group gathers around my kitchen table; Marvin, Hector, Jasper, and Tom Taylor. Van Helden and I remain standing. On the stereo Sly Stone is singing to us about *Hot Fun in the Summertime.* Robert turns the music down below the level of conversation.

"Barry needs to die," Marvin makes the point-blank assessment for the rest of us to distill. "Any ideas how we do it?"

"If we kill him, we better be sure we is right," says Jasper. "Dianne don't know for sure if he the one who done it."

"Who else can it be?" asks Tom. "I never trusted that nigger."

"I never trusted him either, that's no reason to kill him," I say. "Jasper is right. We have to be one hundred percent right about this. Barry's gonna have to somehow let us know he's the one we're after before we whack him." I can't bring myself to say 'kill', although I know that's what we are taking about, killing Barry.

"*What you gonna do, go down to his room and ask him why he done it?*" Marvin's goofy tone makes me feel stupid.

"I got to tell you guys something," I say, with an effort to restore Marvin's confidence in my knowingness. "I caught him once trying to sneak into Sam's room."

"Let's go downstairs now kill that motherfucker!"

"No… We set a trap," Jasper quietly offers. "If we catch him… we kill him."

"You guys aren't really gonna do this?" Van Helden asks, looking at all of us, screwing an uncomfortable smile on his face. "You're kiddin' about this killing shit, right?"

"All right… we don't kill him," says Marvin. "Just hurt him real bad."

"How we gonna trap him?" asks Hector.

We all sit quietly for a minute, pondering the question.

"Barry likes to break into rooms to peek at a little snatch, right?" Marvin smiles at Hector. "So, we spread talk around the building that you left town for a while… Angel is home alone. She keeps her window open, just like Dianne done. Barry comes up the fire escape to sniff inside her room; only Angel ain't there. I'm waiting by the window with a baseball bat. When the nigger sticks his fat head through the window, I smash it with the bat. Simple. Whaddaya think?"

"Maybe that'll work," I reflect on the possibility. "Marvin, what if you miss his head? How good are you with a bat? Barry's a pretty big dude; you don't wanna mess with him if you miss."

"That's why you're all gonna be in there with me," Marvin looks around the table for confirmation.

"What did Dianne say to the police?" asks Robert. "Why aren't they doing somethin' about this?"

"She told them nothin,'" Jasper answers. "She afraid to talk. You got to be careful what you say to the police; it might do more harm than good."

The meeting ends with an agreement that I will speak with Barry tomorrow and drop a few hints about Hector going out of town for a gig, leaving his beautiful Angel home alone; Jasper and Tom will wait in the dark apartment alongside Marvin, who'll be standing beside the window with his bat cocked like Willie Mays at the plate, waiting to slam a homerun across Barry's head.

Joanne spends most of her nights in our room sleeping beside Robert. Julie and I share a lot of bedtime, too, but we never sleep. I'm having trouble making up my mind whether or not I want to keep seeing her. We have nothing really to talk about when we're together, and I have zero interest in that little girl of hers; hell, I don't even know the kid's name.

"It's hard to believe you're twenty-seven," I say, slipping back into my pants.

"Twenty-eight is only a couple of weeks away," Julie smiles, clipping the back of her bra and adjusting the cups firm to her breast. "I don't look my age, do I? Everyone thinks I'm twenty-one."

"I'm eighteen... everyone thinks I'm twenty-one, too. You and me are like ten years apart. Ain't that crazy?"

"Age got nothing to do with it. I know couples who are the same age and they *hate* being around each other."

"But, *ten years*... that's a long time," I roll my eyes up to the ceiling, as if calculating the vast age of the solar system, "Whoa!"

"Ten years is no big deal. We're not so different, you and me."

Friday night, the Four Corners Lounge is packed with Crystal's fans and a bevy of friends. An after-hours party in her honor is planned at Venus's apartment a few blocks away. I sit between the shoulders of Kitty and Julie. Kitty's date, Roger, the bartender from the Downtown Lounge, is seated to her left. Several men connect with Kitty and Julie, lavishing attention, offering drinks and tales of familiarity; the girls soak it up. Roger doesn't seem to care; he actually looks like he enjoys it.

"I got something for you, Lover." Julie opens her purse and begins fishing around, pulling out a midnight-blue handkerchief. "Come here," she smiles and wiggles her finger as my cue to get close.

I lean into Julie and sit still as she ties the silky kerchief around my neck, straightening it just so.

"There, this goes perfect with your eyes and the shirt you're wearing," she smiles and snaps me a quick peck on the lips.

The stage is the focal point inside the lounge the instant a stripper steps up to dance. Perhaps 'stage' is too dramatic a label to pin on the platform that bridges the backspace of the horseshoe shaped bar. A crowd, nearly all men, stands two and three deep behind the backs of us lucky ones seated at ringside. The spotlights above the bar cast a cross of white light on the stage and dim slowly into darkness, permitting no more than a shadowy image of the woman approaching to perform. A chorus of whistles and hoots drift through the smoky air. There is no announcement that Crystal has stepped on stage, unless you call the pulsating beat of *Sympathy for the Devil* a message the show is about to begin. Like a flash of lightning brilliantly transforming night sky into day, the spotlights strike Crystal in perfect syncopation with the Mick Jagger's naughty-boy libretto, and the crowd erupts in a jubilant roar.

I have witnessed countless performances by neighborhood strippers in a variety of venues. Some dancers are boring, pure showoffs with big breasts and little talent, believing that flaunting their boobs is somehow all they need to make it happen. Then there are girls that may not be great looking, but they grab your attention by being creative; you appreciate them more for their style than their sexuality. The best ones, like Kitty and Julie, get noticed because they are both sexy and artistic. There are also a few unfortunate ones that have no business being up there; they're uglier than Olive Oyl, and the dancing looks like their peddling fast on a bicycle, only someone took away the bike. Most of the ladies pull off something in between. One thing I can say for sure: throughout all these experiences, I've found none of the strippers breathtaking. Oh, yeah, I enjoy watching the better ones perform, but I never became sexually aroused by what I was seeing... until now.

Crystal is a voluptuous, haunting, dark skinned beauty from an Arabian Nights fable. I am instantly trapped by her perfection, caught between the languid motion of her hips and torso and the flawless form of her breasts. She looks down and finds me staring up at her utterly captivated; her strawberry lips part, fashioning a French kiss into my eyes. The room is packed with others, of course, but I feel as if this enchanting vision is dancing for me alone. Crystal's body is draped in diaphanous layers of black lace, as transparent as morning mist, inviting my eyes in and over every crevice and curve of her astonishing body. My heart is pounding unbelievably hard. Lifting myself up a fraction, looking closer now, catching my breath, I see a patch of black velvet between her legs held fast by spaghetti-thin flesh colored string. Dark satin dots the size of poker chips cap her nipples. The last pieces of lace drop to the floor as gently as leaves falling from a branch, the deception complete; Crystal appears totally naked to all but those close enough to hear her panting. Too soon, the music stops, the dance is over, the lights go dim and she leaves the stage. I'm completely amazed by how hard I am. Julie said something to me a second ago, but I'm afraid I missed it.

"What'd ya say?" I ask, staring at the empty stage.

"I said, 'Do you like Crystal?'"

I think Crystal is an irresistible princess; a night alone with her would be more precious than Aztec treasure. "She's not so bad. Is she coming back?" I ask, feigning disinterest.

When Julie and I arrive at Venus's studio apartment the party is underway with a flourish. Refreshments are spread out on the kitchen counter. Soul and R&B are stacked high on the stereo. The lights in the room are turned down low. A joint is circulating through a crowd of about a twenty-five, mostly musicians and their girlfriends, and of course, other dancers. I am informed more people are expected, although it's already past one o'clock. The only thing missing is the guest of honor. I haven't been able to get Crystal out of my mind since the instant I saw her on that stage. When I left the bar, I made a promise to myself that before this night is over I would get to know her. I'm leaning against the apartment's radiator holding a can of beer, trying to focus on a conversation with Marvin and Jasper. Dianne is sitting quietly on the couch, her mouth wired shut, sipping a can of beer through a straw.

Marvin's pal Orlando approaches me and asks, "Whut you doing about Barry?"

"I think he split. I let myself in to his apartment. The closet was empty. A few pieces of his crummy shit are still lying around. If he doesn't show up by Monday, Robert and I are gonna hose down his room and rent the place."

I was about to walk over to Dianne and tell her this news when the door swings open and the hallway's incandescent bulbs illuminate Crystal. She is standing at the threshold with her hands on her hips and her legs spread apart, an entourage in tow behind her back. Crystal is wearing a chic, deep blue satin dress cut low on top expressing a revealing tease of cleavage, the hemline perched about five inches above the knee, showing off those glamorous legs. I swallow hard, promising myself to be cool and not trip over my tongue.

"This room is fulla *NIGGERS!*" Crystal yells irreverently into the crowd of staring faces. "What kind of a party did you invite me to!?" She steps inside and throws her head back in a raucous laugh.

I guess her profanity is meant as a bawdy joke… but nobody seems to be laughing, on the other hand, no one appears shaken up by her rude comment either. Crystal stomps around the apartment like a diva on speed, bumping into people, laughing obnoxiously for no apparent reason, her voice shrill and irritating. She rips the joint from Hector's lips and takes a copious drag as she continues threading her way through the room, grabbing food with one hand and a drink with the other. My earlier goo-goo feelings hit the wall with a splat. I just want to go home now and go to bed… alone. I thank Venus for her hospitality, say my goodbyes to my friends, and give Julie a little wave.

The night air is welcoming, a cool refreshment to counter the noise of shouting men and angry horns from taxis in the street. Sidewalks are jamming, still a lot of guys out wandering, some tanked up, laughing, looking for fun; a few others tired, staggering towards home. Turning the corner on La Grange, I pass the bar next door to my building. Cheap chords drone from the organ inside, piping out the open door, following me to my room.

29

Walking on the Moon

"My brother is very disappointed in you, *very* disappointed," Andreus emphasized yesterday afternoon, pointing a finger in my face. I had passed $295 dollars into his open hand, which seemed to soften the edge of his frustration. "My brother would like to see the receipt book, please."

"Sure." I pulled open a cabinet drawer to retrieve it. "It might not be entirely up to speed." I held on to one end of the book while Andreus jerked the opposite corner; we had a mini tug of war going. "Maybe you should let me and Van Helden look at it first, make sure everything's right."

Andreus' yank had a little more oomphh than mine, and he snapped the book free from my fingers, "No, I should take it now… we fix it later."

This morning, Lykos sent his brother to call us on the shit they found in our crummy records. Coming into our room very business-like, Andreus pulls a chair up to the kitchen table; spreads open our receipt book and gets right down to business.

"Here," he says, pointing his long finger into the book, "2B pays every week and then it stops." Andreus licks a digit and flips into the next page, "And here… 2B pays again. What happened to the missing three weeks… where are the receipts? And here," he continues, not waiting for an answer, flipping to other pages he has tagged, "the same thing happens with room 4A. And here, 4B." Andreus looks at Robert and me with suspicious eyes. "Here and here," he chastises, his wet finger flipping and pointing. Andreus snaps the book shut and slaps his big hand down over it with a pounding slap that makes me jump. "You tell me, where is the money?"

"You can't collect rent from empty rooms," I say.

"No, these rooms are rented. We know this!" He holds a stiff, damp finger in the air.

"Sometimes we got problems," says Van Helden. "Plumbing's busted, shit like that."

"Yes," agrees Andreus, "you got problems."

"I admit it… our records stink… what can I say? We forget to write a receipt sometimes, that doesn't mean we didn't give you the cash."

"If you took in money, where did it go?"

"We gave you every penny, unless we had to pay to change a lock, or fix a leak, or a window. They tell us what it cost and we take care of it," I say. "Sometimes they forget to write us a bill, or we forget to ask for one, so kill us… we're lousy bookkeepers."

"That's all that's happening here, Andreus," adds Van Helden. "We're not fuckin' with you, if that's what you're thinking."

Andreus gives us a new receipt book, saying he plans to hold on to the old one. I wonder… is Lykos collecting evidence against us? For our benefit, Andreus goes over a simple lesson in Business 101: "You take money, you give a receipt, always,

always, always. I told you that when you started here. Also, you pay for work, you get a receipt, always, always, always."

"Okay… No problem… We can do that…. That's the plan," we agree, making a string of promises. Robert and I follow Andreus into the hallway. As he waits impatiently for the elevator, we stand quietly in the shade of his funk.

"My brother will be stopping by to talk to you. Please clean the building before he comes." Andreus is tapping his big black loafer on the linoleum. He steps into the box and faces forward, a fierce look in his eyes, posturing like he's got a rod stuck up his ass. We watch in silence as he disappears behind the sliding door.

I toss Robert a resigned look and sigh, "He thinks we're thieves."

Back inside the room, Van Helden and I discuss more important issues.

"Barry ain't coming back," says Robert.

"I know… I think he smelled trouble."

"Those guys gonna whack him?"

"If they can find him… and I won't lose any sleep over it."

"I'm hip."

"I got a line on a job," I say. "I talked to some asshole over the phone. He said I sounded like I got 'real potential'. I'm supposed to show up tomorrow so he can check me out."

"What's the gig?"

"Dig it, encyclopedias," I chuckle.

"Really? You gonna, like, do a 'door to door' thingy?"

"Yeah… pretty weird, huh?

"I can't see you doing that shit around here."

"Don't underestimate me, my man. I'm a pretty good goddam salesman. When I was a kid, I sold Christmas cards in July to my neighbors. I'm sure I can unload a few books inside the Combat Zone."

Boston's air has been suffocating me all summer; it's like breathing in hot paste. Thankfully, the soupy humidity won't touch Marvin and Winky's place. Their room is pure heaven, the only apartment in the building with a window AC unit, cranking out a breeze cooler than Maine in the morning. A cozy crowd gathers comfortably on Winky's white shag in front of the portable TV to catch the most extraordinary event of the summer, the United States of America landing on the moon. Two bottles of sparkling wine from the vineyards of upstate New York State are chilling in a bucket of ice within easy reach. We plan to crack one open when the thing lands; we'll pop the second when the guy jumps from the ship and hits moon dust.

My friends and I sit quietly listening to the space experts and news gurus rap commentary about the mission. Marvin is sitting snug in his comfy chair with a bowl of popcorn in his lap.

"What do ya think of Cronkite?" I ask.

"Ol' Walter's cool," garbles Marvin, through a mouthful of corn. "That dude not only reports history, he *is* history."

We all agree with Marvin's assessment of how cool ol' Walter is. Sam and I are sitting shoulder to shoulder on the rug. Van Helden and Joanne cuddle across a stack of throw pillows; Angel and Hector stretch out beside them. Julie has to work tonight, so maybe she'll join us later. All eyes are collectively glued to a continually expanding black and white image of the undulating moonscape filling the screen, while fuzzy voices from the TV chatter technical jargon we can't understand. The landing craft appears to be gaining speed, dropping faster by the second as it closes the gap between our worlds.

"*The Eagle has landed...*" squawks the voice from the television. Cheers go up from both Mission Control and the gang inside the room. Leaning over, I pluck the champagne from the ice bucket, loosen the cork a couple of twists, place my thumb on the lip of the bottle, and closing my eyes, launch the cork into space. POP BANG... *plop*. The projectile ricochets off the glass shade of the ceiling light and lands in Winky's lap.

"Perfect touch down!"

I stand and pour the cold fizzy wine into paper cups aligned in a row on the kitchen table.

"When are they gonna get out and walk around?"

"Not for awhile... they said it might be a few hours before Neil Armstrong leaves the lunar module," says Joanne.

"Neil Armstrong? I thought the dude's name was Buzz," says Marvin. "Buzz... I love that name," Marvin grins.

"Buzz Aldrin will step out second," says Joanne.

"Somebody ought to go get us a pizza or somthin,'" says Hector.

Darkness fills the room, the evening sky settled in, the sole light being the blue-gray glow of the television screen and the occasional red-hot tip flickering from the joint passing among us. Several hours have passed since anything cool has happened, and we're all about to pass out from boredom. A camera is set up outside the little space ship to record Armstrong's descent, but the images it is sending back are dark, grainy and lifeless.

"Whutzat movin' round there!" asks Hector, coming alive and pointing to the top of the picture screen. "Zat a leg?"

Apparently, things up on the moon have begun to heat up, the cabin door to the lunar module popped open and Neil Armstrong poked his head outside to check on the weather. A ladder is banked up against the side of the ship. We all lean forward, our faces nearly touching the screen, witnessing a Spaceman in a bulky suit lumber backwards, inching his way along the steps.

"Look! He's coming down, he's coming down!" cries Joanne in a loud whisper, pulling Robert's arm.

"Ssshhh!" Van Helden hushes his girlfriend. At once, everyone in the room becomes still as we watch in wonder; the only sound, quiet, indistinct garble from men communicating in the foreign language of precision instruments.

"*That's one small step for man,*" says a voice colored in dark static, pausing now for a second before committing to the unknown and dropping from the ladder, "*one jive heap for man time.*"

Cheers and pandemonium erupt from the folks at Mission Control!

"Whut he say?" asks Winky. "I didn't hear whut he say."

"Somethin' about stepping and jiving," guesses Marvin.

Walter Cronkite answers Winky, "The first statement to come from the moon, 'That's one small step for man, one giant leap for mankind.'"

"Dat's cool."

POP!! "Champagne anyone?"

30

High School Boys

Wishing I was anywhere but here, I tag behind Lykos, stopping beside the airshaft, he cranks open the window and takes a healthy whiff, whips his head back inside and spins the handle shut.

"There is SHIT in the airshaft!" He glares at me like I'm the one taking a crap out there.

"I think that's dog shit?" I shrug.

"Dog shit? Somebody here has a dog?"

"Are dogs against the rules?"

"They are now! Find out if anyone has a dog and tell them it has to go, or they go! Got it?"

"Yessir." I won't name Kitty as the culprit, although I'm sure she's the one throwing crap out the window. Lykos is right about this. I'll have to warn her to bag the shit, or bag the dog. Lykos piles on a long list of duties we're supposed to perform in the next forty-eight hours. I throw him a salute as he marches out of the building.

After talking to Kitty about her crap, I somehow get hooked into babysitting her little runt. What the hell, I hadn't planned on going out tonight, anyway. Josephine is shaking like a leaf, curled up on the floor by the door. I think it's afraid of me. I had to scream at it for peeing on my bed. I stripped the covers and douched the pee spot with mixture of Lysol and Old Spice.

Laughter is coming from the hallway; Kitty's out there yucking it up with some guy. On my side of the door, her little rat dog is spinning and yapping like a bunch of firecrackers ignited up its ass. I get up to let her in, kicking aside the whirling dervish. Kitty enters with a new boyfriend on her arm, a guy I've never seen before.

"How's my little sweetie poo?" she coos baby talk and picks up her pooch, kissing its nose in rapid fire little pecks. The new guy, a tall, slick, fortyish looking dude in an expensive suit, glossy black hair and a chunky gold bracelet, is totally disinterested in the proceedings.

"I hope you was a good girl to nice Mr. Jonny." She continues squeezing affection into the little rodent, who is about to have an orgasm right there in her hands. Kitty turns to me and asks, "Did she pee pee tonight?"

"She pee peed on my bed right after you left."

Without missing a beat, the Expensive Suit opens his wallet and peels out a five-dollar bill.

"Here, kid. This should take care of your cleaning bill."

I stuff the five in my pants.

"*Thank you, Big Mike*" says Kitty in a playful, singsongy voice. "Big Mike, this is the boy I was telling you about that's looking for a job. Big Mike owns Lucifer's," she proudly announces.

"This the guy?" asks Big Mike, pointing at me with his thumb, thoroughly unimpressed.

"You can find something for this child, can't you?" Kitty rubs her long dark hand with its ruby red nails up Big Mike's sleeve.

"Sure," he answers, switching his eyes from Kitty's hand to my face. "I hear you can take care of yourself. We can use someone like you. How'd ya like to be a floorwalker? Ya think you could handle that... uh, I'm sorry... I didn't catch your name."

"It's Jonny. I don't know. I've never done any floorwalking. What would I have to do?"

"Simple stuff. You gotta look sharp, always wear something nice, jacket and tie," he smiles and grabs a hold of his lapels. "Cause ya represent Boston's finest club." Big Mike continues, "Ya keep your eyes and ears open at all times, ya float through the crowd, watching the guests, making sure everyone in the place is enjoying themselves. If someone gets out of line, ya show them to the door. Ya won't be doing this alone, of course. On busy nights, we have a thousand guests and five or six floorwalkers keeping an eye on things. Da ya want the job?"

I look at them both, biting the corner of my lip, thinking of what to say. Big Mike has little patience for slow thinkers, I guess, before I can answer he pulls Kitty by the hand and turns from my room.

"Ya think about it, kid. Let me know."

Kitty purrs against Big Mike's chest as they walk into the hallway, the wooing fading away as they leave me standing alone, thinking about it.

My brother's coming to see me, bringing an old buddy of mine along with him; Kenny Metzler, the most sensible kid I know. He's very much like my brother, levelheaded and reserved without a trace of guile in his veins. Coincidentally, another couple of pals from high school, Richard Smith and Michael O'Donnell, are also headed this way. Richard and Michael are knuckleheads, sexually deviant frat boys on acid, the complete opposite of Jerry and Kenny. If you could read people like magazines, my brother and Kenny would be the *Atlantic Monthly* and *Harper's*. Richard and Michael fall somewhere between the covers of *Screw* and *Mad Magazine*. They're crazy and I love them both.

The 7:55 arrival from Hartford is a few minutes out; I sit waiting on a hardwood bench, people watching. Jerry had said our bus station is a harbor for queers looking for dick, but I don't see anything out of the ordinary; just a few couples with suitcases in various stages of life.

At 8:05, my brother and Kenny enter the lobby and walk past me in a clip.

"Hey, Bozos!"

"We didn't know you'd be meeting us."

"Well, I thought you clowns could use an escort."

Sporting harmonic smiles, the three of us push our way out the double doors into the street.

I catch sight of him standing in the shadows beyond the terminal's canopy, sharing whispers with a pubescent high school boy. The two display the business of an awkward encounter, but whatever their negotiation, quickly conceded, they turn to leave together.

"Ray?"

Raymond's face twists towards my voice, startled; we lock eyes for a fraction before he puts his head down, staring at his shoes. Raymond raises his face again, this time giving me a long look, his expression shameful and scared.

"Let's get of here," I say.

My brother and Kenny catch up with me a halfway down the block. "If you guys are hungry you better get something now, cause I got nothin.'"

"That guy back there, I've seen him in your building. Isn't he a friend of yours?" asks Jerry.

I shake my head, ruling out the uncertainties. "Yeah, I know him. He's a pervert."

We step into the crosswalk and bump into ol' Mr. Eyeballs coming across from the other side, one dark hand outstretched, begging, and the other pathetically flailing in the air, feeling his way through the blackness to the other side of the street.

"Look at that guy!" says Kenny. "He needs help, or something. Shouldn't we help him out?"

"Fuck him," I say. "Just get out of his way."

We round the corner at Stuart and Tremont and cross into a landscape of adult entertainment. Dozens of guys are lolling around the street in front of the strip clubs like chickens in a barn yard; the more colorful cocks, black gentlemen with their equally flamboyant ladies draped on their arms, add a festive touch to the scene. A trio of sailors queue up beneath the spot lights of the Saxon Theater's marquee, displaying the current feature, Midnight Cowboy, Rated X.

"We're home," I say to Kenny, nodding my head in the direction of my building. Kenny grabs my arm and stops me in the street. "Jonny, you *live* here?" he asks, scanning his eyes in a wide turn.

"Yeah… top floor; that's my window," I say, pointing up.

"You got to be kidding."

"You want I should stop in the drugstore and pick up a bag of chips, maybe some soda?" asks Jerry.

"Good idea. And score us a couple of six-packs. We got more people coming."

My lobby door closes behind us, muffling the racket from the street. We stand quietly facing the elevator. The sharp sound of hands slapping on glass makes the three of us jump and turn towards the disturbance. Richard and Michael are in the foyer with their faces pressed up against the door's glass panel. Their distorted lips and noses flattened on the glass present the look of a couple of frogs run over in the road. I walk back to let them in.

"Far out little neighborhood ya got here, Jonny!" says Michael, as the two boys burst through the door, both grinning like a couple of kids passing through the gate of an amusement park.

"Ever go to any of these clubs?" asks Richard, pointing through the door into the street.

"I've been to most of them. Some of the dancers live in the building."

"Dig it!" says Michael. "Ask them to come over and strip for us! Give us a free show!"

"Outstanding idea!" says Richard, giving Michael a congratulatory slap on the back for his prescience.

"I'll see what I can do."

A party of four squeezes inside the elevator, I stand outside the cab looking in. There is barely enough room left over to suck in air, let alone another person.

"Hey, Jonny," says Michael, "if we get on our toes and stand nuts to butts I think we can squeeze you in."

"You guys go up... I'll catch it on the flip side." I reach inside and push the button for the sixth floor. The door closes and the box rattles up the shaft; the sounds of convivial chatter drifts down in its wake.

The lobby door swings opens to the sounds of traffic and nightlife, and Julie's twinkling voice, "There you are!" Dianne and Angel are at her side. "I was wondering what happened to you." Julie and Angel are made up like blonde cupie dolls, bright red lipstick and heavy eye shadow, dressed in slinky miniskirts. Dianne is wearing a casual cotton print outfit and hardly any makeup. "Where have you been hiding?" asks Julie, holding me with a scolding tease.

"I got some friends over. We're having a little party."

"I hope you plan on inviting us."

"Of course!"

The elevator returns to the lobby and I pull open the cage door, "Allow me, ladies," gesturing with a bow, "Your coach has arrived."

Inside the elevator I address Dianne, pointing to her chin, "Ya got that trap taken off."

"Yeah… this morning. It's *so wonderful* having my face back! We were out celebrating," says a bubbly Dianne. "Julie and Angel treated me to my first chewy food in two weeks."

"By the way, Barry is officially gone. We changed the lock on his door."

Dianne clenches her newly repaired jaw, mouthing her words as if it was still wired tight. Her eyes take on fire, "He better not ever come back here again. My friends will kill him dead."

"It's good he's gone," says Angel, "even if he's not the one that did it to you, honey. That guy gave me the creeps."

The elevator stops at Julie's floor and the three ladies step into the hallway. Angel turns and sticks her head back inside. "When's your party?" she asks.

"Now."

"We'll be up in a little while," says Julie.

On the way to my room I stop by Marvin's to see if he'd like to join us. "Marvin doing somethin' tonight with his brother, but I'd love to come," says Winky.

I take the flight of stairs up to my room, pleased with myself. My friends are comfortably sharing the couch, each with a can of soda in their lap. Jerry and Robert are talking at the table over a bowl of chips.

Joanne is standing beside Van Helden, dressed like she's going out for the evening. "I'll see you in the morning, Robert." She snaps her purse shut and straightens the folds of her skirt. He hooks his arm around her waist and walks towards the door, whispering in Joanne's ear before giving her a send-off kiss.

"She didn't have to leave," I say to Robert. "She wouldn't be the only chick. I invited some girls over."

Richard pops forward on the couch, "What's this about girls?"

"It's cool," says Robert. "She's going out with her sisters. It's some family thingy."

"What's this about girls?" Richard asks again, this time more joyfully.

"I just saw Winky… she's coming up. Julie, Angel and Dianne will be here in a few minutes, too." I face the trio of high school buddies, feigning admonishment, "I want everyone to be on their best behavior. These are nice girls."

"Robert, what do you feel like… red lights or blue?" The apartment can use a few designer touches to set the mood.

"I'm feeling kinda blue," says Robert.
"Blue it is!"
"Jonny! Try this pot," Michael offers a joint.
"Put on the radio!"

Oh, Darling, Paul McCartney's plaintive wail fills the room; I begin to sing along… a few bars into it, Kenny joins in. By the third verse, the entire room is belting out the hard-rocking tune at the top of our lungs.

"You boys sound wonderful! We could hear you all the way down to the third floor." Julie gushes as she moves smoothly among us, followed by Angel, Dianne and Winky, Angel and Winky each carrying a healthy jug of red wine by the neck.

The guys spring to attention, offering their seats to the ladies like good Eagle Scouts, standing rigid, except for the wide smiles on their faces, which seem to expand exponentially by the second.

"Help yourself to chips," I say, after introducing everyone.

"How does it feel to have your mouth moving again?" Van Helden asks Dianne.

"I feel like biting Barry." Dianne shares her experience with the group, explaining her lack of faith in the police to take care of things. "I don't trust them… no way, no how."

My guests swap tales of their own bouts with aggravated assault and police response. The girls seem to have more experience in this territory than us boys. The conversation digresses into talk of lawyers, judges and jails. Richard shares his account of being booked in jail for a high school prank involving the theft of a half-dozen cannon balls from our hometown Civil War monument. He packed the balls with potassium nitrate and blew up a few prominent civic icons.

Richard pulls a mug shot from his wallet and passes it around the room; he is smiling above the numbers across his chest as proudly as a kid who just belted a little league homerun.

Someone turns up the music and Julie and Winky break into a dance in the center of the room. Richard and Michael jump up to be their partners. Angel puts her beer down, grabs Dianne by the hand and joins in. I don't know if it's the smoke or the wine, but the blue glow of the darkened room gives the appearance of swaying ghosts dancing in a graveyard. When the song ends, they continue to swoon right though to the next number. Robert and I fold into the mix and partner with Angel and Dianne. We dance for the sheer pleasure of it, song after song; sometimes changing partners, sometimes dancing alone.

Kenny and my brother appear to be struggling to stay awake. They hardly pay any attention to the rest of us. Kenny gets up, goes over to my bed and stretches out. Jerry remains on the couch; but he, too, begins to nod. The pot and the alcohol must have hit both guys hard between the frontal lobes. It seems to have the opposite effect on everyone else. Richard and Michael are fascinated by Julie and Angel since they discovered they dance professionally.

"I don't take my clothes off," says Angel. "What I wear ain't any more revealing than seeing me in my underwear."

"I'd love to see you in your underwear," smiles Richard.

Angel pulls her top off over her head, draws her belt from her waist and wiggles her lolly-pop ass out of her skirt, all to the beat of the music. Richard and Michael howl like a couple of hound dogs. Not to be outdone, Julie removes everything but her ruby-red bra and panties. Dianne does the same as the music continues to play.

"Whut the hell are you girls doin'?" Winky drops her jaw, stands frozen, staring at her nearly naked girlfriends in disbelief.

Michael unbuttons his shirt, pulls the sleeves from his arms and flings it over his head like a cowboy swinging his lasso, letting it fly off into a dark corner of the room. In one fluid motion he unbuckles his belt, zips down his fly... and off come his pants.

"Michael, you're crazy!" yells Richard, before he does the exact same thing. "Come on, Jonny!"

"Yo'all crazy," says Winky, giving them a long look. The other girls laugh; they are enjoying themselves. Winky shrugs, "Whut the hell," and unbuttons her blouse and jiggles out of her skirt, letting them drop to the floor. Winky strikes a pose in her lacy lingerie, placing one hand on her hip, "Come on, Jon," she says, "You next."

I strip down to my underwear. Richard and Michael begin yanking at Kenny's pants, trying desperately to pull them off his prone body.

"Hey, cut it out!" he squawks, "I'm trying to sleep." They drop his legs and return their attention to the girls.

Jimi Hendrix is singing on the radio, wailing a bluesy beat about a man who shoots his old lady. I look over at Julie, dancing alone, her suggestive movements bear a close resemblance to what I've seen her perform on stage.

"Julie," I call out over the music. "Show us what you're famous for!"

Julie pauses for a second to consider my request, stages an approving smile, and steps to the center of the room. My friends form a wide circle around her. Swaying her hips to the music, her flesh glowing an iridescent blue, Julie reaches behind her back, unhooking her bra, stretching the ends free, out tight and straight, sliding the cups over her breasts, teasing a few wicked seconds before tossing it to the floor. Her breasts begin to gain speed, spinning, ice blue orbs, capturing our eyes in a trap of dizzy splendor.

In the interlude following the song, Van Helden begins to undress, but for a different reason. "It's getting late, guys. It's after two… you can do what you want, but I'm gonna crash," he says, turning down the music.

Kenny is fast asleep on my bed. Jerry's propped up on the couch stiff as a mannequin. Robert nudges my brother on his shoulder, "Jerry, you gotta get up… I need to open my bed."

"Huh? Oh, yeah… sure." My brother struggles to stand.

Sleep is tempting me, too; we can't do this all night. I look around at our guests and wonder about their intentions. Kenny is about as easy to move as concrete, "Jerry, why don't you and Kenny use my bed. I'll crash with Robert," I pat the edge of his mattress. Richard and Michael, still dancing and having a good time with the girls, are going to have to fend for themselves.

The music plays on softly. Winky stands at the window looking down at the street. Richard and Michael linger in the kitchen, talking with Dianne and Angel. Van Helden and I face each other on opposite sides of the bed.

"You're getting in bed with me?" he asks, scratching his head.

"I promise I won't touch you."

Julie, wearing only her scarlet panties, comes over to me and whispers in my ear, "I'm sleeping with you, Baby," and wraps her arms around me, kissing my neck.

Robert climbs into bed and slides under the sheets. I do the same, with Julie between us. Julie's face and mine sink deep into the pillow together, kissing. Feeling her hands slide my underwear down to my knees, I help it along, freeing myself completely. Julie slips her panties off and holds them by her fingertips in the air, dainty-like, then tosses them over the side of the bed. I roll on top of her as she opens her legs, guiding me inside.

The mattress begins to roll with the fluid motion of our bodies. Julie moans a dreamy aching pain each time I push down into her.

"Hey, I'm trying to get to sleep here," says Robert.

"Oh, oh… somebody gettin' serious." I look up sideways and find Winky standing tall beside us, looking down with her arms crossed. "Day's definitely gettin' serious."

Sunday afternoon, I feel like someone has taken an ax and chopped it into my skull. My room is nearly empty of bodies; Jerry and Kenny are the last to leave. My brother snaps shut his suitcase and turns to me. "What's going on with you and that stripper?"

"She's got a name, Bro… Julie."

"I found her panties on the floor when I got out of bed this morning. I picked them up and gave them to her. She smiled at me and twirled them around on her finger."

"That was nice of you."

"You got something going on with her?"

"She thinks she's my old lady."

"I thought you were seeing Lara. What happened to that?"

"Nothin'... Hey, if you bump into her when you get home, say 'hi' for me, will ya. Let her know I'm thinking about her."

"Jonny... you're a real prick. You know that?"

I swallow a handful of aspirin. Prick? What the hell is he talking about?

31
Nun of the Above

"Where do you think you're going?" Julie stops me with a stern look as we cross paths in the lobby.

"I'm headed out."

"Out where?"

"I got a job interview."

"You didn't tell me you were going out. When you coming back?"

I speak to her over my shoulder, heading for the door. "I don't know," I shrug.

"Don't be gone too long."

Jesus, Julie, give me a break. I don't need your permission to leave the building.

Charlie is peddling up Tremont Street on a fabulous ten-speed, its polished silver-blue paint glistening in the sun. He slows down and dismounts.

"Dig my new ride! It's an Italian racer. I won't be taking the subway anymore."

"Very nice." I'm immediately jealous.

"I just did ten-miles along the Charles. What are you up to?"

"Me? I'm not doing anything."

"I can use a beer. You want to join me?"

"Sure."

While I take hold on to Charlie's shiny bike, he runs into a nearby liquor store and exits a few minutes later carrying a six-pack. We cross Tremont and search for suitable ground to plant ourselves. The grass inside the Boston Common has just been mowed, bestowing the contented smell of backyards and summertime.

"Dynamite day," Charlie appraises the splendid afternoon, leaning his bike against the trunk of a willow and plopping down beneath its cool shade. He reaches into the bag and fishes out two cans, pulls the tab from one and takes a swig. "Guess who came by to see me last night?" asks Charlie.

"Who?"

"Robin."

"Robin?" I say, quizzically. Her name sounds like a character out of ancient history. She had vanished from my life after our weekend together.

"I got somethin' to tell you," Charlie lowers his voice, sounding as if he is speaking inside a confessional.

"What?"

"I balled her." Charlie takes another slug from his beer. "It was my first time."

"What do you mean... first time?"

"I got laid. It was my first time."

"Whoa!" I'm rocked by this revelation. "Well, welcome to the club, brother." I smile, raising my beer in salute. I'm not sure what manner of fraternity I have in mind: Men Who Sleep with Women, Guys Who Share Sex with the Same Girl, or Boys Who Have Their Virginity Taken Away by Robin, Bless Her Heart. "How's ol' Robin doing, anyway? You oughta tell her to stop by."

My friend looks away from me and stares at his

beer, like he's examining the brand name on the can. His eyes come back to mine, more solemn than they were a second ago. "You remember how spacey Robin was?"

"Yeah, she's a real fruitcake."

"Well, she's changed. She's much more serious now than the way she used to be. You know what was funny... she didn't have anything good to say about you. What'd you do to her, anyway?"

"Jesus," I quietly reply, almost to myself. "I thought we were friends."

"I gotta take a wizz." Charlie stands and places his hands on the ten-speed. "Let's get outta here."

The bike is balanced vertically inside the elevator, Charlie drops it down as the door opens and I follow him out into the hallway.

"*So, you're interviewing for a job, huh?*" Julie steps out from around the corner and blocks our path. Icicles spike her voice. She is glaring at me, legs spread apart and hands grabbing a tight hold of her hips.

"What?" I ask, completely baffled.

"You were in the goddamn park, lying under a tree, drinking goddamn beer. You lied to me!" Julie pushes past us and races down the stairs to her apartment. Charlie and I blink hard when her door slams, the sound reverberating through the building's stairwell.

"Get back Jo Jo, your Mama's waiting," Charlie laughs.

"She musta tailed me."

"Pretty spooky, man."

Charlie relieves himself at my toilet and retreats from the room, wheeling his bike out the door. "Good luck with your girl friend." he smiles.

"She's not my girl friend... I'm breaking up with her. I don't need this shit!"

"You don't need this shit!" Charlie echoes, poking the air with his finger. "When you going to tell her?"

"Tell her what?"

"That you're breaking up."

"I gotta tell her that? I'm thinking I'll just stop seeing her. I don't want to make a big deal out of this."

"Coo-coo-ka-choo," Charlie grins.

The elevator door closes behind my friend, whistling on his way down the shaft.

Lykos wants us to start sweeping the lobby every day, so I came down here to give it a once-over. I lean lazily on the broom handle, staring at the pile of dust beside my feet. Shit... I forgot to bring the dustpan. Maybe I can shoot this crap out to the sidewalk.

"Excuse me, young man." The confident voice of woman is calling from the foyer. I look out through the doorframe's glass panel at the astonishing sight of two nuns, in full Sister regalia, standing sublimely with a little boy wedged between them. The kid's dressed up like he's on his way to his First Communion.

I open up and give them my best altar boy smile, "Hello, Sisters, what can I do for you?"

"Do you know Angel?" one asks, holding me still with her eyes.

"Angel?" I pause, bemused by her question, lost in far away thoughts of Saturday morning Catechism.

"Yes... We're here to see Angel. She's expecting us. May we come in?"

"Of course!" I snap back with a blink. "Angel's

a friend of mine." I step aside, holding open the door. "This must be her son?" I rub the top of the little guy's stiffly combed blonde head, which makes him jerk backwards.

"Would you be so kind and tell us which room she is staying in?"

We walk over to the elevator and I open the cage door. "Take this to the fourth floor, Sister. It's the room opposite the elevator, 4B."

I return to my sweeping duties, singing a little John Lennon, "*Happiness…is a warm gun. Hap-pi-ne-e-ess, is a warm gun, yesitis.*"

A few taps on the door grab my attention. A man, I guess about thirty, is rapping his ring finger on the glass. He's dressed in shiny black bell-bottom pants and a blood-red dress shirt opened wide at the collar, showing off a prodigious gold necklace, as thick as a chain link.

"Hey, buddy, I'd like to get inside!" he says, with a toothy smile. "Can you open the door?"

I walk over and oblige the man.

"Thanks, buddy," he says as he breezes by me in a clip, making a straight line to the elevator.

"Hey, where you going?" I ask. I hold my broom out like a shotgun.

"Not that it's any of your business, but I'll tell you cause you look like a nice kid. I got business in Apartment 3B."

3B? That's the room we rented to the schoolbook salesman. This guy doesn't look like he's in the market for scholarly materials. "What kind of business?"

"What's with all the questions?" The man is obviously irritated. "Who the hell are you, Joe fuckin' Friday?"

"I'm the Super. I run things around here with my partner."

"Oh, I get it." He reaches into his wallet and pulls out several bills. "How much you want? Will five take care of it?"

"Five? You wanna give me five bucks?" Jesus, what the hell is going on inside 3B? This guy is either a John or a pimp. "You going up there to get your rocks off?" I ask.

"What? Listen, asshole, if you're trying to shake me down, I don't appreciate your style. I already paid that fat fuck thirty bucks. He didn't mention anything about you."

"Did he mention Rick Boyko?"

"Who?"

"Detective Boyko, Boston Police. If you leave now, he won't pop you. You go up to 3B, you're going to jail, cause Boyko will be coming up to drag you outta here."

"You tryin' to fuck with me?"

"Me? Hell no… I don't care what you do. I'm just giving you a piece of advice.

"I don't need your fuckin' advice."

"Fine… have fun," I wave him into the elevator.

He stares at me, regarding me hard, "If you're bullshitting me, kid, you got a whole lot of hurt coming your way." He turns and walks out of the building.

I know what I have to do, and I wish Van Helden was here to back me up. I go upstairs and knock on Apartment 3B's door. The perfume smell of incense floats out from inside the room.

"Who is it?" A female's soft voice answers from behind the door.

"Building super!" I bark. A pretty black woman in shorts and a halter-top greets me, clutching a large silver salad fork in her right hand. "Is your old man home?" I ask.

"Who?"

"Lamar, isn't he your old man?"

"Lamar ain't here, and he ain't my old man. He won't be back for a few days." She taps her fork on the door jamb, "Whaddaya want?"

I sigh, pausing to think of the best way to put this. "I want you out of the building by noon tomorrow."

"What!? You fuckin' jokin'!?" Her grip tightens on the fork. "I ain't going nowhere till I talk to Lamar."

"Sorry, tomorrow you're gone. Let's keep it simple. Don't make me call the cops."

The girl's eyes get evil, looking as if she wants to take that fork and make toss salad with my face. I nod a 'good day' and spin around, making a mental note to call the locksmith.

My throat's dryer than a bag of dust. I raise my head from my pillow, open one eye, finding Robert standing in front of the closet buttoning his shirt. A few feet away, Joanne is nestled under the covers, fast asleep. Robert has been investing all of his free time with his new girlfriend. We haven't seen much of each other lately. I come home late most nights after he has crashed, and by morning he's gone while I'm still lying unconscious in bed.

"What's up, Robbie?" I ask, my voice a rasp scraping metal.

"Hey, Jonny... How's it goin'?" Robert steps over and sits himself down on the corner of my bed.

"I found out why we still got Johns coming here." I recount my business yesterday with Lamar's old lady.

"You kicked her out?"

"Yeah, do you think that was the right thing to do?"

"That's cool... we don't need any trouble from the police, or Lykos. You know, he called a couple of nights ago."

"Who called?"

"Lykos." Van Helden scratches his head like he is trying to shake something loose inside. "Dig it... he wants us to cough up five-hundred bucks."

"What?!" My body snaps up into a seated position.

"Shush... Joanne's trying to sleep. Lykos went through his books, thinks we shorted him five-hundred."

"Jesus Christ. What'd you say?"

"I told 'em he was nuts."

"Yeah? Then what'd he say?"

"He said somethin' like... 'I don't want you around if I can't trust you... I'm calling the police, blah, blah, blah.'"

"He can't lay that shit on us! We didn't touch his fuckin' money!"

"I gotta sky," Robert says.

Slipping into my jeans, I follow him into the hallway, dumbfounded by this new development. Robert is speaking from inside the elevator, his voice cut short as the door closes between us. "We'll figure this out later."

"I don't believe this," I whisper to myself

"Mister Renzo in?" I ask the woman on the other end of the line.

"Who's calling, please?"

"Jonathan Tudan. I spoke with Mister Renzo last week about a job. He said I should call before coming by."

"Weren't you supposed to be in here a couple

of days ago?"

"Yeah, somethin' came up."

"I see. Mister Renzo is busy all morning. He should be free to speak with you this afternoon. Perhaps you'd like to come by now and observe one of his training sessions."

"Training sessions... what's that?"

"Before our kids reach out to the communities with our products, they need formal training. That's what we do here." She summarizes a five-day schedule of events that culminate in graduation-day and the crowning achievement of being dubbed a full-fledged representative of Colliers Encyclopedia's crack sales force.

The locksmith I phoned yesterday is waiting for me downstairs. Before heading out this morning, I check on the status of Lamar's room. His old lady's gone, but she hadn't cleaned out their stuff. I gather their clothes and whatever junk not belonging to Lykos, fill a couple of boxes and slide them into the hallway's storage closet. I should tell Lykos we got a room available, but I really don't want to talk to him. Not right now, anyway. I pay the locksmith twenty bucks to change the lock, stuff his receipt in my pants and head back upstairs.

None of my threads hanging in my closet look appropriate for my interview with Renzo. My favorite shirt with the French cuffs is a bit too flashy, besides... it smells like beer. I got nothing business-like to wear. I search for help inside our dresser and uncover my old sunny-yellow polo shirt I wore when I first came to Boston. It's wrinkled, but it will do fine. I slip on a quiet pair of khaki chinos, step into my high school loafers, grab my smokes and hit the street.

The number over the front entry of a prosaic

three-story yellow brick building on Providence Street matches the number on the piece of paper I fish out of my pocket. I wander inside its musty lobby and head for the open staircase. Renzo's office is on the second floor. A wino is reclining with his eyes closed at the bottom of the stairs, stretched across the tread like a bum on a park bench, his shoulders propped against the base of the newel post. I have to negotiate the stair carefully to avoid stepping on him.

"Hey," a tired, scratchy voice speaks to me. I pause, holding onto the railing a couple of risers above the bum. He stretches out his arm, like he's asking for a lift up.

"What's up, man?" I ask, looking down at this mess.

"You got a cigarette?"

Moving back one step, I pull a smoke from my pack, light up, and bend down to hand it over. The wino grabs hard at my pant leg, making me lose my balance and drop my Zippo.

"Gimme!" he barks.

I reach for the rail to steady myself and the cigarette slips from my hand and falls over the side to the lobby floor below. Leaning to retrieve my lighter, he continues to pull at my pants, like a determined attack dog. My balance regained, I flip open my box of Marlboros and dump the contents, raining cigarettes over his head. He releases his grip on me, fingers from both his hands speed over the stairs like wild spiders, picking up the smokes, scooping them into little piles.

Miss Feldman, Renzo's receptionist, leads me into a space that resembles a college classroom, complete with a podium, chalkboard, maps, and rows of desks with tidy looking students. About thirty clean cut, neatly pressed kids, an even representation of males and females, sit quietly taking notes, looking seriously attentive.

"Ssshhh," Miss Feldman holds her finger to her lips and points to an empty desk in the back row; my queue to cop a squat and keep my mouth shut.

At the front of the room, Renzo is putting on quite a performance. Giving sage advice to all the squeaky-clean boys and girls assembled; how to make yourself and your product appear interesting, disingenuous blather for buttering up your victims, followed by a presentation of language to segue the discussion from small talk to sales transaction. Renzo acts out a couple of his bullshit tactics to the class, and then asks for volunteers to try it out on each other. The kids all get hot honing their newfound charm school skills. At the end of his session, Renzo runs a cooling down period where he brags about how much money he made last year as a salesman, how he lavishes diamonds and furs on his foxy girlfriends and all the exotic vacations he's drags them on, how he parks his bigass Cadillac in front of his bigger-ass mansion in Newton. What a phony. Looking at the choirboys and girls all sitting in rapture soaking in every syllable this sham-artist utters, I feel like puking.

The class files out of the room, but not before everyone promises Renzo they will all rush back here tomorrow for their final exams and future assignments to springboard their wallets into the world of financial prosperity. By the expression on some of their faces, they're probably running out now to visit car dealerships to test-drive that new Mustang. I remain seated in the back row. Renzo extends his hand to me and begins jabbering about how happy he is to meet me, and how lucky we both are to be working together. Jesus, this guy ought to run for Congress. I confess my ambition to rake in some of that dough he talked about and promise to return on Monday to join a new class of upstarts on the road to riches.

"Any questions!?" he robustly blurts.

"How soon can I get paid?"

I head home feeling more than a little down. My pockets are empty, and this buffoon Renzo won't commit to a firm date on when I would see something come out of him other than hot air. He threw me a slippery answer, "We will have to wait and see how well we perform, won't we?" What's all this 'we' shit? Fortunately, *we* received a ten-dollar bill in the mail this afternoon from my brother. "Consider it a loan. Go easy, Brother," read the accompanying note. I return to my room and lie down on the bed, worn out. This guy Renzo is taking me nowhere, man. Maybe I should check out the gig Big Mike offered; Floorwalker, my ass, what's with the sugar-coated title? Why didn't he tell it like it is? Bouncer.

The phone starts ringing. I reach over lazily, pick up and mouth a tired hello.

"Who this!" a man barks rudely into my ear.

God, what now? "You tell me your name and I'll tell you mine," I answer.

"Lamar Bashear! You the one who threw my old lady in the street?"

"Lamar," I sigh, "You weren't being straight with us when you moved in here, telling us you sell school supplies. What you and your old lady are selling got nothin' to do with school."

"Whut I do and whut she do is my business. Whut'd you do with my things?"

"I boxed them up for you. They're safe. You can come by and pick them up anytime you want."

"I ain't pickin' up nothin'! You put my things back in my room now and we forget all about this, like it never happen."

"Lamar, take your business someplace else. You're out, man. I'm not letting you back in the building."

"Listen, boy, I ain't through with you. You be hearing from me"... *click*

Lying back down feeling more drained than ever; my eyes close and I start to drift. Fragments of dreams whirl loose through my brain, flailing about in the dark like Mr. Eyeballs; Julie rolls into Big Mike who bumps into Renzo falling over Lamar knocking down Lykos; nobody able to make it across the street. I hear ringing in my ears; everyone freezes and stares at me, waiting for a response, "Whaddaya wanna do, kid?" My eyes pop open. I reach over and grab the phone, "Yeah?"

"Hello stranger."

"Who's this?"

"Lara, that's who," she sounds offended.

"Hi! I was lying down, I'm kinda sleepy. How you been?"

"I miss you. Why haven't you called?"

"I was gonna... I'm sorry... I've been pretty busy."

"I'm sure you have. I hear stories about how busy you are... all your parties," Lara let her sentence hang open for me to stick my neck in.

"What parties?"

"Why are you living in Boston this summer? You're not in school now. There's no good reason for you to be there," Lara pauses and takes a hard breath. "I know about your stripper girlfriend."

"I don't know what you're talking about. I don't have a girlfriend."

"Why are you up there?"

"I got a job."

"Doing what?"

"I'm selling books… and another thing. I can't let go of this building."

"That building?"

"That's right. It's my meal ticket. I can't give this up. It's worth a lot to me."

"Come home, Jonny. You're worth a lot to me, too."

I gotta think about this.

"Goodnight, Jonny. I love you. I don't know why, but I do."

"I love you, too."

I strip down to my shorts and snap off the light. Sleep comes to me in fits and turns.

Tap tap tap …

"Yeah?" my voice croaks, barely audible.

Tap tap tap… I glance at my clock, 2:05. "I'll be right there!" Lifting myself slowly from the bed, I pad over to the door in the dark, stick my eyeball against the door's fish eye, but I am too bleary-eyed to focus.

"Who is it?" I ask warily before opening up.

"It's me," says Sam. She takes a few short steps into my room, wearing nothing but white panties and a man's sleeveless undershirt.

"I bumped into an old boyfriend tonight. He's on his way over here," she sounds like a lost little girl. "I don't want to see him."

"Why not?"

"Can I sleep with you tonight? I just don't want to be around when he gets here."

"Sure…" I stick my head into the hallway for a quick look-see, and close the door behind us.

Sam drops quietly on my bed and slides between the sheets. I lie down beside her, and we face each other on my pillow.

"This guy you're avoiding, he a bad guy?"

"Bad enough… I seem to be a magnet for bad guys."

"This building's a magnet for bad guys. I kicked another hooker and her pimp into the street this week."

"You're kidding? Who was that?"

"Lamar and his old lady. You know, I don't even know her name."

"Lamar? You evicted Lamar?" Sam laughs out loud. "Lamar's not a pimp, he's a pusher. Him and his old lady, her name is Darva by the way, they sell smack, mostly. I scored pot from them a couple of times." Sam laughs again, "Darva's not a whore, not yet, anyway. She's a junkie."

"They're pretty pissed off at me, but I'm not gonna worry about it. I don't think he'll give me any trouble."

"Be careful, Jonny."

"Hey, I broke up with Julie."

"Yeah? How'd she take it?"

"I haven't told her yet."

"Don't ya think she might like to know this, seeing as how you're telling other people?"

"You got any pointers on how to make this easy?"

"No such thing," she sighs.

I turn over and Sam spoons up against me.

"There's no telling how Julie's gonna take this," I whisper. "There's a crazy side to her, I think she might go nuts on me. Where can I score a few downers to mellow her out?"

"If you hurry, maybe you can catch up with Lamar," Sam drowsily mumbles, her face pressed up against my back, as sleep takes her away.

I spend the day brooding over how to make a clean split from Julie. After vocalizing several plausible break-up dissertations in front of the mirror, nailing down an assortment of sincere facial expressions, I decide I'm ready to go downstairs to deliver the news.

Julie is preparing for work, dabbing on makeup, her blonde wig beside her on the kitchen table, a crown of Golden Fleece.

"You coming by to see me later?" she asks, pressing the scarlet tip of her lipstick to her mouth.

"I gotta be honest with you, we won't be seeing much of each other any more."

"Why?" Julie drops her hand in her lap. "You leaving me?"

"This thing we got going... I can't do it any more."

"What you mean is... you don't want me." Julie's voice is scraggly as her bleach-job hairdo. "It's me... go ahead, say it... you don't want to be seen with me." Julie looks frightening, drawn; she managed to color only her bottom lip. Her face is pasty as chalk, except for the dark mascara encircling her eyes. In the last ten seconds she looks as if she has aged ten years. "Why can't you be a man and just say it!? Be honest with me!" she says, her voice shrill. "You jerks are all the same, every last one of you! Why don't I know any better? Why?" Julie cries into her hands, "I find a guy I like, treat him right, and what happens? I get kicked in the face. I'm stupid… stupid, stupid."

"Julie, come on now. Stop it. You're great, you're beautiful… you shouldn't feel this way."

"I'm going to build a wall around me and never, ever, let anyone come inside. Never again!" she sobs, turning away from me. "Go away! Leave me alone."

"Julie…"

"GO AWAY!"

I did the right thing, I'm thinking as I shut the door behind me. So how come it feels so wrong?

PART THREE
HAIR TODAY GONE TOMORROW

32
Cold Fire

Except for what's left of the ten my brother spotted me, I'm flat-ass broke. I've come to the realization it's a good idea to keep my options open. Before I start my sales training with that clown Renzo, I decide to check out the scene at Lucifer's. Sam's been there many times; she knows the ropes. She is sitting on my bed smoking, watching me get myself ready, buttoning my fancy shirt. "When you get to the door, tell them you're there to see Pete."

"Who's Pete?" I ask, looking up.

"He's the bar manager. Tell them you're making a business call. If you get hassled, tell them Big Mike offered you work and you're just following up on his offer; Pete's expecting you."

"He is?"

"Of course not," Sam laughs. "They don't know that, but play it that way. You'll get in without having to pay the cover. They might even comp you a few drinks, if they like you."

"Okay, cool... I ask to see Pete," I shake my head knowingly.

"When you get inside, go straight to the bar and find yourself a seat. The bartender will come by and take your order, ask him what his name is, and say, 'Tom, Dick, Harry'... whoever, 'I was told you would tell Pete I'm here.' Then sit tight. You should be able to handle the rest."

"Why don't you come with me?"

"I don't feel like doing any clubs tonight. I'm thinking about going to see my mother. Now that I'm making her a grandma, all of a sudden she likes me," Sam chuckles, crushing her smoke in my ashtray.

On the subway ride over to Lucifer's, I begin feeling a little shaky about this whole thing. What if I get the job and later they figure out I'm only eighteen? Sam told me not to give that any thought, "What's the worst thing that can happen, they fire you? So what, at least you made a few bucks in the mean time." She's probably right, but I'm still a little nerved out. Big Mike's offer was probably nothing but bullshit. I think he did it just to kiss Kitty's ass, and when I show up, they're gonna tell me to get lost. I jump off the trolley at Kenmore Square and take the short walk over to Lucifer's front door.

The entry scene goes exactly the way Sam predicted. I get through without paying the cover and make a direct line towards the bar, stopping for a second to catch the band onstage. I can see why this place is so popular. The atmosphere in this club is elegant. Lucifer's makes the Combat Zone look like the city dump. Flanking the band are two scantily dressed go-go girls dancing in the spotlight on what appears to be the roof of telephone booths; fashionable men with their hands around attractively attired women dance in tight circles beneath them. I thread my way through the crowd and snatch an empty seat at the bar.

Drumming my fingers on the bar top for a minute, wondering about my next move, I pull a smoke from my pack. A bartender quickly twists in my direction and snaps his lighter to the end of my cigarette, "What can I get you?"

"Hi, my name's Jonny. I wonder if you're the guy I'm lookin' for?"

"That depends, who you looking for?"

I pretend to give his question some thought, "Uh, I was told to see the guy behind the bar... I forgot the name."

"I'm Anthony."

"Yeah!" I snap, "Anthony. They told me at the door to see you."

"What's up?" Anthony asks, sounding disinterested, or perhaps in a hurry to move to the next customer.

"Mike offered me a job. They told me to ask you to go find Pete."

"Big Mike?"

"Yeah. I'm a friend of his."

"Pete's in the office. I'll get'em for ya. You want something to drink while you're waiting?"

"How 'bout a scotch on the rocks."

"You got it." Anthony spins around like a circus juggler, twirls some ice in a glass, flips a bottle upside down and drops a Dewer's in front of me.

"What do I owe ya?"

"On the house."

I tip my glass to Sam and sip my scotch. It burns my throat like cold fire. I don't know why I asked for scotch, it just seemed like a cool thing to say.

I see her seated at the other end of the bar, stretched out on her stool, laughing it up with two other ladies. Jesus, she looks good. I wonder she hates me. I get up and make my way toward her, carrying my scotch in my hand, bumping between bodies like a ball in a pinball machine. The second she spots me she stops talking, drops her glass on the bar, looks me in the eye and smiles, "Hi, Jonny."

"Karen, it's been a while. How you doing?"

"I'm doing great, thank you," she responds brightly. "How about you?"

"Me? I'm cool," I pause, straining my brain for my next line. "I hope you didn't have any trouble finding a new place to run your business?" Perhaps this wasn't the most proper topic to bring up, but she doesn't seem to mind. In fact, I made Karen laugh. This is the only time I've ever seen her laugh and it feels good to watch.

"I'm in a nice apartment on Beacon, thank you very much. I share it with these two girls," she smiles and introduces her very attractive friends.

"Are you still working?" I ask, continuing my brashness about her business, silently wondering if she ever crossed paths with Detective Boyko again.

"I'm still in the escort business, if that's what you're asking." I nod my head for no particular reason, and sip my scotch. I ran out of things to say, and begin to feel uncomfortable.

"Are you still living in that building?" Karen asks.

"Yeah, where else would I be?... How's your boyfriend?"

"My boyfriend? I don't have a boyfriend," Karen looks queerly puzzled by my question. Maybe I should have said, pimp?

"Oh? You left the guy, huh?"

"I haven't had a man in my life since God knows when."

"Weren't you working with some guy?"

"Some guy? A pimp, if that's what you mean? I've always worked alone. I'm an independent businesswoman. I don't throw my money away on some worthless asshole. I'm not stupid."

"That's funny." I remember Sam warning me about Karen's crazy-ass boyfriend.

"Why?"

A well-dressed man with a head as bald as a melon interrupts our conversation, introducing himself, "I'm Peter Brocatelle. Ya wanna see me?"

I look at the guy strange, for a confused second I forget what the hell I am doing here. "Oh! You're Pete. Yes, ah... Mike said you and me need to talk."

"Mike?"

"Big Mike. He offered me a job, and I came in to see..."

"Whaddaya do?"

"I'm a floorwalker. I mean, he said, I could be a floorwalker."

Karen returns her attention to her two friends.

"Well, we can always use another good floorwalker," he says this while looking me up and down, as if contemplating buying a new appliance. "Let's talk." He extends his hand for me to shake. "My friends call me Broccoli. My enemies, and I made a few in this business, believe me, they call me Vegetable. You can call me Mr. Brocatelle. What should I call you?"

"Jonny's fine with me."

"All right then, Jonny. Come… I'll show ya around."

I take a few steps behind Mr. Potato Head, stop and turned back, "Karen!"

She looks up and gives me a little wave goodbye.

"Good seeing you," I smile, and walk on.

Brocatelle takes me to a vantage point where we gaze down on the happy heads of several hundred drinking patrons, all in motion. Like most clubs I've been to in Boston, the atmosphere is dark with ribbons of smoky entrails, color coated by beams of light. Brocatelle begins to explain the main duties waiting for me if I take the job. His eyes gleam as he waves an outstretched hand to the assembly below, "This is your domain. Think of yourself as a shepherd, and these are your sheep."

"How many shepherds you got working here?" I ask.

"Tonight, two; Sunday's typically slow. We have four or five on a busy night. You're here ta serve management, whatever it is we need you ta do ta keep people happy, ya do it; escort guests through the club, socialize, get someone a drink, light their cigarette." He waves his finger in my face, "And keep an eye on the drunks. We run a very upscale establishment, and we don't take kindly ta dickheads messin' up our house. There'll be times when ya have ta show someone the door. When that happens, ya do it quickly and quietly."

"It's kind of ironic."

"What?"

"You want everybody drinking, but you don't want them drunk."

Brocatelle's face opens up with a with smile, like

somebody took a slice out of the melon, "You're gonna do just fine." He raises his nose and scans the crowd like he lost something. "See that guy?" he asks, pointing to a dude down below us wearing a stylish double-breasted plaid sport jacket sprouting a white boutonnière. "That's Thomas. He's dressed the way we expect ya ta look. Ya wanna work here, ya have ta look the part. All our floorwalkers wear carnations." He adds, "We supply the flowers. Ya have a few suits at home, right?"

"Shit, yeah."

"Good. Ya got any questions?" Brocatelle smiles.

"What's this pay?"

"Two dollars an hour, plus whatever tips ya pick off the floor."

"Cool... when do I start?"

Brocatelle drags me around the room and introduces me to a few of his people. He calls them 'My Associates'. "We got us another floorwalker... This is Jonny... he's gonna be working with us." He touts my credentials, "Jonny comes highly recommended... He's a friend of Big Mike." I shake a few hands, encouraging Melon Head's assessment with a smart smile. He starts going over the days he wants me to work and the time to punch in, but I pretty much stopped listening after the rounds of introductions. I'm sure I will never see this guy again. Where the hell am I gonna get the threads for this gig? I got one crummy sport jacket. Anyway, I don't think this scene is for me. I can't see myself wrestling drunks into the street. Of course, I don't tell Brocatelle this. Just in case my deal with Renzo falls through I keep my smiling mouth shut and my options open. Before heading out, I return to the bar to search for Karen, but to my great disappointment, I find someone else filling her seat. I do a quick figure 8, crisscrossing the club, hunting for a sign of her, but come up empty. Karen and her two girlfriends must have slipped away while I was getting my tour. I sigh and turn towards the door.

Robert and Joanne are caught in the grip of a serious discussion. Robert is smoking, sitting in bed on top of the sheets in his underwear. His legs are stretched out straight and he's tapping his feet together nervously like a trained seal. Joanne's is wearing shorts and a sleeveless T-shirt, her bare feet flat on the bed with her knees bent up to her ears, her arms crossed against them making a level plane to rest her head. Joanne glances lazily up at me when I come in; her lovely features are creased with a weariness that belies her nineteen years. It seems I came into the room in the middle of an argument. I pretend not to notice anything wrong, we all exchange pleasant little hellos, and I drop on my bed and try to relax.

After a moment of silence, they continue sniping about whatever it was they had going. I can't help overhearing; there are no secrets between friends in a one-room apartment. The gist of it is, Van Helden's talking about quitting his job and Joanne's freaked out about their future plans, or so it seems.

The mood in the room needs a little boost; I lean forward on my bed and break into their debate, "Dig it… I bumped into Karen!"

"Really?" says Robert. "How she doing?"

"Who's Karen?" asks Joanne, perking up a fraction.

"She had your room before you and Barbara."

"Oh… the prostitute."

"Yeah, nice girl… she looks great! We socialized a little bit. She said she's still in the escort business."

Joanne's face takes on a withered smile, "I bet you wouldn't mind escorting her."

"I don't think I can afford her." I pause, reflecting on the possibility. "So, Robert… you lookin' for a new gig?"

"Yeah, my job's going nowhere, man. The money I make blows."

I flip to my feet and march over to their bed, "Go for it, man, shoot the dice! Quit that stinking job! You'll find somethin' better, no bout a doubt it," I lay it on thick.

"Take it slow, Robert," says Joanne, looking at me stiffly. "It's fine to have big ideas, but make sure there's another door you can go through before slamming the one behind you."

"That's good advice!" I cartwheel over to Joanne. "Don't listen to me… Listen to your girlfriend."

"That's not all, Jonny. Joanne and I are going through some changes." Van Helden looks thoughtfully at Joanne, taking her hand. "We want to find a place of our own."

"You're leaving?" I ask, my voice vacant, "When?"

"We're gonna start looking tomorrow."

"How far you going… you leaving town?" I ask, flattened by this new development.

"Naa…" Robert answers. "We're getting out of this neighborhood. This scene's over for us."

If Van Helden and Joanne want to play house, why should I have a problem with that? I should be happy for them, I guess. I sit down at the kitchen table and close my eyes; a little internal darkness may help me sort out my options. I never planned on running this show alone, but what the hell... why not? I can do it... I *have* to do it... but do I want to? My stomach begins to rumble, the painful consequence of too many Dirty John hotdogs. I hate those disgusting tubers. I laugh sardonically at myself.

"What's so funny?" asks Joanne.

"The shit that passes for food around here is killing me."

"You don't have to eat it."

"I don't have any choice."

The three of us talk on for a little while longer, all feeling uncertain about the path ahead, although their direction seems clearer than mine. They at least know where they want to go. I, on the other hand, sort of whittle things away from my life in order to eventually get to the point I want to be; perhaps not a prescription for success, but it's gotten me this far. I sigh, who am I kidding? I haven't come far at all... and I have no idea where I'm going. The lights snap off and I settle in for another restless sleep.

"GET UP!" A voice blares as if broadcasting through a bullhorn.

Jesus! What's going on? My head blasts high from my pillow, Van Helden and Joanne lift their heads up fast, as well. The three of us stare in disbelief at the figure standing in the center of our room, his fists clench like he's about to throw a punch.

"WHO IS THIS?" asks Lykos, aiming his finger like a gun at Joanne; her mouth a gaping hole to receive the bullet. "She's one of the whores in 2B, isn't she?" Not waiting for a response, he rails on, "Don't think you can fool me, I know she hasn't paid a dime in rent, I know how she pays you, like this," he flicks his gun finger on the bed sheet. "I'm through playing games with you punks!"

"What are you doing in our room?" I ask, incredulous he would pull something like this.

"You owe Joanne an apology," Van Helden speaks evenly, without rancor. "You're full of shit. You know that?"

"*I'm full of shit!?* You lie in bed with a whore where she pays her rent, the bed I provide you to manage my building, you steal from me, and you say, *I'm full of shit!*" All the blood in Lykos' veins runs to his face, his eyes pop out like ping pong balls. "BULLSHIT!"

"You owe Joanne an apology," Van Helden repeats. "You have no right to talk like that... Joanne and I are getting married."

Married? I shake my head in disbelief.

"Married? Ha!" laughs Lykos.

"Married," says Robert.

"WHERE'S MY MONEY!?" Lykos hollers, not exactly ringing Robert and Joanne's wedding bells.

"We're not holding any of your money," I say, frustrated by his accusations.

"I want all of it, every dime, every nickel. You have one week!" Lykos last words hang cold in the air as he turns from the room, not bothering to shut our door on his way out.

My stomachache returns. "You guys getting married?"

"Yeah... it's crazy, I know," says Robert, grinning. Joanne begins to smile as well. "But we're gonna do it."

"When?"

"Pretty soon," says Robert, followed by a happy laugh. "It's crazy, huh?"

"Whoa... congratulations, I guess... Are you jiving me?"

"No," Robert continues laughing, "It's crazy!"

Lucifer's assumes I'm coming back next week to start bouncing drunks out the door. That's my fallback position. Introduction to Sales 101 begins this morning. I have to sit and endure ninety minutes of Professor Renzo's cheap carnie tricks on how to butter up patsies and pick their pockets.

"It doesn't matter what it is you're selling," pontificates Renzo, "if they don't like you, like the man says. 'Baby, you ain't going nowhere.'"

I look around at my classmates, all feverishly scribbling down reams of notes. Renzo has been talking for twenty minutes and I have yet heard him utter a noteworthy syllable.

He continues, "Being liked is Numero Uno, the most important part of the sale process," says Renzo, with an oily smile. "Would anyone in the class care to venture a guess as to what negative character trait in a salesman most people find unacceptable, and thereby the number one deal killer in any sales transaction? Anyone...?" Renzo's eyes scan across the room of clueless faces.

I want to raise my hand and shout, "Bullshit artist!" but think better of it.

"Anybody care to venture a guess... no? Well then, let me tell you. The non-conformist! The guy who wants to be different than everybody else; people don't trust them, people don't like them, and people certainly don't want to do business with them and part with their hard earned money."

The class scribbles away like a pen full of chickens scratching crumbs from the dirt.

"If you want to be liked by the average guy, you got to look like the average guy. We all find comfort in what we know, and are repulsed by the foreign, the bizarre, the unkempt. Any questions?"

I raise my hand, "What if you're peddling books in a neighborhood where most of the people happen to look bizarre, should you try to match their standards in order to make a sale, you know… dress freaky?"

The congregation laughs, but Renzo's hand comes up fast to quiet them down.

"Jonathan asks a very good question. Tomorrow, I will explain techniques on 'knowing who your client is,'" Renzo fingers quotation marks around his words. "But, let me briefly point out another component of success, 'Appeal to the Majority', strike your iron into the heart of Middle America. We do our homework, people, and by that I mean we know our demographics. When you leave Boston representing Collier's Encyclopedia, we won't be sending you off to some groovy, hippy commune." Renzo pauses to soak in the class's polite laughter, "You will be traveling to the upscale communities of Concord, Dover, Amherst, Weston, Exeter… entering respectable homes. You will not have to 'dress freaky' to be accepted. Indeed, some of you may need to clean up your act beforehand." Renzo shoots me a glance.

Looking around the room at my fellow travelers, I feel like I'm sitting here with the Milton Academy Bowling League. Renzo passes out a paper for us to take home and study, spiffy opening lines designed to get our ass in the door. I skim the page and laugh to myself, thinking of a more direct approach, "Stick'em up!"

I decide to skip dinner. I need to conserve my bread; besides, I probably would throw up if I try to eat, my stomach is so jumpy. It feels like I got worms crawling inside my intestines. Van Helden and I made arrangements to meet this evening to go over the new business that dropped on the table; Robert's nuptials and Lykos' plan to put us behind bars. I've been thinking about Lykos. His threats don't bother me; how can we be arrested for a crime we didn't commit? That asshole is nothing but a bag of wind.

"Let's walk," suggests Robert. We take a slow stroll up Tremont on the Common side of the street. The sidewalks are empty. The sun dripped below the horizon a moment ago, and the early evening summer air feels as comfortable as a mother's hug. We sit down on the stone rim of the fountain; behind our backs the sound of gurgling water tumbles like cool music.

"This morning blew my mind, Jonny."

"I'm hip. I felt like jumping up and choking that little bastard."

"I'm not putting up with this shit anymore. Tonight's my last night."

I puff out a long sigh. "I'm gonna miss ya, Robert."

"What are you gonna say to Lykos?" he asks.

"I'm gonna tell him to blow me."

"I told my boss today I'm marrying Joanne. He got this creepy look on his face, like he was trying hard not to cry, then he says, 'Robert... I'm gay'. And I said, 'So am I'. And he says, 'No, I don't think you understand what gay means?' And I say, 'Yeah... you're happy for me... I'm happy, too'. And he says, 'No, gay means I'm a homosexual.'"

"That's pretty funny, Robert."

"I didn't think so... The fuckin' guy started bawlin' right there in his office. He says to me, 'Please don't do it'. He says he's in love with me and can't bear to see me with anyone else."

"Jesus, you're kiddin'?"

"No! It was freaky, man... I didn't know what to say, except I'm gonna look for another job. So, he says, 'I think that would be best.'"

"Are you and Joanne really serious about this marriage thing?"

"Joanne's pregnant."

"Oh, man..."

We sit in silence for the next a minute. I feel like I need to warn him or something, but I'm not quite sure how to put it. "Robert, just because Joanne's pregnant, it doesn't mean you gotta run off and get married. You don't have to top one screw up with another."

"I love her."

"Oh... forget what I just said."

Van Helden rationalized the irrational; when love's involved I guess nothing else really needs to make sense.

"How long does this pregnancy thing take?"

"What? How long do you think?"

"I don't know... ten months, nine months?"

"Nine months, man. Everybody knows that."

"Hey, how the hell am I supposed to know that shit? This stuff was never talked about where I grew up."

"Yeah? Well, I'm sure it takes just as long for the girls in Holland as it does for the ones here in Boston."

Robert offers to treat me to a beer. We duck inside the Downtown Lounge and find Winky sitting alone at the bar; sipping on a coke and watching the band perform. Robert and I drop on the stools flanking her.

"Hiya, Winky!"

"Hey, boys! Whut you guys doin'?"

"We came here to be with you," I say.

The band playing the Lounge tonight is practicing soulful riffs. The lead singer's velvet voice sounds like Stevie Wonder. A few people in attendance, including Winky, are smiling and tapping hands to the beat.

Robert and I are debating the question of teenage love. I'm convinced marrying at such a young age is a recipe for disaster, although I personally have no married friends on which to base my opinion. It just seems like the wrong thing to do. I turn to Van Helden and speak across Winky's chest, "All right Robert, let's just say it doesn't work out. What do you think about divorces?"

"Divorces? I wouldn't do that. When you get married, you're in it for life. How do you feel about them?"

"Me? It doesn't matter what I think. You're the one who may need to deal with it. But if you really want to know, I guess I'm kinda cold towards them, too." I tap Winky on the hand to get her attention; she is biting into her soda straw. "Winky, how do you feel about divorces?"

"Da vorces," says Winky, lighting up an effervescent smile, "day's outa sight!"

"You kidding?"

"Day's cool," she repeats her praise, smiling and pointing to the band with the end of her straw. "Da drummer, da sax, day's cool, too. But, da vorces, day's out of sight!"

Robert and I glance at each other, lifting smiles and eyebrows.

Our friend, Roger, tending bar, drops a pair of bottles in front of us and refuses to take Robert's money. He leans into our conversation, "This group's hot." He nods towards the band. "This is the first time they've played Boston."

"Yeah, we were just talking about how great they sound," I say.

Winky sips the bottom of her coke and twirls the ice in the glass, "Lamar is lookin' for you," she says with a frown.

"Where'd you hear that?" I ask.

"Marvin."

"We had a little misunderstanding," I say, lighting up a cigarette.

"You be careful," Winky speaks slowly, as if she wants to make sure I hear every word, "Lamar can be strange."

"We got more important things to deal with. Ain't that right, Robbieboy?" I look over at Van Helden and smile.

Winky turns to face Robert, "Whut?"

"Joanne and I are getting married," Van Helden announces, grinning silly.

"Heyyy!" Winky hugs Robert hard. "Dat's wonderful!"

"Yep! I'm proud of my boy, here," I pat Robert on the back.

"How you and Julie doing?" asks Winky, turning

to me with bright eyes. "You in love, too?" she smiles.

"I'm not seeing her anymore."

"I thought you like her."

"I do… I mean, I don't. She was always trying to change me… buying me stuff… giving me clothes I don't want."

"Woman like you enough, she gonna wanna dress you," said Winky. "Don't you know dat?"

I return home this afternoon to an empty apartment. Oh sure, all the furniture and shit is still here, pots and pans haven't left the kitchen sink and my clothes still hang in the closet. But Van Helden's gone. I never realized how much of Robert's spirit there was in this place. I lay down in bed till the sky outside my window grew dark, only got up once to throw up in the toilet.

33

Who Am I?

I feel a little better today knowing I just have the weekend to get through before I board the bus on the road to riches. Each freshly anointed sales disciple will be assigned a mentor, a "sales associate" who's been hawking books all summer. Renzo insists on a few days of handholding his "tenderfoots" (his words) to guide us through the "rocky shoals". That's bullshit. I'm ready to hit the ground running. This mentor crap is only going to get in my way. If all goes well, this weekend will be the last time I need to worry about bread. I'm certain to sell my quota of books to those dupes waiting out there in the suburbs.

The buzzer on my wall is ringing like a bumblebee stuck inside a PA system. I stick my head out the window and catch Charlie peering up, waving.

"Throw down your key!"

Charlie comes into the room making a line directly to my fridge, "What do you got to drink?"

"Cherry Kool-Aid."

"How can you swallow that shit?" He reaches in the cabinet and finds himself a glass.

"You don't have to drink it."

"I'm not," he says, opting for warm tap water. "Lykos has our water piped in straight from the

Charles. I'd stick with the Kool-Aid if I were you. Those red crystals kill all the bugs."

My friend holds his glass up to the light, warily inspecting its contents before making a sour face and dumping the liquid into the sink.

"Charlie… where's your bike?"

"Some fucker with bolt cutters rode off with it. I had the thing chained to a lamp post," he shakes his head, dejected. Charlie points to Robert's side of the room, "Where's Van Helden?"

"Robert's gone. He ran off with Joanne to get married."

"Woofa!" Charlie blinks hard, like somebody kicked sand in his face.

"Joanne's knocked up." I volunteer the rationale behind this move, believing it out-trumped their declaration of love.

"Ughhhh…." He shakes his head in a dubious gesture, "I give it six months. What's happening with your girlfriend? She still hassling you?"

"Julie's not my girlfriend… she's not nothin' any more. I broke up with her."

"How she take it?"

"Not too cool… she started cryin' and shit… Said she is gonna build a wall around her body and never let another guy inside, ever again."

"She said that? Unbelievable!" Charlie slaps his legs and howls with laughter.

"I'm happy to entertain you, Charlie, but if you wanna know the truth… the whole scene was kinda of painful. I sort of like Julie… She taught me a lot about women, it really hurt to see her cry."

My buddy's smile fades. He gives me a reflective look. "Well, if you wanna know the truth, I thought you two were kind of a goof."

"I feel like crap."

"You need to get out; a little fresh air will set your head straight."

"Sorry, Charlie… I don't feel much like going out."

"You're all tangled up in blue, cooped up here. Believe me, Jonny; get away from this building." My buddy says goodbye and promises to check in on me in a few days.

I swallowed a couple of gnarly hotdogs for dinner that I'm beginning to regret. The laughing devil inside me is twisting my gut into knots. Maybe I should check into the hospital. As soon as I get paid I'm going to start improving my diet. I'd kill for a good steak and mashed potatoes, or my mother's fried chicken, a juicy polish sausage with a side of sauerkraut, or a plate of her spaghetti and meatballs. Beer goes great with all that good food. I've really come to like the taste of beer. I should go out… I still have a little jing in my pocket. I can afford a beer, or two. Maybe a couple of cold ones will coat my stomach.

On the street, I walk a few yards from my building and stop, standing flatfooted with my hands in my pockets, undecided on direction. I look down LaGrange Street towards Washington and think of the Downtown Lounge. That cool band is playing tonight; I guess I can go see them. Roger will spot me a few beers, I'm sure. Or should I head the other way on Washington and hit the Normandy Lounge? Julie probably is working tonight; she's always a kick to watch. She doesn't have to know I'm there; the room is so dark I can hide in the back where no one will see me. Maybe Kitty will be dancing, too. I could catch them both. I look across the street at the sign above the door to the Four Corners Lounge; Venus is dancing tonight. I wonder if Bruce is working the bar. He's always a fun talker... maybe he'll spot me a freebee.

"You looking for a date, honey?"

"What?"

A skanky looking chick dressed like a cartoon whore approaches me from across the street. "You want a girlfriend?"

"No thanks."

She steps closer into the spotlight of the street lamp. "Whatsamatter, sweetie, you like boys?"

I look at her hard. A shade of five o'clock shadow graces her jaw, framed by the flip of her lacquered black wig; a thick Adam's apple bobs above her open collar.

"Get lost, man," I sneer.

"Did you say you're lost, good looking?"

"Fuck you."

"Oh, would that you could," she coos.

I change my mind; I'm going back to my room. Retracing my steps from a minute ago, I slip my key in the front door. What's the point of pretending to enjoy myself? I didn't want to go out in the first place, not alone, anyway. I sigh and shuffle to the elevator. Inside the cab, the buttons stare back at me on the wall; I'm not sure which one to push. Hell, go back home Jonny, push a button that will take you there. I press number six. On the ride up I fantasize about my hometown; the door opens and I step out onto my street. I'm standing in front of the house where I grew up; my Mom and Dad waving to me on the front porch. The cab jolts to a stop and I open my eyes to the dingy sixth floor corridor.

I snap on the light inside my room and slouch down on the couch, put my feet up and light a smoke. My phone is staring at me from across the coffee table. Maybe I should call home… see if everything's okay.

"Jon… yoohoo, Jon." A soft voice from outside my room nudges me from unconsciousness. Winky is standing in my open doorway respecting my boundaries, graciously waiting for permission to enter.

"Come on in," I say. Standing, I stretch the stiffness from my frame, tucking my shirt into my jeans.

"You sleepin'?"

"No… just resting. What's going on?"

"Will you take me out for a drink? Day don't serve unescorted ladies in da bar after midnight."

"Well, then… I would be proud to escort you, m'lady," I dip a genteel bow. "Where would you care to go?"

"Just across da street," she smiles.

The Four Corners Lounge is crowded for 12:30 on a Sunday night. On the platform Venus is gyrating naked hips to a powerful, soulful version of that Beatle's tune, *With A Little Help from My Friends*. A couple seated in front leaves a tip and gets up from their seats. Winky and I jump onto the empty stools and make ourselves comfortable. A big bear of a guy I've never met is working the bar; tattoos color his forearms, his large face sprouts Groucho eyebrows and a full beard as dark as charcoal. He slides over and presses his face close to mine.

"Whatcha want?"

"Two beers," I say. This guy reminds me of Bluto, Popeye's nemesis.

Venus's finishes her performance, the last show of the night, and several patrons drop money on the bar and file out. The place will remain open for another hour or so, continuing to serve drinks to the beat of the jukebox.

"Jon, when you goin' back to school?" asks Winky, licking her lips after taking a sip from her beer. My body is turned towards her, my eyes trapped by her incredible beauty, enhanced by the room's soft lighting. Does she have any idea how utterly sexual she is?

"You know, Winky, I'm not sure. Classes are supposed to start up in a few weeks. They probably told me when I left, but I forgot to write it down."

"It might be a good idea you call and find out," she says, with a lovely smile.

"You lookin' delicious, Baby… I bet you taste like candy. Why don't you and me take a walk to my place and have us a little party?" A dark voice from a black stranger purrs in Winky's ear, loud enough for me to catch. The man ignores my presence, which annoys the hell out of me.

"Get away from me." Winky shifts uneasy on her stool, turning away from his disturbing come-on.

"Baby, let's get out of here, do a little weed, have us some fun." He sniff's Winky's hair, taking in her scent; his eyes fill with a sense of possession. "Mmmmm, you smell good."

Winky snaps her head away.

I hate this guy. Christ, if this jerk doesn't back off, I just might have to do something.

"What you got against me, Sugar? I'm the

sweetest thing you ever had. I got somethin' big and pretty you gonna love."

"Didn't you hear the lady? Get lost!"

The words come across clear and hard; I can't believe they came from me. Instantly, I go from being invisible to becoming Winky's White Knight.

Mister Big and Pretty gives his head a little shake, acting as if his ears aren't working properly. He steps in my face, giving me a menacing grin, like he's about to enjoy what comes next. The stranger tightens his eyes, sizing me up. "What did you say?"

"Leave the lady alone, asshole."

The man drops his grin and braces his face… I stiffen my fists. We lock eyes for an eternally long second. To my unbelievable surprise he turns away, walking fast around the front of the bar and out the door.

"Thanks, Jon." Winky breathes a deep sigh, "I was sure he would do somethin' bad… I'm surprised he run off."

"He didn't run off," I suddenly recognize what just happened. "That guy had murder in his eyes. I've seen that look before. He's coming back to kill me." I whistle for Bluto, wiping down the bar. He gives an annoying grunt as he works his way towards us.

"We need to use your back door," I say, talking fast, standing and grabbing Winky by the hand.

"What?"

I point down the only hallway in the place. A door marked 'PRIVATE' stands opposite the entry to the toilet. "Is that it down there?" I ask, anxiously.

"Can't you read? You can't go in there."

Holding on to Winky and running for it, I ignore the shouting bartender behind my back and disappear into the private room. Across a tight little space cluttered with boxes we find another door flanked by a file cabinet. I turn the knob and pull hard. "Fuck!" The damn thing is locked! A dead bolt with a thumb-turn secures it from the inside. I spin the little knob to free the bolt and try the door again; it swings open the instant Bluto bursts into the room, his fat hand gripping a billy. Winky and I jump across the threshold into the dark alley that runs between the strip club and the movie theater. I slam the door behind us.

The narrow alleyway opens onto Tremont Street, less than one hundred feet from the entrance to the club. We creep to the side with our shoulders against the wall until we reach the mouth of the alley where the building meets the sidewalk. I motion for Winky to wait behind me while I poke my head around the corner's brick edge. Standing under the light at the intersection of Tremont and Stuart is my newest enemy. Mister Big and Pretty is having an animated conversation with two of his buddies. I make out a word or two, 'Motherfucker this and motherfucker that'. The talking stops, and the three men, sharing the same serious expressions, march through the front door of the Four Corners Lounge.

"Let's go!" I grab on to Winky, holding her tight by the hand, racing across the street to the sanctuary of our building.

Winky and I stand together in silence riding the elevator back to our rooms. The cab stops at the fifth floor and Winky steps into the hallway.

"Thanks, Jon," she says, looking back at me over her shoulder.

"My pleasure." The elevator door closes and the cab continues on its way up; I can feel my heart pounding. I walk inside my room and drop into bed, too wound up to bother to get undressed. Pulling a smoke from my pack with shaking hands, I light up. I'm not going to forget that guy's face, and you can bet he won't forget mine. I look up at the ceiling through the smoke I exhaled and picture a very different conclusion from the action in that bar. Tonight, I was lucky.

Standing naked in front of the mirror, my face staring back at me… I feel so strange. Who am I supposed to be today? I wish Van Helden was around. I'd raid his closet for a sport jacket and make it over to Lucifer's; at least there I blend. I hate my new job and it hasn't even started yet. What was it that asshole said? "If you want to be liked by the average guy, you got to look like the average guy." Well, I would have given him my opinion about being liked if he had bothered to ask, "You want people to like you, you first gotta like yourself."

I step into a well-worn pair of bell-bottom jeans, pull a black T-shirt over my head, one with a front pocket to hold my smokes, and slip on my brown leather vest with the antelope horn buttons. The only question I have regarding footwear, should I wear socks with my buckskin moccasins, or go sockless. It's summertime… fuck the socks.

The phone starts ringing. Picking up… I glance at my watch… 8:15.

"I came by this weekend! Where were you?!" Lykos screams.

"I don't know. I don't hang around here all the time. Why didn't you tell me you were coming?"

"Don't play funny-boy with me! I told you last week I would see you Saturday morning."

"You did? Sorry I missed ya."

"You think this is some kind of joke? I looked for you again yesterday. I'll tell you what I did find, a goddamn filthy building! The place looks like a sewer! There was puke on the sidewalk by the front door!" Lykos stops to take a breath, "Do you have my money?"

"Hey… I did some sweepin'… I never saw any puke."

"My MONEY! Where is it?"

"Look, Lykos, I'm on my way out. Can't this wait until tonight?"

"I'm coming over there *right now*! I want you to be in your room when I get there!"

"I won't be here."

"Oh, *yes* you will!"

"I gotta go," I say, hanging up.

I walk through Park Plaza and enter Renzo's building feeling desperately optimistic my fortunes will change today. Taking a seat at the back of the room behind the freshly minted sales team of sparkling boys and girls, I'm thinking about the hole I blew in my wallet last night, dropping three bills at the bar. Renzo enters the room with all the fanfare of an evangelical revivalist, towing along six of his seasoned sales associates; our mentors. He explains to us new recruits how the process will work. We will break up into teams selected by the mentors. They'll be walking up and down the rows of seats choosing novices by tapping them on the shoulder.

"Any questions?" he asks, turning his head

around the room. "Okay, then," he claps his hands, "Let's get started!"

A stream of a half-dozen fresh cut All-American faces drift up and down the rows as we sit still with sheepish smiles and our hands folded properly on the desk. The whole scene takes less than thirty seconds. They return to the front of the class and stand alongside Renzo.

"Well, are you all clear on who you're working with?" asks a grinning Renzo, "Any questions?"

I raise my hand.

"Yes, Jonathan!"

"Um… I didn't get picked."

Renzo studies me with a contemplative eye, and turns to his crack sales force, "Would any of you care to explain why you did not bother to select Jonathan?"

A half-dozen hands shoot up at once.

Renzo directs his question to the one nearest him, "Francis, can you tell Jonathan why you do not want him to join your team?"

"His hair," answers Francis the Dupe.

"Is that the consensus of the group?"

"Yes!"

Renzo puts his studious glare back on me, "Well… I see. What can we do about this?"

"I can get a haircut," I volunteer. "But I got a big problem. Haircuts cost money, money I don't have."

"How much do haircuts run these days in Boston?" Renzo asks, solicitously.

"Five bucks," I answer, without hesitation.

Mr. Magnanimous reaches into his back pocket and pulls out his fat wallet, fingering a five and waving it in the air.

"I will loan you the five dollars!" he announces proudly, "Will you get yourself a haircut this afternoon and come back here first thing tomorrow?"

"Sure."

"All right now," Renzo turns to face his groupies, "Who wants Jonathan to join their team?"

The same half-dozen hands shoot up straight in the air. Renzo, with an idiot smile on his face and the five spot in his hand, approaches me from the front of the room.

"Here you go," he says, handing me the bill like it is some kind of winning ticket. "We'll see you back here tomorrow morning." He adds in a whisper, "And put on some decent clothes."

I stand up, straighten my vest, and tuck the money in my top pocket behind my smokes. I say thank you to Mr. Renzo and all the fine people in the room and leave the building.

On the walk back to my place, I pass the Trailways Bus Station. Displayed on the storefront windows are pictures of all the scenic places to visit in America. Disneyland, Niagara Falls, the Alamo. I stop and stare at the posters, stick my hands in my pockets, absentmindedly fumbling a few nickels and dimes while gazing at the Statue of Liberty. Turning on my heels, I walk inside the terminal making a direct line to the ticket counter. An older gentleman smoking a cigarette and dressed in a white shirt and tie sits on the other side of the counter behind a narrow cage of steel bars.

"Can I help you, son?"

"How much is a one-way ticket to Hartford?"

"That would be five dollars and sixty-five cents."

I fish change from the pocket of my jeans, spreading the contents on the countertop, and pull out Renzo's five, slapping it down on top of the pile. "When's it leaving?"

"The next one's at 4:55 this afternoon, young fella."

I can't go without saying goodbye to my friends. "Do you have one going out tomorrow morning?"

He pauses and looks at a chart beside him on the wall. "We have a ten fifteen."

"I'll take it." I shovel my cash in close to the man.

Riding up to the fifth floor hoping to find Marvin, I knock and wait beside his door. Winky appears within a few seconds.

"Hi, Winky, is Marvin around?"

"He be home soon," she smiles, "You wanna come in and wait?"

"No, that's cool. I just wanted to stop by and tell you guys I'm leaving."

"Leaving? Leaving where?"

"I'm going to Connecticut. I'll be back in Boston when school starts, but I won't be coming back here."

"Oh. Jon…" Winky lightens her voice, "When you going?"

"I'll be gone tomorrow morning. I couldn't leave without saying goodbye to you and Marvin." I pause, finding my emotions grabbing me by the throat… "I want to thank you for being my friend."

Winky struggles with a smile, steps forward and hugs me hard, placing a soft kiss on my cheek, "Thank you, too, Jon."

At the opposite end of the hallway, Little Joe Cook has his door open. I stick my head in. A couple of musicians are setting up speakers and amps; others busy tuning their instruments. There must be dozen people crowded in his room, counting the band members and their girlfriends. Joe's bass player, Carlos, is a tall, good-looking dude with an Afro the size of a blueberry bush. He is shirtless, save for his black leather vest opened to his hairless chest. Carlos is sitting on the couch with Julie on his lap. She has one arm slung over his shoulder. We make eye contact and she gives me a smug smile, pulling Carlos in tight. I throw her a little wave and continue on my way. I guess ol'Carlos must have poked a hole in Julie's wall.

Packing up my things takes less than five minutes. I have a couple of posters on the wall that I'll leave behind. I only want to keep one. I roll up Lee Van Cleef with Julie holstered in his gun belt and snap a couple of rubber bands around them. My books and drafting tools stuff into my ammo bag and what I can't squeeze in I throw into my suitcase beside my crumpled clothes. I stare at my cheap collection of plastic plates and aluminum pots and pans stacked in the cupboard and spilling into the sink. I'll leave this shit for Lykos. *Lykos? Damn!* I better give him a call. I shouldn't just evaporate from the scene; that might look suspicious. I'm clean, I've done nothing wrong, but I guarantee that bastard won't see it this way. I'll call him tomorrow morning before I split. I should phone my folks, too, and maybe Lara. They might be happy to know I'm coming back.

I spot the building's passkey lying on the corner of the kitchen table, pick it up and flip it in the air like a coin, catching it in my palm. I remember how obsessive Lykos was when he first handed it over, and laugh at the thought of what he'd do to me if I disappear with his precious key. "This cost me $5,000! Don't drop it, don't lose it, and don't ever give it to anyone." I hold it in the air, inspecting its fangs, sunlight beaming through my picture window glints off the brass finish. I can leave the key with one of my friends, I think, before stuffing it into my pocket.

The phone starts ringing; I blink at it… almost afraid to pick it up, grabbing it on the third ring, "Yeah?"

"Who's this!?" the man hollers rudely into my ear.

"Is that you Lamar?" I ask, acting happy to hear his voice.

"Yeah! I'm in the building, asshole… downstairs! You and me got some business to deal with, you dig?"

"Listen Lamar, you wanna live in this building?"

"Whut? I don't have any time for more of your jive bullshit!"

"No, I'm serious. Come on up. I'll give you back all your things. I got you a new key," I say, trying to sound sincere. I finger the passkey inside my pocket. "You can move back in right now. Like you said, we can forget this shit ever happened… pure misunderstanding. I'll even give ya two weeks free rent for your trouble."

"I knew I could reason with you," he says, with satisfied arrogance.

"By the way, Lamar, where you calling from?"

"Your friend, Raymond, he letting me use his phone. He know how to treat his neighbors with respect. Ain't that right, Raymond?"

"Hey!" Marvin walks in and catches me lying flat on top of the bare mattress. He points an accusing finger at me, "What the hell are you doing?"

"Staring at the ceiling."

"Winky said you're leaving. That right?"

"In the morning."

"You got some reason for going?"

"I got no reason for staying." I sit up and look my friend in the eye. "I went out last night with Winky..."

"Hey, I got no problem with that. You and her wanna go out and have fun, that's fine with me."

"There was this black dude in the bar... he came on to Winky..."

"She told me about it. I want thank you for looking out for her. I think what you done was way cool."

"The whole thing scared the shit out of me."

"Don't you let some coke-bottle pimp scare you! You're a better man than he is."

"He didn't scare me. I scared myself. I was ready to kill that guy. I woulda done it without thinking." I shake my head and stare back up at the ceiling, "That scares me, man. What the hell am I doing here?"

"You're livin', ain't nothin' wrong with that."

"I show up for a new job today and the guy in charge sent me home because I didn't fit in."

"Fuck him!" Marvin jabs his index finger in my face.

"No… it was cool. He actually did me a favor. I wasn't right for that scene." I pause, looking at my friend, "It hit me this morning on my way back to the building, I don't feel right being here, either. That's become real clear to me the past twenty-four hours. I'm an eighteen-year-old kid, Marvin. What the hell am I doing here?"

"You're a man, Jon… you're not a kid. You're a man."

"I'm not sure I like the man I'm turning into."

Marvin sits down beside me on the bed and lets out a healthy sigh. "You got nothin' to be ashamed of, Jon."

"I'll miss you, man."

"You gonna come back and visit?"

"Sure… I'll check in on you." I smile.

"Think I can have your room?"

"I don't see why not. But, that's not my call… I guess that's up to Lykos."

"He's gonna need a new Super. Maybe you can put in a good word for me?"

"I don't think Lykos wants to hear anything I have to say."

We sit through a minute of sober silence.

"Well," says Marvin, slapping my knee, rising from the bed. He stands looking down at me with a warm smile. "I'll miss you, too, man," he confesses, before walking out of my life.

Shortly before midnight, I hear Sam step off the elevator and open her door. I make a quick line to her. I have been sitting around for the past few hours hoping she would come home.

"Where've ya been, handsome? I haven't seen you in awhile," says Sam, turning the key in her door. "How'd you make out at Lucifer's?"

"They offered me a job. Your advice was right on."

"Well, you're welcome," she smiles.

"Thank you."

"When you gonna start?" Sam kicks off her shoes and unbuttons her blouse, tossing it on the bed in exchange for a sleeveless T-shirt she picks from her dresser.

"I'm not. I went with the encyclopedias."

Sam pulls on the T-shirt, her head pops out laughing, "You think you're gonna like that action, huh… selling books door to door to housewives? I guess it does have its possibilities."

"They wouldn't give me the gig unless I got a haircut." We both share a laugh over that one. "Dig this, I told them I was broke, so they gave me the bread to go do it."

"I see you must have spent it on something else," says Sam, stepping over to me and running her fingers through my locks.

"I bought a bus ticket. I'm going home."

"What?" Her question a near whisper. "You're leaving?"

"In the morning."

Sam slips her bare feet back into her shoes. "You feel like taking a walk?" she asks.

The darkened path through the Common looms ahead as foreboding as the trail in Sleepy Hollow. A short distance away between the moonlight and the deep shadows of a grove of trees, four black teenagers are rolling a guy across the grass, kicking him in his sides, going through his pockets. They look like crows picking on road kill. I reach out for Sam's hand and pick up our pace.

"Tell me something," says Sam, stopping and pulling me over by my shirt. "We've known each other for quite awhile. How come you never hit on me?"

Her question knocks me off balance, like she pitched a ball at my face and I'm standing with my hands in my pockets. I duck, "I don't know."

Sam let go of my shirt and folds her arms, looking at me, posturing impatience.

"You're my friend," I fumble. "I never thought of you as anything else... and you always had some guy on the line. I wasn't gonna get in the way."

"You're a good boy, Charlie Brown," Sam smirks.

Hands dropped to our sides, we continue walking in silence together, apart, and enter the Public Garden, taking the central path leading to the bridge. We stop and sit down on the top step of the stone staircase that guides you to the dock where the swan boats are tethered. Milky-glass globes perched on top of cast-iron spindles shine above our heads like lollypop moons, casting a cool glow into the water. Sam lowers her head onto my lap and closes her eyes. The city surrounding us has settled down for the night. The muffled sound of a single passing car hums through the warm night air. A few feet away, I hear scratching of a small animal; a well fed fat rat skulks along the edge of the step below my feet. I watch as it moves on its way into the shadows.

Sam's pretty face looks so soft and peaceful, as if she has fallen into a dream. I gently brush her hair with my hand.

"Jon," Sam whispers my name, "don't leave." She pleads faintly, "Don't go, Jon, don't leave."

"I have to," I say, believing with all the certainty I possess, "I gotta get away."

Sam sits upright and looks at me with swollen eyes, "Why?"

"I don't belong here." I turn, looking into the pond.

"Let's go home," says Sam, her voice drained.

It sounds strange to me now, calling that building 'home'. It no longer fit. Taking the step up to the bridge, I stand beside her on the path and take her hand.

"Sam, you scared?"

"Scared of what?"

"Having your baby, alone."

"No… let's go."

Sam's face hardens; the helpless look she gave me seconds ago vanishes, tucked away in a flash.

"I'm leaving a few things behind, maybe you want something?" I slip in my key, swing open the door and follow Sam into my room. She gravitates to a poster I put together months ago; a large black and white silhouette of a tall ship, its sail riggings an elaborate spider web dominating the scene. I had several pictures of myself taken inside one of those twenty-five cent photo booths. I cut out my head with scissors and glued them to the mast, boom and main sail's riggings, the faces lost in the maze of ropes and beams. You had to search hard to find me. I love it.

"You want it?" It's yours."

Sam climbs up on a chair, reaches to the poster's top corners and pulls out the tacks, handing them to me. She steps down, holding the artwork in her hands.

"You can rummage through my kitchen, take anything you see."

"This is all I want," she jiggles the poster in the air.

I look at my watch, surprised to find the time close to two in the morning. "It's getting late, Sam. You'll probably be sleeping when I split tomorrow."

"Probably," she says.

"Come on," I smile. "I'll walk you home."

The distance between our doors is four simple steps. I've taken this easy walk hundreds of times. Now, the steps feel complicated... confused. She works her key into the door as I stand behind her hesitant, unsure of myself. Sam turns to face me, her eyes reveal nothing.

"Have a nice life, Jon. Drop me a postcard."

"I'm not saying goodbye... I'm coming back."

"Sure," she says, her tone blunt, its effect razor-sharp.

I'm not Sam's lover... so why do I feel like I'm running out on her? I step in close and hug her tight. Sam's arms droop to her side like wilted stems. I'm afraid to let go, but holding on doesn't feel right either. I squeeze hard before stepping back. Sam kisses my face and turns quickly into her room, closing the door, leaving me standing alone in the hallway; it never looked as dismal as it does to me now.

"Goodbye, Sam," I whisper.

"G'morning," I speak warily into the phone.

"YOU!" Lykos snaps. "I came to the building yesterday... I told you to be there, didn't I? I said no more games, didn't I? I warned you there would be severe consequences if you tried to avoid me again, DIDN'T I!" The man is a boiling, loud mouth loony. I pull the phone away from my ear; I can feel his voice vibrating through my hand. If we weren't separated by miles of telephone line, I'm certain he would be wrapping the phone cord around my neck and strangle me blue.

"I told you I wouldn't be here. I was straight with you. I didn't try to ditch you."

"I'm having you arrested! Do you understand me? When I hang up I'm calling the police."

"So arrest me, I don't care... I'm leaving today."

"You can't run from me!" Lykos laughs. "I'll catch up with you and have you thrown in jail! You and your buddy, Van Helden! You stole my money and you're going to pay for it!"

"Blow me, Asshole! We didn't touch a dime of your goddamn money."

"Yeah? Why are you running?"

"You think I'm running? Listen, you want me? I'll make it easy for you. I'll tell you exactly where I'm going. You can come and get me, or send the police." I shout out my home address into the phone. "Ya got that!? I hope you wrote it down, cause I ain't gonna repeat it."

Lykos begins seething in my ear, but I cut him off in mid-seethe, yanking the chord from the socket. I grab the phone and throw it hard across the floor; the solid plastic casing smashes against the wall, chipping a dusty chunk of lime plaster unto the linoleum tile. I stare down at the mangled telephone; smoking in the dust.

"Goodbye, Lykos."

Beautiful sunshine greets me as I step outside and stand on the sidewalk in front of the building's diner, peering through the glass at the three Greeks behind the counter waving their arms in the air at one another, communicating breakfast orders like a fire drill. I enter and approach the harried trio, saying hello. They grunt a response; ignore me, going about their business. My stomach has a sick grumble happening inside. I'm not sure if it's from hunger or some kind of involuntary spasm reacting to the greasy slop they're shoveling on a line of porcelain plates. I address the toughest looking one of the bunch who is barking the loudest; the brains of the outfit.

"You know Lykos, don't you?"

"Yes, of course, the Big Boss," he answers in clipped English.

"Do me a favor, will ya. Give this to him, okay?" I hand the man a sealed envelope with Lykos' name printed on it. "He's expecting it," I lie. "So, don't go losing it."

He snatches the envelope from my hand and waves me away, pissed-off by my lack of trust.

"Thanks."

I gave serious consideration yesterday to handing my passkey over to Lamar when I got him settled into his old room; he would be clueless of the secret power his magic key possessed. I loved the irony of it. But, I got to thinking… if Lykos wants me behind bars for a lousy five hundred, he would probably have me whacked for lifting his golden key. I considered leaving it with one of my friends, but that seemed a bit dicey. Rather than take any chances, I slipped the key inside the envelope I entrusted to the hands of strangers.

Wandering through the terminal I see that my ride to Hartford leaves in ten minutes, so I have a little time to kill, pull the morning paper from a trash can, and park myself on an empty bench to read the news. It's been a long time since I followed current events; a quick scan through the pages tells me nothing much has changed; Nixon's peace plan is working like a charm; Ground attacks north of Saigon, one hundred and thirty Americans killed so far this week. Craziness out in California; police on a manhunt for a suspect in a bizarre "ritualistic" mass murder at the home of some Hollywood big shot, one of the dead is that honey-blonde actress Sharon Tate. More trouble for the Kennedys; someone's claiming Teddy concocted a phony alibi when he drove his car off some bridge on Martha's Vineyard. Local yokels in upstate New York are freaking out; caravans of hippies are showing up early for a concert planned this weekend in some little town called Woodstock. I flip to the sports page; the Celtics have just been sold for a NBA record price tag of $6,000,000! Whoa… now that's news!

A voice on the PA system announces my bus is ready to board. I slip a hand in my pocket and pull out my ticket, reading 'HARTFORD' below the word, DESTINATION, and begin to feel anxious about where I'm headed. I need to be back in Boston in a few weeks and find a new place. I have no idea how I'm going to pull this off.

My bus parked beneath the canopy is spewing stinky gas into the air. I hand my bag to an attendant, who tosses it inside the luggage bin, and step on board with Lee Van Cleef and Julie rolled up in my hand. The driver sits hunched behind the wheel reading the sports page. He gazes indifferently at the ticket I wave beneath his nose. I pause for a second, scanning dozens of empty seats ahead of me; finding a choice spot to be alone for the next couple of hours will be easy. I walk up the aisle viewing my options when I pass her sitting alone, Miss America, reclined in a window seat with her face inside a paperback novel. Backing up and placing Julie and Lee Van Cleef in the overhead bin, I slide down beside the beautiful stranger, decked out in a sensible college-girl blouse and skirt. The right makeup and some tighter clothes and she would look as hot as Crystal. Making a big display of myself, I flip my seat back and forth before coming to rest at the exact angle as hers. She lowers her book a fraction and turns her lovely face towards mine. I meet her bored expression with a smile. Ignoring me, she drops her eyes back into her business. Her tepid reaction is less than thrilling. Never mind; we have the next two hours to get acquainted. With my newspaper folded across my lap, I settle back and light a cigarette to relax.

"Excuse me?" My luscious seatmate closes her book, finally acknowledging me.

"Yes," I answer pleasantly, putting as much social grace as possible into that three-letter word.

"Your cigarette." She fans a hand in front of her face, her other hand pinching her nose between her fingertips. "Would you mind blowing your smoke someplace else?"

AFTERWORD

Like the poet says, "To live outside the law, one must be honest." Robert and I were honest kids. Lykos, on the other hand, was a shady thief, and by no account a fan of jurisprudence. He never did send the police to bring us in. In later years, he would be convicted of bank fraud involving a prototypical check kiting scheme that masterminded an intricate and sophisticated plan of passing bogus checks between numerous interstate bank accounts to the tune of over one-million dollars. On top of this little misstep, the Massachusetts Attorney General sued Lykos for posing as a phony mortgage broker, orchestrating a mortgage scam targeting Boston's Asian community.

Robert and Joanne Van Helden were married in a civil ceremony on the same day the Woodstock zeitgeist danced in that jam-packed meadow, and nine months later a healthy baby boy, Armand, entered their lives. The Van Helden's and I saw little of each other after going our separate ways at the end of the summer in 1969. I would discover thirty years later Robert had joined the military, and he and his family, which soon included a daughter, Vanessa, spent twenty years traveling the world with the U.S. Air Force, living in Turkey, Italy, Latvia, and the Netherlands before returning to the States. In 2003, my friend Charlie informed me that Robert's son, Armand Van Helden, had grown into an international phenom house musician and remix artist. I reconnected with Robert and Joanne through Armand's website, leaving a cryptic message about this book I'm writing that involves his parents. We happily reunited and today continue to thoroughly cherish our time together. A funny footnote to the intersection of our lives: I spent a decade practicing architecture in the town of Prescott, Arizona, before leaving that scene in 1990 for a new life in the Pacific Northwest. Five years later, unknown to me, Robert and Joanne had left the Pacific Northwest and moved into Prescott, just a few blocks from where I had lived, and purchased a home I had remodeled.

The character of Charlie is actually a fusion of three close acquaintances. My editor believed I had confused my story by saturating the action with too many of my friends and advised me to limit their number, so I condensed a trio of buddies into the single character of Charlie. However, my descriptions of Charlie are ninety percent Charlie; my apologies to Al and David. Charlie eventually received his bachelor degree in psychology; but he shied-away from mental health in favor of physical fitness and a life in construction. Charlie became an artist with a backhoe. Today, our mothers live across the hall from one another in the same Senior Living facility.

With a "General under Honorable Conditions Discharge" below his belt, Donnie Pyle left the Marines and moved back home to live with his parents. One morning, upon my return to the neighborhood, I stopped by his house to confront him and demand the forty dollars he stole from me. I found him lying in bed watching Saturday morning cartoons. "I ain't got it," he shrugged. We stared at each other for several long seconds, the only sound between us, his TV, turned down low. I yanked the plug from the wall socket and left his house with my arms wrapped around his television. Years later, after Donnie's parents had passed away and he was living alone, a relative found Donnie dead, lying in bed. The coroner's report listed methadone toxicity as the cause of death.

Upon my return to Boston, in the fall of 1969, I made one last trip back to the Combat Zone to pay my respects to Marvin and Winky. They were now occupying the coveted room Van Helden and I had vacated. I felt uncomfortable standing by their door, looking in. There was a hub-bub of activity all about the place. Lykos had recently installed Marvin as the new Building Superintendent, and my friend was busy discussing terms with a couple of new tenants while his brother, Lenny, pushed Winky's furniture around the room, arranging stuff just so, to her satisfaction. You caught us at a bad time, Marvin had said, and asked me to come back later, "Don't be a stranger!" That was the last time we saw each other.

Sam had left the building and moved to the suburbs. When I heard she had gone into labor I hurried over to Mass General Hospital and found the new mother in bed with a baby cradled in her arms. Sam looked flush and content, and her baby girl, immaculate. We drifted apart soon after, but not before I paid a final visit to Sam and her three-year old at their home outside of Boston. Toys, dollies, stuffed animals and coloring books were scattered about the living room floor. Sesame

Street was playing on the TV. The poster I gave her the night we said goodbye tacked to the wall. Sam looked good. I wanted to sleep with her, but knew that was impossible. I couldn't go back, and… after all, I was married.

Following graduation from Wentworth, I was accepted into an architecture program at Arizona State University. Lara had just turned eighteen and I was a few weeks shy of my twentieth, the two of us were inseparable and crazy in love. We fought like maniacs to convince our parents to let us marry, and unbelievably, they agreed. The day after our wedding, in Hartford, Lara and I flew on an airplane for the first time in our young lives, taking a one-way ticket to Phoenix. Like most teenage marriages, it was a constant struggle to keep a life of promises, and ours together went down in flames after eight tumultuous years.

My professor, C.T. Pederson, spent his last days teaching structural engineering at Wentworth Institute. The college features a laboratory where small cylinders of concrete are tested to gauge the structural composition's ultimate strength. The concrete sample is placed in a hydraulic crushing devise, subjected to several thousand pounds of force per square inch before the mass explodes in a pile of dust. C.T. committed suicide one very dismal day when he placed his head in the device, pushed the switch and crushed his skull.

During the 1950's, Little Joe Cook sang in Alan Freed's early rock-and-roll shows and appeared at the Apollo Theater in a line-up that featured The Drifters, Big Maybelle and The G-Clefs. In 1957, he appeared on American Bandstand to sing his hit, "Peanuts," which would remain on the Billboard Top 100 chart for 15 weeks, peaking at number 22. Little Joe possessed a five octave vocal range, with a piercing falsetto that would become his trademark, and pave the way for singers like Frankie Valli and Lou Christie. The popularity of his hit song "Peanuts" continued over the years. The Four Seasons covered the tune, and it was used in a Skippy Peanut Butter commercial. After Cook moved from the Combat Zone in the late Sixties, he landed a regular gig at the CanTab Lounge across the river in Cambridge and performed there for over 25 years. In 2002, Little Joe performed with Harvey Robbins' Royalty of Doo-Wop and Rock 'n' Roll show at Symphony Hall in Boston. In a music poll conducted by the *Boston Phoenix* newspaper, Little Joe Cook was voted the 2002 Best Local R&B performer.

Close to thirty years had passed before I returned to Boston as a member of a prestigious architectural firm. I was fortunate to be appointed project architect for the restoration of the Massachusetts State House atop Beacon Hill. One of my challenges was coordinating the installation of a new memorial on the State House grounds commemorating the Commonwealth's valiant police officers who had fallen in the line of duty. It was my great privilege and heartfelt honor to have participated in a convocation honoring the memory of Patrolman Francis Bucky Johnson, thirty-five years after his death.

In the decade following my departure, the Combat Zone became more hardened, gritty and dangerous. Pasties and G-strings came down, murder and felony rates went up, and City Hall got busy. Boston's Planning Commission officially mandated the district as an exclusive adult entertainment zone to corral the burgeoning sex trade. The scene's reversal of fortunes, or misfortunes, climaxed from a combination of forces: market factors, real estate investors, civic, church and institutional players. Walk through these streets today, you'll see no trace of the neighborhood's nefarious past. It's all gone. Well, almost, anyway. When I began writing this story, I found among the flashy, new high rise development two strip clubs residing quietly, although now euphemistically called, Gentlemen Clubs, both located on the block I called home forty years ago.

Jonathan Tudan

2008

Support

I recall a joke from Lilly Tomlin I heard many years ago; "Remember, we're all in this alone." With all due respect, Lilly, I couldn't disagree more. Without the support of my precious family and valued friends and the grateful contributions I received from knowledgeable colleagues this story would never have been published. Directly upon leaving the Combat Zone I began an oral history of the events I witnessed, recounting the best of these vignettes to anyone willing to listen, usually over a bottle of wine or dinner conversations, always evoking an enjoyable reception. As the years turned, I filed these tales away in a drawer inside my mind with the thought that I may, someday, open that drawer and scribe them to paper. This opening came with the encouragement and inspiration of Mary, my beautiful wife, life partner, and the fiercest critic. I could never have undertaken this effort without her. I am also enormously beholden to my cherished friends Robert and Joanne Van Helden, who shined a bright light across the path of my darker memories. For accuracy in matters dealing with crime and punishment, I received invaluable assistance and communiqués from the Boston Police Department Archivist, Donna Wells and a former Commander (c. 1969) of the Vice Squad, Eddie McNelley. I wish to express my indebtedness to the *Boston Phoenix* newspaper for Joe Cook's biographical information, and *Architecture Boston* magazine's Executive Editor, Elizabeth Padjin, for publishing a piece of my work and introducing me to the brilliant Jerry Berndt, who captured the emotion of my story in his transcendent photography. Without the discerning advice of the capable and gifted author Gini Sikes this memoir would never have left the gate. Thank you, Gini, for your incredible thoughtfulness. I am blessed with supportive friends and talented associates who offered a wealth of ideas and encouragement as they suffered through this story's countless iterations. I want to express my deep appreciation for indulging me and granting permission to enter their life: David Howard, Richard Martin, Iris and John McNerney, Misty and Bruce Rutter, Paul Pressman, Joan Goody, my sister Christine and her husband Bob Byerly, Barry Porter, Suzanne Kellett, Joshua Ben-Nun, Barbara Nichols, Nan and Al Gagne, Richard Smith, Michael Donohue, Tom Coleman, David Lang, Ken Metzler, Charlie Backus, Paul Peters, Fred Garrett, Walt Pollard, Skye Wentworth, Sorche Fairbank, Adam Stumacher, Jon Marcus, Mose Allison, Armand Van Helden, and Shelly Lauterbach. Special thanks to my sister, Linda Tudan, for her perceptive comments. And, most importantly, I am grateful to the forces in the universe for bringing Maxim and Leah into my life, bestowing the precious joy of love at first sight each time I lay eyes on them.

The Author

Jonathan Tudan AIA has an extensive career as an architect stretching from Boston, Massachusetts to the Central Mountains of Arizona, across Puget Sound, through the Pacific Northwest and down the west coast to southern California. Jonathan lives with his wife, Mary, and son, Maxim, in Calabasas, California.

LaVergne, TN USA
11 February 2010
172826LV00001B/158/P